Seeking Oz

My Twelve-Year Journey in a Cult

Makena McChesney

BALBOA
PRESS
A DIVISION OF HAY HOUSE

Copyright © 2018 Makena McChesney.
Photo Credit : Jacob McChesney

All rights reserved. No part of this book may be used or reproduced by any means, graphic, electronic, or mechanical, including photocopying, recording, taping or by any information storage retrieval system without the written permission of the author except in the case of brief quotations embodied in critical articles and reviews.

Balboa Press books may be ordered through booksellers or by contacting:

Balboa Press
A Division of Hay House
1663 Liberty Drive
Bloomington, IN 47403
www.balboapress.com
1 (877) 407-4847

Because of the dynamic nature of the Internet, any web addresses or links contained in this book may have changed since publication and may no longer be valid. The views expressed in this work are solely those of the author and do not necessarily reflect the views of the publisher, and the publisher hereby disclaims any responsibility for them.

The author of this book does not dispense medical advice or prescribe the use of any technique as a form of treatment for physical, emotional, or medical problems without the advice of a physician, either directly or indirectly. The intent of the author is only to offer information of a general nature to help you in your quest for emotional and spiritual well-being. In the event you use any of the information in this book for yourself, which is your constitutional right, the author and the publisher assume no responsibility for your actions.

Scripture taken from the King James Version of the Bible.

Scripture quotations marked (NIV) are taken from the Holy Bible, New International Version®, NIV®. Copyright © 1973, 1978, 1984, 2011 by Biblica, Inc.™ Used by permission of Zondervan. All rights reserved worldwide. HYPERLINK "http://www.zondervan.com" www.zondervan.com The "NIV" and "New International Version" are trademarks registered in the United States Patent and Trademark Office by Biblica, Inc.™

Scripture quotations marked (NLT) are taken from the Holy Bible, New Living Translation, copyright ©1996, 2004, 2015 by Tyndale House Foundation. Used by permission of Tyndale House Publishers, Inc., Carol Stream, Illinois 60188. All rights reserved.

Scripture quotations marked (TLB) are taken from The Living Bible copyright © 1971. Used by permission of Tyndale House Publishers, Inc., Carol Stream, Illinois 60188. All rights reserved.

Print information available on the last page.

ISBN: 978-1-9822-0619-2 (sc)
ISBN: 978-1-9822-0617-8 (hc)
ISBN: 978-1-9822-0618-5 (e)

Library of Congress Control Number: 2018906813

Balboa Press rev. date: 06/21/2018

This book is dedicated to the ones I love the most—the ones with whom I traveled the Yellow Brick Road. They are also the ones who suffered unnecessarily as we journeyed through the Dark Forest. They are the ones with whom I celebrate liberation and freedom of choice never to be taken for granted. They are my three sons.

Contents

Preface xi
Acknowledgments xvii
Introduction to Dear Reader xix

PART 1
LOOKING BACK
Formative Years 1
      Why?
      Unnecessary Guilt
Later Childhood and Adolescence 7
      Early Church Indoctrination
Adolescence and Early Adulthood 11
      No Blame—Just Lessons
      Infatuation at Sixteen
      Relational Red Flags
      Unequally Yoked
      Cowardly Lion
      A Move and a Snowstorm

PART 2
THE CULT YEARS

Year One 33
- I Like It!
- A Safe, Happy Interval
- Marriage Focus and Decline
- Settlement

Years Two and Three 43
- Survival on the Homefront, and Church Doctrines Emerge
- The Royal Family
- Introduction to Community Living
- And More Community Living

Years Four and Five 57
- A New Relationship
- Next Steps
- Second Marriage and an Untimely Tragedy
- My First Paranormal Visitation
- Decisions and Choices Unapproved

Years Six and Seven 77
- A Difficult Move to Horseshoe Court
- Terrible News
- Move into House on Horseshoe Court
- Church School and Expanding, Expanding Household

Years Eight and Nine 105
- More Leave the Fellowship
- Focus on the Positives
- Legalism to the Max
- Synergy and Projects
- Changes and More Changes
- Negatives and Hidden Negatives
- Phil's Labor Contributions and the Church Building Project

Years Ten and Eleven 137

    A Community Sharing Company
    Final Straws and the Big Questions
    Straw Number One
    Straw Number Two
    Straw Number Three
    Straw Number Four
    Straw Number Five
    Straw Number Six
    Straw Number Seven
    Two-Year Countdown
    My Secret Ally
    New and More Extreme Doctrines
    Relentless Work Expectations and Imposed Restrictions
    Secrets Kept by the Royal Family
    Accidents and Fatalities
    The Beginning of the Shock Waves
    Second Shock Wave

Year Twelve: In and Out 211

    The Beginning of the End—Tell Phil
    Teaching Second Grade
    Change in Household
    A Compassionate Revelation
    Imminent Angels
    Third and Final Shock Wave
    A Message from the Other Side
    More Suspicious Behavior
    The Wedding
    Steps and More Insights
    Three-Month Wait
    Out but Still Tethered
    The Wait Is Over

Preface

How is it that I am called to write a book, and I haven't a clue what it will be, other than my spiritual journey? And how is it that I am to share something that seems dear to my own heart but now will go out to others I don't even know?

And how is it that I know I will be guided step by step as to what to write and when to write? Shouldn't I have a direction, an outline, or a specific impression instead of this wide, huge amount of information that has had chronological order but spills in all directions in my mind so as to make it difficult to gather it together to know what to write and what not to write? But then, that is my mind chatter, and that is not the purpose. So best I leave it to what comes through from the Other Side. They know.

I recently experienced another birthday milestone. I am now up to seventy-one years. That doesn't necessarily make me wiser, but as with most seventy-year-olds, it definitely means I've accumulated numerous life experiences. As I draw closer to the final phase of my life—the golden years—I marvel at how complex we make life, when in its purest form, it is simple, consistent, and purposeful, as exhibited in the cycles of nature. Change is inevitable, and it all happens quite naturally, just as the wind blows and the seas ebb and flow—sometimes furiously and sometimes softly. Nature can be brutal at times, but most often, the purpose is evolution.

We are all experiencing together, and we are all evolving. Always, change is inescapable during the process. The purpose of change is to learn, grow, love, and, eventually, go home after our journey is complete. The journey is important, and what we learn and how we develop on that journey are important.

As I was on my daily walk this morning, I pondered what I would write in the preface to my cult experience narrative of the late 1970s to the early 90s. I had to ask myself again, "For what purpose am I writing this book? Who is my audience?"

When I reflect on the pain I caused myself and my children during the cult years, my most immediate reaction is to put out a warning to those who might take a similar life detour—a sidestep that eventuates in needless heartache. I want to warn those of sound mind and heart to heed those who would convince them otherwise and to consider that the aggressors might not have their best interests at heart. The target audience is not necessarily just those individuals trapped in a cult. The audience can be anyone who finds him- or herself a victim of bullying. The bully could be hiding behind a religion, a corporation, a marital tie, a place of political prominence—any number of institutions that lend power to position.

My twelve-year cult experience, from my perspective, can be reduced to two opposing attitudes coming together—those who desired to control and those who allowed it, or you might say the bullies and the victims.

Throughout the years since May 1990, when I have dared to mention that I was in a religious cult for twelve years, the first response I have gotten from the listener is "Why? You seem to be a rational, intelligent individual—actually quite strong in your person. Why would you allow such control?"

I could probably answer that question in a few words, but I will attempt to answer that question in two hundred, fifty-plus pages. However, if you care to search deeper than this simple narrative of my life experience, you might find that actually, many are controlled in one form or another. Many do not challenge some of the deeper questions in life, and though they might be searching for something to bring significance to their lives, they accept what has been handed to them by parents, spouses, corporate leaders, political authorities, movie stars, religious figures—all men and women with their own belief systems, thoughts, and prejudices. Often, the result is less than satisfying.

What if in the deepest part of each person exists a divine nature that can safely and completely lead the individual to a common goal of love that doesn't want to control and doesn't want to be controlled? What if we all ask ourselves, "What if I am capable of the greatest goal—unconditional love?"

Sometimes we have to go through the fire of difficult experiences like the phoenix who rose from the ashes. Sometimes we simply have to trust our inner guidance, our inherent higher self, our gifted divine nature, and listen and follow. Some evolve quickly, and some evolve slowly. Does it matter how or when if we are all ultimately going the same direction on the Yellow Brick Road? If we take the detour through the fearful Dark Forest, we can choose to come out thankful and more determined to keep going, and we can ask questions in order to experience the most edifying answers that subscribe to a rather simple moral code: to love ourselves and our fellow man.

The main objectives are to keep our eyes on the goal, avoid following someone or something through dangerous and damaging detours, and recognize and appreciate that we are all one in the evolutionary process.

My experience took place in a nondenominational Christian fellowship of believers with a charismatic pastor. However, the same experience could have taken place in any religious group. I liken my experience to a microcosm of what the world experiences when it blindly follows narrow, exclusive doctrines and divisive belief systems that are capable of some of the most heinous crimes—reducing the goal to "The end justifies the means" rather than the goal of loving unconditionally.

Whose responsibility is it to maintain a worthy goal and not be used and manipulated? Whose responsibility is it to ask questions, research, gain knowledge, and listen to a loving heart that supports the basic laws of love of self and others? It is mine. It is yours. It is a choice.

The purpose of my narrative is not to condemn the offenders but to encourage victims to be strong and take personal responsibility. We can let go of our end of the rope when battling in a tug-of-war with bullies who are determined to pull us in their direction when our heart tells us otherwise. What happens to the bullies when we let go and walk away? They fall, and they are faced with their own responsibility. If every victim were to relax fear and take courage, the bullies would have no recourse but to face their own demons of insecurity and fear and move on their own toward wholeness or destruction—also a choice.

I retained religious vernacular throughout the narrative, typical to my status as a Christian at the time, such as is evident in the original document I presented to members when I left the cult. I have traveled several years since, asking questions and researching, and I currently prefer not to limit my belief system to any one religion, mainly because all religions embrace the same basic moral principles. Additionally, my understanding and acceptance now are not exclusive to those who are averse to religion entirely or even those who prefer not to define or believe in a higher power.

I personally hold to a belief in a loving Divine Source, but the more I travel, the more mysterious is the concept of God. I prefer to refer to God as a Source of Love. I also believe that enveloped in that love are all those who have moved on beyond the veil to higher dimensions far less restricted than our third-dimensional planetary existence. Additionally, I accept the understanding that our loved ones are close to us and watch over us. But that is my current belief system, and I don't intend to impose my perspective on anyone. There are many perspectives and always will be. There is no harm in different belief systems, provided our overriding goals are to be tolerant and to love and not harm our fellow man.

My narrative is primarily addressed to a third person: dear reader. Sometimes I share self-talk or my thoughts current to the experience. I relived the experience from my memory pulled forth from several years past. The more painful the memory, the more vivid the recall.

I changed all of the names in my narrative for an obvious reason—to protect those who were involved.

Until we go home, we travel together in an extraordinary school to gain knowledge and understanding, seek love and be loved, and exercise the courage to travel the Yellow Brick Road that actually doesn't stop at Oz. I believe the travel is a privilege and a responsibility.

Acknowledgments

I acknowledge all those on this side of the veil who know the truth of the cult journey and who patiently listened to me and collaborated while I relived the pain of twenty-eight years ago. Again, I acknowledge my sons—the two eldest for their intelligent cooperation and contribution to the writing and my youngest for his many philosophical conversations.

I acknowledge all those on the Other Side who journeyed with me as I applied my life narrative to documentation—some who experienced the cult and some who are my champions in camaraderie—to help others avoid the missteps due to unnecessary and unfounded guilt, fear, and shame.

How can I say how much I love you?

Introduction to Dear Reader

I came out of the cult in May 1990. I was forty-three years old. It took me about three years to deliver myself from rage. During that three-year period, I attempted several times to write about the cult years, which were from 1978 to 1990. Surrounding those writing attempts, I would have what I refer to as "naked dreams"—nighttime dreams of trying to move about in public life bereft of either clothing or the necessary means to fit in to society.

In my dream, I could be walking down the street, crossing busy intersections, and suddenly realize I was wearing inappropriate clothing—like just a bra and underpants with no shoes!

"Yikes! I want to run and hide!"

Sometimes the dreams were more subtle, such as attending a formal affair wearing tennis shoes, while most ladies were in dress high heels. In those dreams, my hazy dream mind would struggle with how to deal with the inappropriate, when all the while, I was miserable with the knowledge that I was not okay.

Other dreams would surface as well, such as forgetting to study for a test or not remembering my gym locker combination and being unable to get to my gym clothes. My worries would be "I will be late for class," "I will be marked tardy," "I am exposed," or "I am ill prepared."

Yes, it is pretty obvious. I wasn't ready to tackle writing a book about my cult experience in the early 1990s. I felt too naked, too vulnerable. I had too much anxiety. Those were years when I needed to understand myself and look for the reasons that I allowed myself to be entrapped and imprisoned by another person's or group's belief system.

There is one major difference between the book I would have written twenty-eight years ago and what I want to express here. That first book would have been primarily about entrapment and blame: *Watch Out for the Bad Guy Who Lurks About*, a fear-based literary endeavor. In contrast, and with several more years of life experience, this current book focuses on freedom of choice, personal responsibility, and listening to our divine guidance—our birthright from the first day we arrive on this planet: *Nurture and Listen to the Good Guy Within*, a documented work about love.

The Yellow Brick Road through the Dark Forest

Yes, dear reader, it looks like we are going to start with a reference to the fictional story of L. Frank Baum's *The Wonderful Wizard of Oz* in order to provide you a definition of a cult. It's funny because I was going to start with a dictionary, but it appears that Spirit says otherwise.

So if we follow the story at the point where the tin man (who needs a heart), Dorothy (who wants to get back home to Kansas), and the scarecrow (who needs a brain) are journeying down the Yellow Brick Road through the Dark Forest, we find that they are confronted with notions of fear. Fear! Yikes! The road is obscured, the trees darken the sun, and occasional deep growling sounds in the forest evoke notions of large, scary animals hidden among the trees.

They continue on because they seek the Wizard of Oz to help them acquire what they need (heart, home, and brain) to be whole and complete, and guess what? Fear enters their consciousness! What could happen on this scary journey through the Dark Forest? Their worst fears are realized when a huge lion bounds out from the woody darkness and onto the road with a deafening roar.

Unbeknownst to the journeying threesome, the lion is really a coward. But he puts them on the defensive with his loud, intimidating growls and bullying behavior. With his strong paws, he strikes a blow to the frail, flimsy scarecrow, sending him hurling; and he knocks down the tin woodsman with his sharp claws. He is a bully. He is also a coward, because he then goes after the smallest and most innocent victim of all to show his prowess: Dorothy's little dog, Toto. Big mistake, Mr. Lion Bully. (As a sidenote, the dog is not intimidated by the lion and barks at him, most likely because his instincts are pure and not doubted.)

Dorothy, who loves her little dog and already feels defensive of her newly acquired friends, grabs Toto and, without fear, smacks the lion square on the nose. Dorothy tells the lion he should be ashamed of himself for trying to bite a poor little dog. "You are nothing but a big coward!"

It's a turning point. The lion breaks down and cries and reveals that he is really a coward. We could carry an analogy further and also point out that Dorothy, a merciful soul, melts with the lion's confession that he is cowardly and afraid, and her love and compassion triumph over and erase the fear.

That's what a cult is. A cult is a belief system that bullies and disempowers those who journey toward wholeness, intimidating them with an overpowering voice, keeping them off balance, and putting them on the defensive, thereby keeping them in subjection and fear, when in reality, the cult (or leader thereof) is a coward.

The analogy carried out would indicate that only love can break the cycle of fear that unnecessarily causes us to become victims of bullying. We need to love and believe in ourselves and understand that the Source of Love can give us all the help we need in our quest for wholeness.

Does that make sense? Well, it will make more sense as we journey together, dear reader, because don't we all seek a heart that receives and gives love, a sense of home and belonging, and a brain that gains knowledge and understanding and makes proper choices? How many times in our seeking has fear put us on a path that has caused us to doubt ourselves and make less-than-positive choices for ourselves—choices that brand us as victims to someone who senses that fear and insecurity and capitalizes on it?

We give away our power. Our quest to be loved, belong, and be in control of our lives becomes instead imprisonment and a nightmare. We are bullied into subjection, when we are really being held unnecessarily by cowardice—perpetuating fear and eliminating love. It's just a detour. We have the power and the birthright to release ourselves from being victims and propel ourselves into freedom. It sounds easy—why wouldn't we? But first, we need the courage to change our thinking and possibly our outdated belief systems. We need to ask ourselves the big questions, such as "What if I am believing a lie?"

PART 1
LOOKING BACK

✝ Formative Years

Why?

One of the first questions I asked myself when I came out of the cult was "Why did I let the cult leader and his family bully me into a community lifestyle that was cumbersome and devoid of joy and personal choice?"

This question took me back to childhood. Where did this all start—this insecurity that caused me to be in a cult?

I remember getting out an old baby picture of me, taken when I was about ten months old. I was prompted to ask myself some questions: "Who is that? What do you note about this baby you call you?"

Since I had loving parents when I came onto the scene in the late 1940s, my photo revealed me as a happy, wispy-haired, chubby little blonde girl in a silky, plain off-white gown. My wide-open eyes and big smile said, "Hey, here I am! I am open to the world and pretty darned happy with everything so far."

When I think of the formative years, birth to five or six years old, I have several outstanding remembrances.

I can picture myself in my backyard, wearing a mustard-yellow terrycloth bathing suit as I ran through the sprinklers. Immediately following the war years, our entertainment in those days was simple. To romp through the grass barefoot on a hot summer day and feel

Makena McChesney

the consistent *splash, splash, splash* of cool water was a delicious memory of joy and power.

I felt in command of myself. My joy had no bounds, and I felt as if I were one of the monarch butterflies in abundance among myriad garden flowers planted by my mom. I liked to kneel next to her and experience the damp, squishy earth as she troweled through the dirt bed, discarding weeds and uncovering long, wiggly pink worms. Then I was off again to bathe in magical water sprinkles that refracted silvery rainbows. I can almost smell that backyard when I close my eyes: the grass, the earth, and the unbelievable scent of roses and calla lilies.

I was happy and free.

Another formative remembrance took place when I was about six years old, as I walked home alone from school through the back alley. I came across what I later understood as a hydrophobic dog. He approached me with sharp bared teeth and was foaming at the mouth. He seemed huge and was probably a German shepherd or something of that size and nature.

He growled and snarled at me, and with those sharp, intimidating teeth, he grabbed the scarf I was carrying in my hand. Though I was crying and afraid, I would not let go of the scarf. The scarf was mine, not this monster's! I was all about justice, and this wasn't going to happen! I have many recollections of praying for and manifesting my heart's desires at early ages, and that was certainly no exception.

I cried, prayed silently, and tugged at the scarf as if playing tug-of-war with a rope. I planned to win. I can't say how long that went on. My guess is not long, because I wasn't all that brave—just stubborn. I remember the dog releasing the scarf, turning, and walking away. I had a habit of saying thank you when prayers were answered, so I'm sure that utterance was sent to heaven immediately following that experience.

As a young girl, I enjoyed engaging in what my sister and I called "pretty-tend" world. When we got together with our cousins of similar ages, we would put on our mother's (or aunt's, depending on which home we were at) high heels and costume jewelry. We were acquainted in those early years with watching the romantic movies of the 1950s, so we would name ourselves the favorite actresses of the time. My sister and I were the blondes—Betty Grable, Bette Davis, or Doris Day; our brunette cousins were Linda Darnell, Esther Williams, or Ava Gardner.

We would roll paper into "cigarettes" and pour ourselves "champagne" from the water faucet. We would use words like *dahling*, and we were undaunted if we decided to take a stroll down the street, our lips painted ruby red, while clopping in our oversize high heels. We knew we were beautiful. We knew we were awesome. Pretty-tend.

Okay, so far, the profile of this victim is joyful and powerful; tenacious, strong-willed, stubborn, and principled; and imaginative, creative, and confident. This description doesn't sound like someone who would someday become a victim.

Unnecessary Guilt

What else? Guilt ridden. I was guilt ridden. I came into this world feeling guilty. My mother and older sisters would say that while I was sitting in my infant high chair during a family meal, if I spilled my milk, no one dared to look at me with any accusatory or even surprised expression, or I would burst into tears.

I was highly sensitive. I cried easily. I was perfectionistic. I hated sticky hands and the snow that was too cold. I cried over the cats who were found dead in the street and travailed over the dog chasing our car on the way to church, dodging traffic.

If anything went wrong and I was in the vicinity, I would immediately own the blame, logically knowing I wasn't at fault. In one incident, when I was about five years of age, my sister, five years senior to me, plugged in the vacuum cleaner. The plug shorted out at the receptacle, causing sparks that left a black circle on the wall and blackened my sister's hand. Crying, I followed her to find our mother while screaming, "I killed her! I killed her!"

On another occasion, when I was six, I reacted the same with my little brother, who was about three years old. I built a swing with rope and an old board in the willow tree behind the house. I wrapped the rope around the lowest tree branch and tied it further to some free-standing fencing that leaned against the shed nearby. He grabbed the rope near the fencing and pulled it down on himself. It resulted in a broken arm. Once again, I ran with him to Mom while yelling, "I killed him! I killed him!"

So I either had an overworked imagination or brought something forward from a past life for which I felt guilty. I'm not sure, but I was definitely and unnecessarily guilt ridden. I had a psychic friend tell me years later, "Guilt nails you to the wall."

Okay, so now we are getting somewhere. It isn't difficult to imagine that an oversensitive, self-blaming, self-doubting person could be a victim if the bully knows what buttons to push, particularly if that bully can point out something specific to accuse.

I am now going to move along to a period that underscored that guilt and embedded it into my overactive conscience. Before I do, I want to let you know that I will eventually describe more about the cult. Please bear in mind, however, that the cult can represent any type of victimization whereby a victim becomes prey by choice.

We can choose an abusive spouse. We can succumb to a tyrannical employer. We can choose many experiences that place us in what seems a prison of sorts. I am not speaking here of the victimization of innocent young children or the helpless elderly, though abuse at an early age can certainly lead to choices throughout life that require a change in thinking in order for one to experience freedom from entrapment. In these instances, for the young child and the elderly, choice is not an option.

Seeking Oz

Please travel with me, dear reader, as we follow Dorothy down the Yellow Brick Road. "Who is Dorothy?" you ask. Dorothy is you, and Dorothy is me.

We all seek Oz.

✝ Later Childhood and Adolescence

Early Church Indoctrination

I remember being somewhere beneath my eldest sister, who was probably standing on a chair while my aunt hemmed her hand-sewn 1950s prom dress. My sister had to have been about fifteen or sixteen years old, so that would make me four or five years old. We are still talking about the formative years, but this memory stayed with me during my later childhood years and adolescence.

My sister was beautiful. She was also mature for her years, unlike my middle sister and me, who would eventually be what you would call "late bloomers." The dress was full length and huge and billowy. She must have had on a hoop skirt or crinoline petticoat. The dress was a sight to behold, and in those moments, I believed my sister was a princess. The material was some kind of taffeta or satin that was bright turquoise blue with pink material flowers sewn about the bodice and lowered neckline.

My aunt was a talented seamstress, and she created a vision of excitement and wonder as I watched my sister stand quietly. My sister easily could have been Cinderella, and my aunt was the fairy godmother magically transforming her from the ordinary to the magnificent. The feelings I felt were also magical, stirring within me something to which I aspired for myself someday.

Why is that memory significant? Because the possibility of preparing for the ball was not an option for me as time went on.

Something changed from that time period to my later childhood years and adolescence. Childhood is interesting because experiences, processes, and timelines are not necessarily significantly understood at the time. You just remember feelings tied to experiences.

Unbeknownst to me, a timeline emerged whereby my parents became more involved in church—a Pentecostal church. Sometime between my sister's princess dress and about eight years of age, I was not allowed to consider dancing or going to movie picture shows. Somehow, those activities, along with playing cards using the euchre deck, were associated with the devil. Those activities were not filled with wonder and excitement; they were sinful. Though my parents weren't necessarily against dance and the theater, they were honest people who followed rules, and since they had joined the church, they believed they needed to uphold the doctrines.

I remember a few confrontations in my earlier childhood years, around seven or eight years of age, when I challenged my parents about going to church. I didn't like the hard pews, and the environment in the evening meetings was particularly disturbing. Nearing the end of what seemed to be an interminable, boring session, people would go to the front of the church and wail and cry. Being empathic, I absorbed feelings that were dark and unwelcome. I cried and asked that I not have to go to church in the evenings. My dad was rigid and adamant in that regard. He was not an unkind man, nor did he ever punish us physically in anger. He was a good father. He was generally cheerful, smiling, and optimistic. However, his word was law, and there would be no argument. I would obey.

After a few of those confrontations, I felt guilty—that I was bad for not wanting to go to church. I was bad to question my dad's authority. Church was a holy place, a place where God met with us and expected us to be sorry for our sins. I had fond thoughts of God, who was huge, awesome, and sacred, but more so of Jesus, who was portrayed in my Sunday school stories as being close to people, walking among them, healing them, and encouraging them.

However, God, at times, seemed distant and was easily angered. He was capable of throwing his children into the fiery depths of hell. Best I obey and not question. Right?

So thankfully, I did derive feelings of well-being in my child mind in relation to Jesus, who was there for me in spite of my distaste for the church life. I prayed to Jesus on a regular basis and felt comfortable asking him for even the smallest thing:

"Please help me with this test."

"Please help me not to be afraid of the dark."

"Please help me find the dime I lost."

Rarely did he let me down, for which I was thankful.

But in spite of my relationship with Jesus, throughout those years, I felt guilty. Eventually, I was one who made my way to the altar on many Sunday evenings. The pastor or visiting evangelist, following a sermon, would present an altar call. The altar call was for publicly confessing sin, which was, in my mind, anything not perfect or, as defined in the Bible, "falling short of the glory of God." Tall order!

The plea was always accompanied by somber hymns about how unworthy and wormlike we are, full of sin. We would sing the words over and over while we were presented a frightening visual: we could walk out the door with remaining sin, get hit by a car, and go to the eternal fiery pit of hell. These altar calls were my biggest introduction to a shame-based, fear-based religion that I didn't dare question.

To make matters worse, I wanted to dance. I really, really wanted to dance. I begged my mom to let me take ballet. The answer was always an emphatic no. I am not sure I originally understood that her reasons for turning me down were related to church doctrine. We children were accustomed to being told no due to the economic times. Anything that cost money was met with a no.

At any rate, in time, I knew that not only would I not be able to dance, but I certainly needed to keep any of those desires to myself—they were shameful in the eyes of the church, whatever that meant. Deep down, I knew my mother had no aversion to dancing.

Makena McChesney

She told stories of how she used to dance as a young girl. All I knew was that we needed to obey the church rules and not question them. We needed to be above reproach among our fellow churchgoers.

The same required obedience pertained to going to the movie theater. We knew that Mom had been an usher in the theater in her younger years, and she loved to tell us stories about the old movie stars. Then, one day, we were not allowed to go. Again, I knew that my mom and dad knew better, but we needed to obey the church's rules. Somehow, the church knew better than my mom and dad. The church was associated with God, and God was all-powerful and not to be questioned. I stood guilty for not agreeing in my heart. But I obeyed—mostly out of fear, not love. I never questioned whether or not God was love. Instead, I questioned and doubted myself. I was guilty.

† Adolescence and Early Adulthood

No Blame—Just Lessons

Before we continue down the Yellow Brick Road, dear reader, please let me insert here that when presenting the background explanation of why I became involved in a cult—became a victim as such—I want to steer clear of blame. As mentioned earlier, this is a document to establish the need for personal responsibility when we find ourselves entrapped in a less-than-positive experience on our journey to wholeness. You might even say, in some cases, such experiences might be a necessity, a catalyst, to break us open, to apply pressure in order to bring us closer to wholeness.

I place no blame on loving parents who guided me the best way they understood to be an upstanding person. How could I possibly blame them for raising me in a fear-based, shame-based religion, when I eventually took the baton from there and imposed an even more confining belief system on my three sons?

I also don't blame the religious institution from which I came, nor do I blame the subsequent religious cult, as those structures, though toxic to me, might have been perfect stepping-stones for some who sought security in a more controlling environment. But as individuals, we all know when we are in those dark valleys and experience loss of peace. We need to acknowledge that and have the courage to go ahead and ask the questions. We will get answers.

So as I journeyed toward adulthood, I was pretty well entrenched in a less-than-satisfying religion and even acquired some judgmental attitudes toward those who didn't share my beliefs.

Beneath the repressed layers of my soul, however, did I really believe that the sweet, kind neighbor next door who never stepped foot inside a church would, after this lifetime, burn in hell?

Didn't I have thoughts, even as a young child, that would emerge occasionally, such as *I have always been and will forever be*?

Didn't I crave to have innumerable biblical questions answered, such as when reading the story about a snake tempting the first woman ever created?

A talking snake? Really? And how could multiple ethnicities come from one man and one woman? If the flood destroyed all mankind except Noah and his family in the timeframe proposed in the Bible, how did so many ethnicities develop from there? If everything originates from God and God is pure love, why and wherefore came evil and the devil, or Satan?

The answers were all supposed to be in the Bible—God's final word on any subject. In order to balance out the disappointment I often felt regarding the Bible, I absorbed and put to memory many beautiful, positive scriptures that resonated with me and kept me intact where my religion was concerned.

I loved that Jesus was a friend to the imperfect people— the sinners—and he would eat with them and spend time with them. When the religious leaders questioned that alliance, Jesus responded, "They that be whole need not a physician, but they that are sick" (Matthew 9:12 KJV).

Jesus loved children. Great! Children, to me, were the embodiment of transparency and authenticity. My observation growing up was that generally, children had no guile—no premeditated, malicious agenda. They spoke their truths and quickly shed grievances. They grabbed on to unconditional love and reciprocated with warmth and adoration. They also recognized the difference between the genuine and the contrived. When the religious leaders disallowed the children

Seeking Oz

to come close to Jesus, he responded, "Suffer the little children to come unto me, and forbid them not: for of such is the kingdom of God" (Matthew 10:14 KJV).

To me, the soundest ideology of all was in the following: "Do to others as you would have them do to you" (Luke 6:31 NIV), and "Love your neighbor as yourself" (Romans 13:9 NIV).

In stark contrast, there were scriptures in the Bible that were less than positive. They bludgeoned all my thoughts about a loving God. There were innumerable scriptures about hell. Hell was a place to which God would banish the less-than-perfect person—the so-called sinful person or the person who rejected God's sacrifice of his son, Jesus. Those scriptures were haunting and disturbing, such as "And if thy hand offend thee, cut it off: it is better for thee to enter into life maimed, than having two hands to go into hell, into the fire that never shall be quenched" (Mark 9:43 KJV).

In my mind's eye, hell was to be avoided at all cost. I thought, *Hell is an unending, burning, painful existence. Best I cut off anything offensive in my life—anything that does not appease the God of the Bible.*

Also, there was the following verse: "And [the angels] shall cast them [those who practice lawlessness] into a furnace of fire: there shall be wailing and gnashing of teeth" (Matthew 13:42 KJV).

My child mind told me, *The blessed, beautiful angels will cast the sinners into a fiery furnace (ouch!). The burning sinners will not just cry; they will wail! They will grind their teeth in utter determination to endure the everlasting, burning torture.*

According to scripture, it appeared the odds were in favor of entering hell rather than heaven: "Because strait is the gate, and narrow is the way, which leadeth unto life, and few there be that find it" (Matthew 7:14 KJV).

Not encouraging!

Clearly, there was to be no mercy for the rich man. His destiny was hell: "And again I say unto you, it is easier for a camel to go through the eye of a needle, than for a rich man to enter into the kingdom of God" (Matthew 19:24 KJV).

Those were only a few of the scriptures that troubled my questioning and imaginative mind.

But faith was supposed to be the answer to all questions related to my religion because how dare I even question? After all, the Bible was the infallible Word of God.

Hanging on to the positive while enduring the negative was generally the formula I used to reckon with a fear-based, shame-based religion. I carried that formula forward, as you will learn, dear reader, as a victim journeying down the Yellow Brick Road.

Infatuation at Sixteen

Journeying on to age sixteen, I met the man who would become my husband and the father of my two eldest sons.

At that time, how did I stack up with the tin man, Dorothy, the scarecrow, and the lion on this side of Oz?

I could relate to each of them. My heart yearned for completion, to be fulfilled by receiving love from this man who captured my attention entirely. My greatest desire was to create a home and have a family so I could give and receive love. I would have a sense of belonging, an arrival of some kind of my own liking. My thoughts were clouded at that stage, ruled totally by my own impulses and hormones. My brain could have used more logic, but I felt quite adult in my decision to move forward in marriage. Was I afraid? Not yet, but I was soon to be. Again, the brain was not fully engaged.

This man was the antithesis of the stereotypical churchgoing young men I was exposed to in the young people's groups. I guess you might say the attraction I had for him overpowered any caution provided in my upbringing. The rebellion I repressed in early childhood surfaced in the form of an infatuation that couldn't be extinguished. Steve was six feet four inches tall, strong and athletic in his build. He was twenty-two years old and had been a high school basketball athlete who made his mark six years previously. He was serious and intelligently intense in his demeanor, and somehow, I had captured his attention. It thrilled me completely!

I met him when a tire exploded on my old 1950 Ford. I was still in high school but on my way to an interview for a part-time job. As I made a right turn onto a main road near our neighborhood corner gas station, my front passenger-side tire blew. I thought there was an altercation at the bar across the boulevard because the startling blast sounded just like a gunshot. Not until the car lunged and jerked to a slow halt did I realize it was my tire.

Steve came running out from the gas station to the car. I assumed he worked there, so I quickly complied when he suggested I move over to the passenger side so he could drive the car into the gas station parking lot. Within a short time, he replaced my tire with the spare in the trunk. When I offered to pay him, he smiled and said he didn't work there; he was just stopping in to get gas. Instead of payment, he said, he would like my phone number. Though I'd been taught not to entertain strangers and never to give away personal information, I knew in my heart, which prevailed over anything else at the time, that this man was a good man, and I thought, *Wow! He is very good looking indeed!*

Dear reader, please understand at this point in time what my self-image was in my mind's eye. I believed I was unattractive and somewhat of a misfit. I got straight As throughout most of middle school and all of high school. I received awards for my academic achievements. I was respected by my peers but not included in any popular inner circles. I later learned that exclusion was my own doing as I created my own blocks, envisioning myself as square or overly studious in everyone's eyes.

My youngest son made a comment to me not long ago when he saw my high school photo: "Mom, you said you were homely when you were in high school. I don't see that at all in this photo. You were really pretty." Well, I guess if I was, I was the last to know that, because I felt I was too skinny, overly tall, and somewhat awkward.

I dated Steve for a short period and was totally smitten. He then stopped calling. But for some reason, I didn't let go of him in my mind. I didn't give myself the negative talk I was so accustomed to in those early to late teen years, such as "He decided he didn't like me. I am not pretty enough. I am not curvy enough. I am too shy."

I held him in my mind. I pictured him; I drew pictures of him on my binder and notebooks. I prayed for him to come back into my life. Yes, I knew where he lived, and I knew his phone number, but I was old school. A girl never called the boy. The boy initiated—always! There were no exceptions! Long before I knew the meaning of the word *manifestation*, I was intent on manifesting this man back into my life.

Relational Red Flags

Were there red flags that this man would not necessarily be good for me? Yes, but I blocked them out. Instead, I thought, *Steve is older and not silly and obnoxious like the high school boys. Besides, the high school boys are not interested in me. He had to be interested. He wouldn't have pursued me at all, even though the time was short.*

For some reason, I would not give up.

There was some indication that he drank alcohol—not when he was with me, but I noticed his speech would be slurred on occasion when he called me on the phone. My parents were teetotalers, but I had uncles who drank; so I did recognize the signs.

Steve had had several previous relationships with women. I had no experience with male suitors whatsoever, just unreciprocated crushes. That profile made him, by the church's definition,

Seeking Oz

worldly—something I craved. I had been living on the outside perimeters of experimenting with life.

The biggest red flag of all was the fact that Steve was not what the church called "saved." He hadn't invited Jesus into his life so that he would be free from eternal hell and damnation. Per my religion, there was one way only for a person to enter into the gates of heaven after crossing over from the earthly plane.

Even as I write this, I marvel that anyone would think that the Source of Love would slam the door shut on his or her creation based on a particular belief system.

I thought, *But the Bible does say the way is narrow, does it not? And the Bible, of course, is not to be questioned. But what if ...?*

But that is a conversation for much later.

At that time in my life, some part of me—the brainwashed part—believed the biblical references to the narrow way to be true, yet I would ignore that Steve was not walking the same path as me, possibly because some part of me wanted to believe that the way was not that narrow, our love for each other would cover any differences in our belief systems, and he would eventually become a Christian like me. Wrong!

Steve did eventually call me, and the rest is history. We dated for two years. Toward the end of that period, because I felt guilty about premarital intimacy, Steve offhandedly suggested we get married. He said I reminded him of his mother. That comparison didn't exactly strike me as a romantic notion, but I was intuitive enough to realize that he was being influenced by his parents to go in my direction. Because I was so in love with him, I took that as a proposal. We talked of marriage and became engaged two months prior to the wedding in January 1966. I was always thankful for the newspaper engagement announcement in November 1965 because almost exactly nine months later, our first son was born. I was nineteen years old, and Steve was twenty-five.

If you've ever watched the 1961 Natalie Wood and Warren

Makena McChesney

Beatty movie *Splendor in the Grass*, you can understand a little of the shame that accompanied premarital sex and, particularly, a pregnancy before marriage in that day.

My mother was a nervous wreck when planning the wedding as I started showing signs of pregnancy—mainly vomiting two to three times a day. At first, I thought it was the flu, but my mother, who was paranoid that any of her girls not be virgins prior to marriage, picked up on my symptoms and was quick to confront me, taking me to the doctor immediately. Needless to say, my guilt overwhelmed me and was accentuated by my mother's reaction. Her foremost concern was that her church friends and the pastor not know I was pregnant.

However, I remember feeling angry with her. I was already ashamed. I was prepared to admit the truth—to stand up before the church and confess my sin. However, I was trapped with feelings of concealment in order for my mother to save face among her friends. Did I confront her? Of course not. I kept my guilt and shame stuffed inside while dealing with her condemning attitude during the wedding plans and throughout the wedding.

I remember glancing at my dad just prior to his giving me away. Daddy stoically kept his feelings to himself. I had no idea where he weighed in on the terrible situation I had caused, but something inside me reminded me that I was carrying a precious baby, and that baby was a blessing—a little bit of me and a little bit of this man I loved deeply. I was on a journey in which we would be a happy unit, moving toward Oz.

I was wrong.

Within six months of our marriage, and at a time when I was about to give birth, I knew Steve was an alcoholic. He didn't just have a beer now and then, as he'd told me before we got married. He consumed many, many beers and staggered, swayed, slurred, and delivered abusive speech to ensure I didn't oppose him. Because I was overwhelmed by that behavior, he hid it from me by staying away from home for several hours at a time after work and on the weekends.

Because I was embarrassed and ashamed, I kept his behavior a secret and did everything to make sure my family was unaware. I am sure it is no coincidence that my two sisters, having been raised to be submissive wives, similarly hid their husbands' poor behavior, as I learned many years later.

How could our husbands possibly live up to the example that our dad provided us? Why did we choose husbands who were less than kind and verbally abusive, when we had a perfect example in our father?

After ten years of living with an alcoholic husband and experiencing hints of his unfaithfulness and another child later, I turned to what I knew best: God and the religion introduced by my consistent and loving parents.

During that marriage, I regularly attended church and took my two young sons, making sure they received the teachings I had received. However, nearing the ten-year mark, I became weary, unhappy, and disillusioned with my marriage. I wanted in the worst way to divorce this man and walk away to raise my sons on my own.

However, I was an at-home mom, as was popular in that day, and the thought of going into the workplace and leaving my children with day-care providers broke my heart. My children were everything to me. I would have left Steve much earlier if it weren't for that concern, and of course, I didn't have proven Bible grounds, adultery. I felt trapped and imprisoned.

What I'd believed to be my road to wholeness instead became failure, and I stood guilty. I married a man who ultimately caused me and my children pain. There was no physical abuse, but we endured plenty of verbal abuse and neglect, which can be just as damaging.

We are getting close, dear reader, to where I was the perfect candidate for the cult life that presented itself. I not only chose a wrong path for myself but also chose a difficult path for my children.

I thought, *I messed up. My journey down the Yellow Brick Road so far has proven that I didn't get the loving heart I sought to complete me; my sense of belonging and creating a warm, stable home is shattered; and my brain repeats to me that I am at fault and don't make good choices.*

Now I was prey to fear and vulnerable to a label that accentuated my apparent insecurity: "unequally yoked."

Unequally Yoked

According to my religious upbringing and the Bible, I had entered into a marital relationship that is summed up in the admonishing scripture "Do not be yoked together with unbelievers. For what do righteousness and wickedness have in common? Or what fellowship can light have with darkness?" (2 Corinthians 6:14 NIV).

To my understanding, the only hope for my marriage and a positive home environment for my sons was that my husband become a Christian.

So I prayed for Steve to become a Christian. I prayed for myself to be able to cope. I prayed for my sons' protection. At that time, I was attending a small church of the same Pentecostal denomination of my childhood in a rural area approximately forty miles from the large city of my upbringing. I was away from parental scrutiny and chose not to attend any formal services in the morning or evening but took my children to the early sessions of Sunday school, where they could receive the same education I had received.

The parishioners were friendly and kind and only pressured me now and then to attend more services. In time, they allowed me to teach a kindergarten Sunday school class without making any other demands that I participate in the other services.

I chose not to integrate further into the small rural church for several reasons. I didn't want them to know that my husband was an alcoholic. I didn't want to experience any of the dreary altar calls that took place on Sunday evenings and weeknights during revivals when guest evangelists were brought in, nor did I want to expose my children. In general, I wanted to keep my life private.

I didn't share my situation with anyone. My parents had an idea that Steve was a drinker but didn't know he was an alcoholic or absent from the home a great deal. They liked him because he was a hard worker. He made good money, and they knew the children and I would be well cared for in that regard.

Steve worked as a welder in the trades, and when he was out of work due to a lag in construction, he did auto bodywork on the side. He also bought old vehicles and fixed them up and sold them. We both participated in flipping homes, which, at the time, wasn't as popular an idea. We bought and sold two houses that were in disrepair and fixed them up. The second home was in the foothills, as mentioned, about forty miles from the city. He did the construction, and I painted inside and out and added to the decor in the way of sewing curtains and hanging wallpaper—making the home appealing. We made extra money that way, and we eventually bought some acreage and built a home, doing as much of the work as possible. Steve was actually a workaholic, and that was partly why he drank—because he couldn't relax.

Steve was definitely what you would call a "working alcoholic." During the early years of our marriage, when we worked on the houses, he would start drinking early in the afternoon and continue until he was not functional. That was often when he would get in the car and go to a bar or hang out with friends whom I never met. We lived together, but we had separate lives other than the sideline of working on the houses.

As is the case with living with an alcoholic, there were emergency situations. He received drunk driving citations, and I would be called to pick him up. Twice he was in auto accidents, and the vehicles were totaled. I have been thankful many times that the consequences of his reckless behavior when intoxicated didn't involve any innocent victims or touch the children and me—at least physically. Also, he was unreasonably possessive and controlling. If I went anywhere for any length of time, he would call me and angrily insist I get home. Of course, by the time I got home, he would be in a drunken stupor or gone.

But, dear reader, though living with Steve was extremely difficult, I loved this man. I still love this man, though he crossed over to the Other Side several years ago. His body succumbed to diabetes at age twenty-eight, he was on insulin by his midthirties, and he died of heart failure at age fifty-eight, eighteen years after I divorced him.

I learned a great deal from him. I learned not to feel sorry for myself. I learned to be emotionally strong for my children and to put their feelings and safety uppermost. He taught me what it was to work hard physically and not give up.

I recall one occasion early in our marriage, when he was battling the effects of the flu while putting in a sprinkler system in the front yard. Though he was perspiring from fever, he manually shoveled through layer after layer of hard red-clay earth, creating the trenches that received his flu-induced vomit. As I watched him, admiring his perseverance, I travailed over a man who couldn't truly love himself or anyone else. This was a man who created a void in his life because he was escaping from the pain of a dysfunctional family life during his formative years.

No matter what I did to create a happy home and provide well-behaved children, nothing seemed to keep him from his self-destructive path. I long ago forgave him of his abusive behavior and unfaithfulness. I have since asked his forgiveness for my inability to relate to his pain and my intolerance for his drinking. Unequally yoked? Yes.

Cowardly Lion

About ten years into the marriage, I found that I was unhappy and feeling trapped. I was living with an alcoholic and essentially acting as a single parent, raising my children on my own and hiding my pain and embarrassment from everybody—family, friends, and the church.

One Sunday during that period, when I was responsible for my kindergarten Sunday school class during a special church program, I sat in one of the first few pews in the main sanctuary with seven or eight little guys and gals who all had what we call today attention deficit disorder. I considered and still consider that behavior normal under the circumstances. As mentioned earlier in my narrative, I had an aversion to hard church pews as well. It was perfectly normal.

At any rate, whoever was officiating at the time asked if anyone wanted to come forward to lead one of the church songs listed on the church bulletin. Someone behind me whispered in a forceful male voice, "How about you? Why don't you go forward?" I froze in my seat. I had flashbacks of being called to the front of the class to spontaneously do a math problem on the blackboard or being required to sing in the teen church choir, when I could barely carry a tune.

I thought, *Now I am an adult and am able to avoid any such uncomfortable situations, and here is a man behind me, prodding me to get up and do something I am entirely unequipped to do. I haven't the inclinations or the talent!*

I immediately mistrusted that person. *How dare he invade my space and tell me what to do, when he doesn't even know me or anything about me. But this is a churchgoing person. Why then is he so brash and insistent?*

Enter the lion—the cowardly lion, the bully, the later-to-be cult leader. No subtle foreshadowing here, dear reader. You have to know how I felt about that intrusive man from day one. Did my intuition warn me? Yes. Did I listen? Yes, but only for about a year. Had I not eventually doubted myself, my journey down the Yellow Brick Road would not have taken a major detour. But was it a detour or a necessity? I can say now that if it hadn't been that detour, it would have been another, because I really needed to learn something. I needed to listen to my inner divine guidance and not turn my God-given choice over to someone or something else.

To continue with the church scenario and the lion man sitting behind me, I was surprised when I turned around to see a rather pleasant, handsome, prematurely white-haired man about fifteen years my senior mischievously smiling at me. I'd never seen him before, but I never attended the regularly scheduled Sunday morning services. I quickly dismissed the subject with a somewhat weak and frightened "No, I don't sing," and I promptly turned back around, hoping he wouldn't say anything else.

I avoided the man when I would see him in the church parking lot after Sunday school and before Sunday service. He made me feel uncomfortable.

On another occasion, after Sunday school, when I prepared to leave for home, he introduced himself and then confronted me. His stocky, muscular stature of about five feet nine inches, along with his intrusive behavior, was intimidating. He asked me why I didn't attend all of the church services. Though he was smiling and was seemingly friendly, again, I felt as if he were pushing past a safe boundary I maintained for myself, and it made me want to run.

I honestly can't recall what I said. Whatever it was, it must have been truthful because I was transparent and could never get away with telling a lie; however, I am sure I tried to keep it brief and simple. What I do remember was his accusatory demeanor. I could sense the intention behind it—to shame me. Again, my intuition was entirely correct. At that point, there was no need to fear, however, because I knew that all I needed to do was stay clear of him.

Dear reader, again, I must pause. I have been eager to introduce the cult leader to you because every good story needs to bring the antagonist out in the open fairly early in the story. Isn't that what makes life interesting? The light and the dark. The yin and the yang. The good and the bad. The victim and the bully. The antagonist and the protagonist.

At risk of spoiling the story early on, I will tell you that the cult leader is not the antagonist. The antagonist is fear. Reference again the scene on the Yellow Brick Road. All three characters are afraid of what they will encounter on the road through the Dark Forest. The cowardly lion would have been able to convince them they had reason to fear and were inferior to him had Dorothy not challenged the lion by letting go of her fear and smacking him on the nose, exposing his cowardice.

But as mentioned early on, this is my spiritual journey, and unfortunately, it was quite a long journey through the cult before I gained Dorothy's courage. You will be reminded occasionally that fear, in the form of self-doubt, was the problem throughout, fueled by a fear-based, shame-based belief system. At any given time, I could have smacked that man on the nose—figuratively, of course—and gone on my merry way, but unfortunately, the more I ignored my inner warnings, the more deeply I became entangled. However, I am getting ahead of my story.

A Move and a Snowstorm

As time went on, I became aware of trouble brewing in the little rural church I attended. Since I stayed clear of the adult services, I didn't witness any of it firsthand. However, the agitation among the members was evident, and it spilled over in the between-service parking lot gatherings.

The complaints and murmurings described the lion man as being angry and vocal in the main church service. Somehow, I could see that happening since the man was bold and outspoken. However, having attended church all my life, I understood that the formal service was no time to express opinions or grievances, and the man was certainly inappropriate. If anyone had issue with anything or anyone in the church, the matter was discussed either privately with the pastor or possibly during the adult Sunday school sessions.

Evidently, this man was challenging the old and traditional ways and making strong suggestions for change. That was all I knew, and frankly, I didn't care. I was safely removed from all of the uncomfortable confrontations and accusations taking place in the after service. I just wanted to go to Sunday school, do my part to teach young people the happy stories about Jesus, and make sure my two young boys were getting educated in the church. Besides, I had enough drama in my own private life.

Around that time, Steve and I sold our remote country home and bought property within twenty miles of the large city in which I was raised and where we'd originally met. We planned to build a home on our newly acquired property. We hired a contractor to do the framing and managed subcontracting for plumbing, electrical, and sheetrocking. We lived in a small travel trailer during the early construction and eventually moved into an unfinished house, undertaking all of the finish work ourselves over a period of a year or so.

I did dishes in the upstairs bathtub, cooked on a hot plate, and did many of the household chores the hard way while construction was still in the works. Of course, domestic life continued; Steve went to work daily, and I tended to home chores, managing the children and the household in general.

Steve's drinking continued, and tempers flared. I tried to keep confrontations away from the children, but the tension increased, and I prayed with desperation that God help me. I did not have Bible grounds to leave him (adultery), yet I knew he was probably unfaithful to me. By then, the children were older, both in primary school, and I could work outside the home and only have to cover a few hours with after-school care.

Seeking Oz

During that time, I became acquainted with a neighbor who also attended the remote rural church twenty miles from our homes. Her name was April. She was close friends with the lion man, his wife, and their five children. She was only about ten years my senior but took a motherly role when talking to me. She also encouraged me to attend later services and was insistent that I do so because she suspected my private home life was less than happy. Mainly, she recognized it because her husband at the time was also a drinker, and she was still raising a family as well. She would make phone calls to check on me periodically, and eventually, I confided in her that my husband was an alcoholic and opposed to attending church with me and the children.

April told me that the lion man was a good-hearted, wonderful Christian who wanted to make the church a better, more authentic representation of our faith, but he was receiving resistance and opposition from the pastor and parishioners in the little rural church up the hill.

One day she called and said she had wonderful news. As it turned out, the lion man was to receive a small plot of land in our town as a place to build a parsonage, and he would be starting his own church. At the time, I didn't question how he'd come to acquire the land or money to build the parsonage, but I was led to understand that it was to be part of the same Pentecostal denomination. Somehow, the transaction was an extension of the same church of which I was a member.

April was excited about the new church to be pastored by the lion man, and she encouraged me to attend. The services, for the time being, would be conducted in a neighboring campground just off the main highway. That campground was popular in the 1970s. Besides the camping provisions, there were many happy events held on the weekends. There were hay rides for the young campers, and the grounds included a man-made lake. The campground was appealing, with its oak trees, ducks, squirrels, and other wildlife.

Somehow, the lion man was able to acquire the large, open barn for Sunday morning church services.

Did I stop attending the small rural church twenty miles farther up the highway when I could attend church services within two or three miles of my home? No, not for at least a year or so. Why not? Because again, I didn't trust the lion man. I guess I should give him a name. His name was Bud Collins. Everybody called him Bud—not Mr. Collins, just Bud.

My initial impression of Bud was that he was intimidating and invasive, and I wanted to remain exclusive. Besides, I was faithful to teaching my kindergarten Sunday school class, and my children were familiar with their classes. Also, as I attended the rural church up the hill, I continued to hear murmurings of how Bud had caused division in the church, and some people left to join his group down the hill. They frowned when they spoke of him. I had no intention of attending his church.

Then, one Sunday, it snowed in our little town. We were at an elevation where it rarely snowed, and if it snowed at our elevation, we could count on the fact that it was snowing heavily twenty miles farther beyond the foothills. I could not attend church. There was no way I could travel uphill in the snow. I was unaccustomed to such traveling.

Of course, up to that time and for the past year, April had been calling frequently, inviting me to the local church services at the campground barn and raving about how wonderful it was to worship there. "Bud is such a humble, God-fearing man," she said. "He wants only for everyone to experience the love of Christ." She spoke glowingly of how he gave up his own career to take a risk and start a church. "He uprooted his entire family because he trusted God to sustain them as he launched out to follow God's leading."

By then, I was suffering in an unhappy marriage and had only the welfare of my children in mind. I received a call from April that snowy morning, encouraging me to attend the services in the barn. "Bring the children, and come to the services, Makena. I promise you; you will enjoy it!"

So I went.

PART 2
THE CULT YEARS

† Year One

I Like It!

I was pleasantly surprised. I still have fond memories of that Sunday morning. The barn was large and roomy. The space was open, high-ceilinged, and rustic. Folding chairs were set up across about half the area, and a small table was set just inside the door for what appeared to be the offering plate. I really liked that.

That scenario was unlike my formal church experience since childhood. There were no ushers standing at the ends of the long pews with their hands folded behind their backs, watching expectantly as the plate made its way down a long row. The ushers would wait patiently for everyone in the row to deposit money or not deposit money. I always felt the act of giving anonymously was ruined by that formal ritual. In this case, the plate was there for whenever the giver was so inclined.

The next thing that caught my attention was that most everyone was dressed in jeans and warm jackets. Bud was sitting in the front row in a plaid flannel shirt. No one stood in the front of the small congregation. The singing was informal and upbeat. The songs were happy and mostly about love—no somber hymns. Though the crowd was smiling and happy, there was a certain reverence among the group that felt mostly like sincere thankfulness. There were no dramatics or outbursts of regret or sadness—just joy.

I instantly felt comfortable. The place felt like home. I could be happy there. The environment resonated with the deepest part of me, which was joy—sheer joy that I knew I was and wanted to forever be. The feeling could transport me from the void provided by my unhappy marriage. What attracted me the most was that I could sense that my children felt the same way. They were now eight and twelve years old. They also felt what I felt.

Another surprise was that Bud did not deliver the message. A young twenty-year-old in the audience delivered the message while Bud sat in the audience. I say *message* because that was what it felt like. It wasn't a sermon. It wasn't an admonition. It was a message. It was just a sweet note about who Jesus is and how much he loves us. It was similar to my Sunday school message to my young kindergartners.

I thought, *I love this! Not a dull, boring sermon! This message is for both young and old. There is no need to travail over sin. We just need to recognize the love available through a Friend who knows how we really feel. Jesus is awesome. He understands! He is there for us!*

Afterward, some in attendance came up to me and introduced themselves. Altogether, there were probably about five or six couples from the church up the hill and several young people in their early twenties. I was to learn later that some of the young people were friends of Bud's children, and a few were from some type of detention camp for troubled young people who were previously under Bud's authority when he was a law enforcement officer. Evidently, his career had to do with detaining and rehabilitating wayward young people who were not old enough for formal detention.

Bud approached me with a smile of approval and charm. Sorry—did I say *charm*? Yes, charm. Everyone knows that a cult leader is charismatic. According to *Oxford American Dictionary*, the definition of *charismatic* is "exercising a compelling charm that inspires devotion in others." He was pleased that I'd finally attended the services of which he was in charge. Previously, this man had given me nothing but looks of "Shame on you," and now he was beaming with "Well done, my child. You finally are doing something right."

As I write this, dear reader, I am chuckling. How naive of me. I knew better. But in my state of mind at that time, dealing with a negligent, alcoholic husband, it felt good to get that look of approval and acceptance. Couple that with everything I had felt since the moment I stepped inside that barn, and needless to say, I was hooked.

Once I made the move to that local church, it just seemed to get better. However, the move didn't happen right away. First, I needed to give my notice to the Sunday school department up the hill that I would not be able to teach the kindergarten class any longer. They begged me to stay until they could replace me. Months went by, and that didn't happen. I was conscientious enough that I didn't challenge their delay; however, in the meantime, I received pressure from both Bud and April, who would say, "You need to give them your date of departure and stick to it. They are not wanting to let go of you."

I felt there was more behind the reluctance of the kind people to let go of me, but nevertheless, I eventually followed the admonitions of Bud and April and gave the church my final departure date. By that time, cold winter had left, and warmer weather approaching summer was on its way. I made the change to worship in the neighboring campground barn and established my allegiance to what I was told was not an affiliation to my former church after all but a nondenominational, independent church—actually, a fellowship. I liked that. I was tired of dogma and have-tos and shoulds.

I just wanted to be part of a happy, young group of people who gathered together purely because of a like-minded faith in Jesus.

A Safe, Happy Interval

I looked forward to Sundays, and my children were happy as well. After the morning message, we moved the rows of folding chairs into a large circle and sang fun, upbeat choruses. Sometimes we acted out songs, such as "Father Abraham," who had many sons. It reminded me of the hokey pokey, in which you put one arm in and one arm out. Regardless of the meaning of the song, there was action, laughter, and a little silliness.

There would be a sharing time, and I was fascinated by the variety of young people in the group who would share encouraging stories of how God was present in their day-to-day lives. One young lady, probably around twenty-seven years old, who had been hooked on a highly addictive illegal drug, exuded thankfulness and often shared that she felt free of the bondage caused from her addiction and gave credit to God, who'd delivered her. The testimonies were genuine and transparent, always happy and upbeat. There was no wailing or crying. The changes those young people were experiencing were real, and it gave me hope that my husband could be delivered from his addiction to alcohol and that my children and I could enjoy being a happy unit.

It didn't take long for me to feel a unity with the group, and children from a few of the older couples bonded with my children. In addition to Sunday morning services, we planned different events, such as Halloween parties, pumpkin-carving contests, outings, picnics, and more. The activities were always group events, and it was a fun, creative, intelligent group at that. There was a lot of humor, plenty of laughter, and sharing of great food and good times. We participated in folk dancing; put on short plays; and celebrated all of the important holidays—Easter, Christmas, Thanksgiving—all with creativity and fun activities.

On the first of May, the younger girls dressed in beautiful white dresses, wore flowers in their hair, and performed the maypole to lovely classical music. We read the same books, written by wonderful authors—both old and contemporary—and we discussed what we read and learned. We applauded the good and condemned what we deemed as the bad. We upheld everything ethical and denounced everything destructive.

It seemed that whatever we did together as a group, we threw ourselves into it as young children do at play—happily and creatively. For example, when we decided to plan and carry out an old-fashioned Victorian picnic one summer, we went all out. We divided up tasks—someone was in charge of menu and food assignment, someone was in charge of accessing the venue, and someone would research authentic Victorian outdoor games. We had to prepare costumes, and everyone dressed for the occasion, right down to the toddlers and babies. The games that required props were made to be authentic. It reminded me of when I was a child—when I would work hard and play hard with my cousins and siblings. We spent hours building outdoor forts or raking leaves just to jump in them.

The Victorian picnic took weeks to prepare for, and the joy was not just in the actual execution and picnic participation but also in the planning and preparing as well.

Needless to say, my doubts about Bud subsided.

I wondered, *Is this happy gathering of like-minded people what Bud envisioned and suggested to the formal church up the hill?*

I stood corrected. This man who'd appeared to me at first as pushy and invasive was actually proving to be bold in his convictions.

Bud challenged the dull, tired dogma of the rural church, and they were unable to relax into a freer and more joyful congregation, I thought. *In actuality, they were wrong, and Bud is right!*

I felt I was leaving the darkness of my former church and evolving into a lighter version of what it meant to be in the family of Christians.

Marriage Focus and Decline

During the first year or two, Bud conducted a class on a weeknight evening for unequally yoked wives. There were only four or five of us ladies, and I quickly came to learn that the other ladies were experiencing the similar pain of an unhappy marriage. Their husbands were entirely averse to being a part of the church, most of them were verbally abusive, and a few were alcoholics also. April, of course, was in the group. After having kept my uncomfortable situation to myself for several years, it felt good to be in the company of other ladies who shared my concerns.

We didn't focus on the negatives, however. With Bud as teacher, we instead read and studied a book together that gave us helpful instruction on how to win over our husbands. We were to be submissive, loving wives so they would see Christ in us and want to become followers of Christ. The formula for success, of course, was backed by scriptures, and it did ring true to me.

I just needed to be a perfect wife and pray for Steve's soul. In many respects, I was already submissive and was a good wife and mother. However, I disapproved of his drinking, and though I knew not to challenge him, especially when he was drunk, I felt hatred in my heart once he changed from Dr. Jekyll to Mr. Hyde. I couldn't hide my feelings. He knew. I hated his drinking, and I hated him when I saw his personality change to, what seemed to me, that of another person. That emotion of hatred had to change. I had to change those feelings. Wow! Now, that was difficult!

Actually, looking back, it was impossible for me to feel love for Steve during those times of his personality change. What I thought was success was actually my being someone else when he walked in the door late and staggering. I had to be a person who could love him unconditionally when he was in that state, so I had to smile and act as if I didn't notice he was unbelievably drunk, obnoxious, and insensitive.

After two years of spending a lot of time on my knees praying and playacting that everything was just fine, he cracked. He broke down and told me he was unfaithful. Not only was he unfaithful, but he had been in an affair with another younger woman for two years. I blew. Though I was an uptight little Christian girl and didn't curse, he had taught me quite a vocabulary of expletives, and I let loose and used them all on him.

Then I told him to get out and go to the other woman. He did go to her that night. He stayed for a couple days and then called me and told me he'd left her and was staying in the small office of a commercial building we had acquired during our marriage. At the time, he said nothing of wanting to return to the marriage, and for that, I was grateful. I felt bad that he was staying in the commercial building, but I knew we would have to work things out financially—fifty-fifty—in fairness to both of us.

Now I had Bible grounds for divorce—marital unfaithfulness, or adultery. I had wanted desperately to escape the bondage of living with a verbally abusive man with a drinking problem, though I felt that metaphorically, I would be giving up an arm or a leg in the process. I told you, dear reader, that I loved this man and still do. It was true. It is true. However, as many know, it is difficult to endure staying with someone you love when he or she is returning abusive treatment.

Additionally, it had become impossible for me to protect my children from experiencing a dysfunctional environment, and I loved them too much to continue. Moreover, I couldn't hold inside of me the opposite emotions of love and hate—loving one moment and hating the next.

One notable thing was present also. Evidently, I did possess some love for myself. I wanted to be respected and loved in return, and I felt I deserved it. Looking back, of that I am proud. Though I had carried a great deal of self-doubt and a lack of self-worth due to a strict, shame-based religion, I had some inner strength that validated my thoughts of

I don't deserve this treatment. I don't deserve unfaithfulness. I have been a good, submissive wife and a loving, nurturing mother.

For that, I thank God; my loving, supportive parents; and my divine inner guidance, to which I clearly gave my attention at that period in time.

In some respects, I felt that after twelve years of hell, I could escape on wings so as to soar like an eagle. Thoughts of being like Superman came to mind.

I feel as though I could leap over tall buildings. I am free—gloriously free!

I was to be free from the awful feelings I had kept inside for so long. Blessed freedom! I could walk out of prison and not look back. However, it wasn't that easy. Remember, I loved this man. Plus, he was the father of my children.

I confided the separation situation, first to April and then to Bud, who was now officially my pastor. I got opposing viewpoints. April counseled me to consider taking Steve back and to continue to work with him; he might see his wayward ways and still become a Christian. My response to her was "Absolutely not! I have Bible grounds. I am finally free from the alcoholism. I will, of course, continue to pray for Steve, but no way can I return to a broken marriage."

She insisted it would be the higher road to take him back despite the unfaithfulness. "Consider how much more loving pressure you could apply, Makena, by staying with him?" she said. Again, I stood my ground and disagreed. Besides, I knew April's past. She had been promiscuous in both of her marriages and was not someone I would necessarily be able to take counsel from in that situation.

I was pleasantly surprised with Bud's response when I told him what had taken place—that upon learning of Steve's unfaithfulness, I'd insisted he leave the home. Bud was quiet, pleasant, and understanding. I told him April's viewpoint and said I couldn't accept her opinion because my life was not the same as her life.

Bud was a discerning man and well educated in behavioral science. He knew my background and my life to that point. He agreed. I was not April, and I did not deserve the abusive treatment and unfaithfulness from Steve. I appreciated Bud very much in that moment. I could see he did have a good heart, and his counsel was the same as the advice

I'd received from my mother and father. I needed to follow through with the divorce and focus on raising my children.

As it turned out, in a short time, Steve was penitent and wanted to return home to me and the children. I had no remaining faith that he would be able to turn away from his drinking or his unrestrained lifestyle. Over the course of the twelve years, I had hoped the accidents and drink-associated incidents would bring on that life-changing wake-up call. However, I was repeatedly disappointed. The incidents eventuated in short periods of remission, and then he would resume his way of life as always.

Steve was willing to attend church with me in the barn. He talked briefly with Bud, and Bud recommended he meet with one of the men in the fellowship to participate in Bible studies first. I vaguely recall Steve attending one service during which he sat across from me in the circle. The look on his face was painfully sincere. He seemed to be genuine in his desire to change. However, I still couldn't take him back for fear of the negative pattern returning.

I wanted to pray for him but not be married to him. I also recall him coming to the house to talk to me and then turning away in shame, saying, "I want to come back, but I don't know if I can be faithful to you." Perhaps that was why I loved Steve and still do. He cared enough for me at that time that he didn't want to fail and hurt me all over again. He was a man who didn't love himself. How could he love me?

Eventually, Steve did return to his drinking and had several short-term relationships with women. He didn't spend much time with the boys. Again, he carried on with his lifestyle, and that included not spending quality time with them. I moved forward with divorce proceedings and went to work in an engineering firm close to home.

The properties were split such that I received the home and the remaining mortgage. Steve assumed the majority of the commercial property, which was paid for, and eventually, I received a portion of the commercial property as additional compensation, resulting in an even fifty-fifty proposition.

Settlement

My dad was helpful in loaning me the money for the divorce, for which I paid him back over the course of the following two years. Bud also was involved in coaching me to be sure to get my share of the commercial property, which originally was not discussed in the first meeting with me, my dad, and the lawyer.

Bear in mind that I now faced the prospect of supporting my two sons, with a mortgage payment and food, clothing, and school costs. I received a small support payment from Steve but not necessarily consistently. If I hadn't been so drained from the divorce and being a single parent, I might have picked up on some foreshadowing from the discussion with Bud about the commercial property. He insisted that I go after it—that I deserved it. Everyone knows that when going through emotionally draining situations, the last thing you want to do is fight. To try to acquire part of the commercial property was a struggle because Steve was resistant, but eventually, I won out because the numbers were fair.

Bud said to me, "Makena, just think: you may be responsible for our setting up a church on that property." Inwardly, I recoiled from such an idea—not because I didn't have an appreciation for the need but because I had my children to think of, and to give up that property would reflect on their futures since my ability to be the primary wage earner was limited. However, I didn't say anything, because inwardly, I thought, *Surely he wouldn't expect such a thing from me.*

I had more to learn about skipping past red flags. Bud's way of thinking—"The end justifies the means"—shows up more clearly a little further down the Yellow Brick Road.

✝ Years Two and Three

Survival on the Homefront, and Church Doctrines Emerge

As a single mom, I often referred to the first part of that phase of my life as "survival." I was so busy. Not only was I busy with keeping up with my domestic life, raising the children, helping them with their homework, and participating in their sports and school activities, but I also worked outside the home full-time and had an exceptionally active life in the church fellowship.

Of course, I was old school, so everything I had done before as an at-home mom I continued to do as a single working mom. Home-cooked meals and a clean and tidy home were musts for myself and the children. Simultaneously, the church requirements started amping up. By that, I mean there were more Bible studies, more meetings, and more church members coming to my home for occasional evening meals.

Also, around that time, somehow, the fellowship lost the privilege of worshipping in the barn at the campgrounds and started meeting in a large commercial building that had been recently converted to low-income housing. We had access to a large room and a couple of smaller rooms upstairs. We started out with meeting for a couple hours on Sunday, and by the end of that two-year phase, we were assembling all day. We brought our food and spent the entire day together, worshipping and sharing fellowship by eating together, studying together, and praying together. I had only one day of the weekend to prepare everything for the boys' school week and my work week.

Also, during that time period, the church environment was changing considerably. Bud was doing all of the teaching on Sundays, and his agenda included many admonitions to live a more dedicated and practically applied Christian lifestyle. He admonished us to be more sacrificing and less private and self-serving, to be like the early Christians in the Bible's New Testament book of Acts. He often used references to the first Christians as those willing to give up their possessions and property. He emphasized the calling to be bold witnesses for Christ, as the early Christians had been, by showing how much we loved and cared for each other. It was said of the early Christians, "Behold, how they love one another" (Tertullian's *Apology*, chapter 39).

In other words, our witness to the world that Christ was Lord of our lives was our love for each other.

Early on, those teachings made sense to me, and by then, my sons were approaching early adolescence and able to understand the teachings as well. At that stage, it wasn't difficult to grasp and appreciate Bud's invitation to a dedicated life of service. We enjoyed each other's company, we were growing by learning together, and we were there for each other. If someone was sick or in need, we practically served in love by providing meals, cleaning the home, and taking care of the children. In general, we did whatever we could to help out.

However, also during that time, I started to notice Bud's teaching becoming narrower and stronger in nature. There were three areas of our lives that he felt we needed to examine so that we held the church as a priority in our lives: (1) our preoccupation with what the Bible calls "mammon," (2) our strong ties to family, and (3) our allegiance to the dictates of our government.

The scripture "Ye cannot serve [both] God and mammon"

(Matthew 6:24 NIV) was fairly self-explanatory. We were not to allow our pursuit of material wealth to interfere with our devotion to God and the church. We were, in fact, to challenge anything that interfered with the devotion to the church, including our family ties.

We were to put our brothers and sisters in Christ above our earthly brothers, sisters, mothers, and fathers. This Christian ideal was backed by the scripture also, referencing when Jesus responded to his disciples after they told him his mother and brothers were waiting for him outside. Jesus's response was "My mother and brothers are all those who hear God's word and obey it" (Luke 8:21 NLT). If that were true, then conversely, those who did not obey God's Word were not necessarily true family, as was the body of believers, the church.

That teaching eventually evolved into a lifestyle that excluded those who did not live as we were living, in community. We were strongly influenced, per the scriptures, to give up our individuality for the sake of the whole. Bud also indicated that we must always be true to our faith, even if challenged in some way by the government.

Somehow, it became more evident through Bud's teachings that we all had issues and were in need of each other or, again, in need of the church. In time, we found we were labeled. My labels were that I was a divorcée, was too private an individual, and was too much of an individual, period. I know there were others being challenged for not conforming to some of the ideals that Bud was putting forth. On some level, the very fact that the individual did not yield to Bud's way of thinking was becoming a label of insubordination to the true way of following Christ.

Whereas the teachings initially had centered on God's love and forgiveness through his son, Jesus, now the focus seemed to be our lack. We lacked the correct way to conduct ourselves, be strong, and follow the narrow way. We weren't doing enough; we weren't doing it right. Sometimes subtly and sometimes not so subtly, Bud or Bud's family seemed to know what was best.

Since Bud was becoming more and more present in our lives,

he would infuse his teachings into what might appear to be small, insignificant teaching moments during times of casual get-togethers, such as summer picnics. Those occasions were always happy, with lots of laughter and lots of great food in the way of home-prepared side dishes and from-scratch desserts. Almost always, the fair-weather occasions were followed up with a fun outdoor activity of some kind since the fellowship was predominately young people.

For example, one summer, our entire group participated in an outdoor barbecue, and Bud used grilling hot dogs as a lesson. There were three or four grills set up for everyone to prepare his or her own frank for the main course.

When it was my turn to place the raw frankfurters on the hot BBQ and turn them on the grill, Bud tapped me on the shoulder from behind and said in his solemn voice, "Makena, you know you aren't doing that correctly. The franks should be placed lengthwise on the grill, so when you turn them, they cook uniformly. Do you see?"

Of course, I understood what he was saying, but I didn't think the direction of the franks was necessarily going to be a problem in my ability to cook my franks. Though I considered it a somewhat petty request, I knew it was delivered with a strong intention, so I did as I was told and repositioned my franks per Bud's directive.

No sooner had I finished grilling my franks than Bud again appeared behind me and said, "Makena, you aren't watching the others. They are grilling their franks incorrectly. It is now your responsibility to teach others how to do things the right way." I felt embarrassed, and I didn't want to admonish anyone for doing something that I didn't perceive as being wrong. However, the next person who placed a frank on the grill placed it just as I had initially—per Bud, the wrong direction. Ugh! I knew Bud was watching, so I leaned over and, without a great deal of conviction, meekly said, "Ellie, you are supposed to place your franks this way so they are easier to turn and cook evenly." It shouldn't surprise you, dear reader,

Seeking Oz

that Ellie, one of the young singles, with head still down, raised her eyes and eyebrows as if to say, "You are kidding, right?"

Though Ellie and I were able to use that anecdote much further down the Yellow Brick Road as an inside joke and funny wisecrack—"Be sure to get your wieners lined up right"—it wasn't funny at the time. Somehow, in the midst of all of our joviality and having a good time at that particular barbecue, there was a subtle but pervading seriousness to do things right, and doing things right equated to Bud's way of doing things—even turning franks on a grill!

To further underscore Bud's teachings, during the all-day sessions on Sunday, we would break into assigned small groups and discuss a certain topic provided by Bud. We would discuss some thought-provoking subject, always relating to what the church would do and should do. Bud's teachings centered on the collective church, the bride of Christ, as indicated in the scriptures. The topic itself encouraged us to parrot what Bud was teaching from the pulpit.

A familiar phrase emerged: to make determinations and choices without the collective input of the church was "fuzzy thinking." Who did we think we were to make all of our decisions on our own? Could we really trust our own inclinations without the collective weigh-in? Another phrase Bud repeated often was "There is no such thing as 'me and God.'"

My initial thoughts regarding that phrase were *I have always understood that our relationship with God is personal and private, and we can go directly to him. However, I also understand what Bud is suggesting. After all, look at all of the religious crazies out there who make bad decisions and do terrible things in the name of God. Okay. I see that by submitting our decisions to the collective church, we are more apt to get validation if we are on the right track, and conversely, we will receive admonitions if we are veering offtrack. This makes sense. There can be no harm in entrusting our deepest concerns and difficult decisions to the church—to the people who love God and who hold to the highest calling in the Bible: to love each other.*

Hence the small groups. While eight or ten adults met in each of the groups, the children met separately under an adult's supervision. At the time, the fellowship numbered around eighty-five, including children. Throughout the twelve-year period, with the fluctuation of people leaving and people joining, we averaged in number anywhere from 85 to 120.

We adults could discuss anything in our private lives—work or home—and put forth consideration for help or counsel from the group. We were learning to depend on each other. We were not individuals; we were a group. We were the church—Christ's church.

The Royal Family

In time, I started to note there was always a member of Bud's family included in each small group. That arrangement wasn't difficult for a family of seven since typically, there were about six or seven groups. Since Bud's children ranged from ages fifteen to twenty-three, they were able to be valid representations of what I later referred to as the Royal Family.

Bud frequently referred to the fact that his children were exemplary. Per Bud, he and his wife, Sandra Sue, "did a fine job"—didn't they? They disciplined their children, who were "all well behaved indeed." There were two boys—the second-to-eldest child and the youngest child. The three girls were all beautiful redheads and had incredible singing voices; they often sang in a trio. I noted that they were far from humble. They certainly held themselves in high regard and with confidence. To be honest, I pretty much felt their overall behavior was one of haughtiness. I remember questioning myself.

Am I jealous? But there are many beautiful young ladies in the group, and they are all genuine and sweet-spirited. I don't feel any jealousy toward them. I enjoy being around them. However, Bud's girls are not sweet. Sometimes they appear to be downright disdainful. I don't like being around them.

I have to say, though this self-questioning about the arrogant Collins girls came to mind on a few more occasions, once I settled it and realized it wasn't me, I dropped the unnecessary guilt for thinking that way. It wasn't me. They behaved as haughty young ladies. I never drew close to any of those girls throughout the entire twelve years in the cult, though by the end of the twelve-year period, I had many close, loving relationships with several women in the group, both young and old.

Breaking into small groups seemed to be the beginning of getting closer to each other as individuals, but in time, I realized it was a way for Bud to familiarize himself with our weaknesses.

One Sunday, Bud had us break into groups of two, and the following question was put forth: "What is your greatest fear?" We were to share our answers with each other and talk about it. I remember Bud moving from group to group. Though I had gained a measure of trust for him by then, that activity somehow activated a warning in me: *Where is he going with this question? Why is he going to each group and listening in?*

I got the same uneasy feeling I'd had when I first encountered Bud. From the corner of my eye, I watched as he moved from group to group to find out each individual's answer to the question. My initial thoughts were *Why is he interested in our greatest fear? Is this exercise revealing some vulnerability that he could use against us? I feel invaded like I did when I first met Bud, when he appeared intrusive and pushy, reaching beyond my personal boundaries.*

However, then my thinking would change to *But why would I question his motives? After all, he is a dedicated man, not just a pastor who speaks on Sundays. He is participating in all of our lives to help us and encourage us to do the same. We are like one big family. It is a beautiful thing.*

I admonished myself for thinking such thoughts and dismissed the uneasy feeling—for the time being. That certainly was not the last time I would question Bud's motives. It was just the beginning.

If I had doubts, why didn't I leave? Many of us in the fellowship, I am sure, did have doubts, and some people, even families, did leave. Initially, we did express our concerns and thoughts regarding Bud's teachings. However, alongside Bud's teachings of complete sacrifice in service, we were made to feel incomplete and unworthy. Our goal was to set aside our individualism for the sake of the whole. Anything less was not Christian.

As I learned after leaving the fellowship much later, mind control, or brainwashing, is a process. A patient leader who systematically breaks down a person's sense of self can eventually brainwash an entire group of people.

Further, you have to understand the basic tenets and emphasis of the Christian faith: "God so loved the world that he gave his one and only Son that whoever believes in him shall not perish but have eternal life (John 3:16 NIV). We are loved by a sacrificial yet punishing God who actually threatens death unless we believe in his son. So how do you serve such a God? It often turns out that you return the same type of love—sacrifice in service.

A perfect example of early Christian sacrifice in service is the church in the book of Acts. There you have it. Take a leader, and add eloquence and lots of time spent in gaining trust and working with the people. Voilà! Cult. Did I think it was a cult at that juncture? Of course not, but I was getting close, though I would spend an additional seven years first challenging the idea of community living and then, eventually, giving in because I doubted myself and felt guilty because I was too private, too much of an individual. What did I know? I was a divorcée. Guilty! I was facing the lion on the Yellow Brick Road. I received his accusations that my brain was fuzzy, and my heart could deceive me. Therefore, I had best belong to that group—otherwise, what might I encounter through the Dark Forest to Oz?

Introduction to Community Living

On one occasion, when I had several of the young people at my house, one of the single fellows, a man just five years younger than I, passed through all of the rooms in my house and said my home would house more people quite nicely. I was taken aback. He was a young fellow almost my age who had lived what I would call a hippie, laid-back bachelor life. He knew nothing of what I had been through and accomplished in the twelve years of my marriage or the strife of being a single mother to two growing boys.

Is he suggesting I invite others to live in my home? I thought.

Again, I got that vague, familiar feeling of being invaded. Unbeknownst to me, Bud was starting to talk to some of the young men in the fellowship about community living and extended households. Being a somewhat private person, I found the idea frightening. I didn't want to think about having to share my home. My home was my sanctuary. It was a place where I could relax and enjoy solitude when needed. As it was, I didn't have much time to relax, because I willingly devoted what time I had left after work and church to my children and my home. How would it be to have the house full of a variety of individuals who all had their own demands for attention and interaction? Even as a young girl, I had several young school friends vying for my attention. I learned to step back and allow myself times of solitude. An extended household situation would put undue pressure on me—a single woman supporting her two sons.

Shortly after that incident, Bud approached me to ask if I would house the fiancée of his eldest son, Curtis. Curtis's fiancée, Linda, was a delightful young lady in the fellowship. She had a jovial countenance and laughed easily but conducted herself in a no-nonsense fashion. It would take the tougher part of her personality to cope with someone like Curtis, who, though somewhat good-natured, was strong-willed and opinionated like his father. Curtis was a little rough around the edges and intense, though likable. He closely aligned himself with his father's teachings, but on occasion, he would challenge something and end up burying his opinions in favor of his father's lead.

The situation Bud presented to me was that Linda needed a place to stay for the next six months previous to the wedding. Though Linda was young, about twenty-two years old, she had been working as a waitress and living independently outside her family's home in an apartment. I never fully understood why she needed to stay with me for those six months, but it had something to do with her family's disapproval of her marriage to Curtis and the need for a more protective environment during the few months prior to the wedding. Maybe there was some advantage also to saving rental money. I wasn't sure.

Since it was a temporary situation, I didn't object, and Linda moved in. My two sons shared a room and gave up one of their rooms to Linda. Along with Linda, unbeknownst to me, an apartment full of furniture accompanied her into my dining and living rooms. She was apologetic, but I really liked Linda, as did the boys, so again, I figured we could certainly handle the temporary situation.

Curtis would visit on occasion, and I recall him propping his feet up on my coffee table. That doesn't sound so terrible in itself, but we lived in red-dirt country, and most new homebuilders in the area had guests remove their shoes. That was the habit in our home, and it was evident, as we all removed our shoes just inside the door. Guests always followed suit without being asked—all guests except Curtis.

Curtis wore his construction boots inside the house and, shamelessly and without hesitationm propped them up on the coffee table. I remember thinking, *This bothers me. This bothers me a lot.*

Is this a statement that mammon doesn't matter—that relationships are more important? Am I supposed to not care if he gets dirt on my table and carpet, because they are just material things? What about the behavior? Isn't this rude? What about that? He is certainly old enough to know better.

I have been in his parents' home, and his mother is very tidy like me. Is he supposed to be testing me since his father's teachings speak often of sharing and relinquishing ownership—not giving in to our obsession with mammon?

Did I say anything? No. By then, I was beginning to bow to the members of the Royal Family as well as the dictates of Bud's teachings, and I said nothing.

Linda fit nicely into our home life, as she was a mature young lady, and in return for room rental, she taught my children how to swim at the local pool. They knew the basics, but she was a taskmaster at teaching physical sports and tutored them on the level of competitive swimming. She also helped out in the kitchen when her waitress shift allowed her to be home at dinnertime.

I missed my privacy, so I was glad when Linda married Curtis and moved in with him, but I had developed a fondness for her that remained until she met tragedy. However, that is later down the road. Since we have not been paying attention to the detour signs much, we are continuing on the same path of the Yellow Brick Road, and as you know, when you ignore detour signs, death and destruction are possibilities.

And More Community Living

Not long after Linda moved out, I was approached by Bud again—this time to consider housing one of the new-to-the-group teenage gals who was having trouble at home and needed a stable place to live. According to Bud, I would be able to help her by example. I would be a good role model, and she could help by paying me rent and helping out around my home.

Believe me, the small rent payment was not enough of an enticement, though my wage was still fairly low. I valued the sanctuary of my home and needed to have as much quality time with my sons as possible. As it was, to run a household as a single mother to two young sons was a pretty hectic lifestyle; and I really didn't want to be responsible for another person in my home.

Shortly after Bud queried me about taking in the young girl, a couple of the other young people also approached me with the same suggestion: "How wonderful it would be for Monica to have a nice home." According to them, I would be the perfect person to show by example what it is to run a Christian household, and she could be of help to me.

The old guilt trip reared its ugly head, and the next thing I knew, Monica moved into our home. She was a somewhat moody, troubled girl—about nineteen years old going on twelve! She didn't cook or clean, and it was supposed to be my job to teach her to do those things. I had to remind her to pay her small amount of rent, so I also had to teach her responsibility. Consequently, instead of getting help, I got more work.

At the time, a few of the young married couples were also moving into larger rentals and including some of the young people in their homes. Again, the objective was to combine households advantageously—coupling some of the stronger leader-type individuals with some of the needier individuals, further emphasizing our caring for each other and setting positive examples for spiritual growth. Plus, weren't we saving money and being practical also?

I was the only single head of household who took in someone, but I was often referred to as being a strong role model with positive ideals and values. I knew I was respected, but I felt lonely in some respects. I was getting tired, and no one seemed to understand. Again, most of the fellowship members were people ten years

Seeking Oz

younger than I, unmarried, and single. The other few extended households were run by couples.

My children understood. My children were mature for their ages. They knew what I had gone through in the marriage. My eldest son, Joseph, loved his dad, but he knew how much his dad had hurt me. Joe was wise and intuitive for his young years and picked up more than he should have. He also inherited my unnecessary guilty feelings. He felt responsible for his dad's alienation and, at the same time, protective of me.

I tried to help him understand that he needn't feel divided. He was free to love each of us—no sides necessary. His dad made choices in life that left him outside our family unit. But I understood why Joe felt that way. He was empathic like me. I felt it too. I felt bad for Steve. He had so much, yet he continued to destroy himself and everything good in his life in the process.

My second-to-eldest son, Matt, was very young when his dad became more absent and less sober, and consequently, he didn't bond much with his dad. He was bonding with some of the young men in the fellowship, which was another reason I valued the group. Bud encouraged us all to be role models, and that worked well for a single mother and two young sons who lacked a father.

That was another reason I felt I should not complain about sharing my home and helping young people who needed a home. After all, I thought, *I made a poor choice when I married Steve. I failed by dragging my children through a divorce, resulting in the loss of a father. Shame on me for complaining about being tired and helping out.*

By the summer of 1980, I had been divorced for approximately two years, and I was a busy, single thirty-three-year-old lady. My sons, Joe and Matt, were fourteen and ten years old, respectively. Monica lived with us and added to the noise level by running through the house like a young adolescent. I fed three children and mentored the oldest. My sons didn't need mentoring. I already had done the hard work with them during the formative years. I chuckle when I write this, because I sound a bit sarcastic. My sarcasm, dear reader, is aimed at myself. What should I have done differently? I should have said, "No! Emphatically, no! I do not want to raise an adult young lady when I already have my hands full!"

But this is a journey, a chronological narrative down the Yellow Brick Road about an individual who doubted her own mind. It probably didn't help that I had built up my endurance muscles to be long-suffering. I still hadn't learned to build my strength in standing up to opposition. I certainly was not well tutored in listening to my inner guidance. I wasn't a Dorothy smacking the lion on the nose—at least not yet.

✝ Years Four and Five

A New Relationship

A year earlier, Winnie, my sister eleven years senior to me, had wanted me to meet someone she thought I might be interested in. She lived in the big city where I was raised, as did Phil, a long-standing friend to her and my brother-in-law. Phil was exactly one year to the day older than I was. He was single, never had been married, and claimed he wanted to marry someone like my sisters. He also knew my next-eldest sister, Carol, who was five years my senior. Phil was acquainted with both of my sisters' husbands.

Phil observed and learned that all three of us girls waited on our husbands, as we were raised to be submissive in our roles as wives. We thought that viewpoint was humorous and were oblivious to the fact that it was not necessarily a virtue or a compliment. For us, we understood it as a way of life.

Our mother and father had distinct roles. After two months of courtship, my father proposed marriage to my mother in 1941 with "If I bring home the bacon, will you cook it in the pan?" Nowadays, that proposal would be an insult, and the young woman would laugh her suitor right out the door. They had been married for sixty-five years when my dad passed away at age ninety. My mom, an exceptionally strong widow, passed just shy of ninety-nine. After Daddy crossed over, we girls often commented on how well he provided for and protected Mama all those years of marriage and well beyond his death. Mama had a home paid for and sufficient wealth to cover her for the rest of her life due to Daddy's plan to ensure her well-being should he go first.

Our husbands overlooked the fact that Daddy adored and respected our mother, made a good living, and made her life as comfortable as possible; and she returned the favor by providing Daddy with a warm, well-cared-for home and home-cooked meals three times a day every day of the week. Though their roles were distinct, they came together to agree on all of the important issues in raising a family, and they shared any additional workloads. Their model of marriage was based on mutual respect and practical caring.

At any rate, I hadn't been ready to meet Phil a year earlier, and I'd told my sister I wasn't interested.

However, by that summer of 1980, I was ready for something I felt was missing. I wanted a normal life as a family unit. I wanted someone to come alongside me and love me and my children. Instead of being loaded down with more responsibility, I thought, *Wouldn't it be nice to be a family with a husband who is supportive instead of me being both mother and father, not to mention a tutor to adult children?*

I needed to consider dating.

I remembered that Winnie had told me the year previous that Phil reminded her of Daddy—pleasant, ethical, and, in general, a good guy. And he had the same birthday as me.

That has to mean something!

I called my sister and told her I was ready to meet Phil.

Within a month or so, Phil rode up to our country home on a large Gold Wing motorcycle. It so happened that the males in our family were all motorcyclists, on either street or dirt bikes. My brother, who had recently finished his four years as a Navy SEAL during the Vietnam war, rode a street motorcycle as well as a dirt bike. My son Joe, then in high school, raced motocross. (I might mention here that since I couldn't afford to buy Joe his motorcycle or any accessories,

Seeking Oz

he paid for everything by working nights and weekends for two years as a janitor at the engineering firm where I worked.) Matt followed in his brother's footsteps by riding a smaller motorcycle around the country roads.

Phil had become acquainted with my brother-in-law and my brother several years earlier when riding motorcycles at a park near their homes, and they all participated in off-road enduro racing, along with my nephews. A couple of the young men in our fellowship also were into motorcycles.

So it was no huge surprise that when Phil roared up the driveway of our home, my youngest son, Matt, bolted out the door, ran up to Phil, and gave him a big hug. Matt was not in the least bit intimidated by the stout young man sporting a full red beard and propped on the oversize bike. Wow! I took that as a good sign. Phil was, as my sister had described, a pleasant, laid-back young man. He had a quiet, dry sense of humor. Unlike our boisterous, jovial family, he rarely laughed; he just smiled.

Our first couple of dates included the children. We went to a popular theme park on one occasion, and on another occasion, we took a day trip to the ocean, to one of Phil's favorite coastal locations. We took Monica along as well. She had never been to the ocean. It didn't seem to bother Phil that I had a young female roommate, along with my two children. He settled into our family unit nicely.

On our first date alone, we went by motorcycle to a Renaissance fair while my mother watched the boys. It was in the foothills and included typical activities of the medieval culture, such as blacksmithing and jousting. There were men, women, and children dressed in the costumes of that time period, acting out the medieval lifestyle as well as providing entertainment and theatrics. There was a lot of laughter and joviality. I have referred to that occasion many times when I think back on my time in the cult. That event proved to be a pivotal point for me. Once again, it caused me to doubt myself and allow someone else's thinking to take precedence.

Makena McChesney

I remember standing just outside a circular, primitive, open-slatted fenced area where a family scene took place. Inside the circle were women in long dresses and aprons, cooking and stirring with long wooden spoons what appeared to be soup in large pots. The familiar and welcoming smell of barbecued pork ribs, flipped by men on a nearby open fire, added to the ambiance. The men were laughing and chugging drinks from large mugs while little children ran barefoot among the adults, playing games with sticks and small wooden swords.

It was more than a family scene. Actually, that was community living. Phil stood smiling for a long time, observing the scene, before he commented. I'll never forget what he said: "I really like this. This is community living—something I always wished I had, since my family wasn't like that. We never did anything together."

At that particular moment, I realized that not only was I looking for a person to fill the void in my family unit—a husband to me and a father to my children—but I was looking for an out. I was contemplating leaving the fellowship. What had started out as a wonderful improvement to my Christian upbringing—leaving out the pomp; formality; and dark, depressing music—was changing. Not only was the environment changing, but the teaching was getting more confining, and the community living ideas were fearful to me. Bud's ideas were becoming invasive to my way of living. I had a need for privacy. But he ridiculed that need, which made me believe I was too private, even though a large part of my life allowed for little, if any, privacy with just myself and my boys.

So what did I do with that statement from Phil, whom I was beginning to like more and more? And, I might add, I noticed that he was taking a serious interest in me as well. In that instant, I doubted myself and figured that might be a sign from God. Just when I was thinking of leaving, God sent me a sign through this man that I was selfish and should be as the early Christians were—sharing their lives and homes with each other. Actually, they shared everything.

They owned nothing. I stood self-condemned in that moment. That was what I did.

Next Steps

After a few more dates, including attending one of our fellowship's fun activities with me, Phil expressed a serious intention to eventually marry me. I knew I was going to have to let the pastor know I was dating Phil. Mind you, there was only Saturday to see Phil because my Sunday was completely full with the all-day fellowship activities, and the work week was out of the question, as I had to take the boys to their sports commitments and help them with their homework, not to mention all of the domestic chores associated with raising a young family. Plus, we were starting to have Bible studies and special meetings and classes during the week as well.

Bud accepted my announcement with a somber countenance. "You know, Makena, that you are vulnerable to making the same mistake you made in marrying Steve. Do you really believe you can trust yourself to know what is best in this situation? How much do you know about this young man? Is he a Christian?" I had to answer no, but I knew Phil was interested because we had been discussing my faith and the fellowship I belonged to. Phil was intrigued by a fellowship of young people who were becoming increasingly more integral in each other's lives—not only worshipping together but also having fun together, helping each other out when needed, and caring for each other. Also, he had already indicated an interest in community living.

I shared all of this with Bud, and his response was that if Phil was interested in me as a possible mate, he would definitely have to participate in the fellowship lifestyle and be tutored in the Word of God by joining in the Bible studies and special meetings we were starting up during weeknights. The men in the men's club would be informed, and they would come alongside Phil and get to know him. They would ultimately make the decision as to whether Phil was suitable for me and my children. Furthermore, Phil would need to experience community living. He would have to move in with Bud's eldest daughter and her husband; become a part of their family; and, of course, pay rent and help out in the household.

Some part of me processed Bud's plan as being sound. I thought, *Bud has my best interests in mind. After all, I made one terrible mistake. I could do it again. He is being protective and also helpful to ensure that Phil will become a good Christian and be the perfect husband and father.*

Another part of me reasoned differently. *Would I really make the same mistake again, when this time, I have not only my happiness to consider but also my two sons' welfare to consider? This decision is vitally important not only for my well-being but also for the well-being of my children. Phil has known my sisters and their families for quite some time and comes highly recommended. Isn't this enough? He has also expressed an interest in becoming a Christian. I believe I know this decision is right. Do I really need the entire men's group and Bud to make this decision for me?*

I had a good example in my mother and father. I knew the difference between a functional family and a dysfunctional family. Phil wanted to spend time with all three of us—even with Monica thrown in for good measure. This man was not like Steve at all. He didn't drink, he didn't smoke, and he didn't curse. He was a good, decent man. I was going to have to tell him that he would have to move from the city and live in our rural town. Not only that, but he would have to move in with one of the young couples and participate in their home life as well as the fellowship in every aspect of our living.

I thought, *When I make this proposal to Phil, he may do a 180-degree turn and run for his life!*

Well, somewhat to my surprise, Phil was agreeable to Bud's proposal. He moved from his apartment to Caryn Sue and Ben's

Seeking Oz

home, a good twenty miles from where he worked as a concrete forms carpenter. Now, I have to tell you something about this young couple. First of all, Caryn Sue was, as mentioned, Bud and Sandra Sue's eldest daughter. I have already designated her as haughty. Of the three girls, she was indeed the haughtiest. Microsoft Word synonyms for haughty are *proud, arrogant, conceited, self-important, snooty, stuck-up, puffed up,* and *overconfident.* That just about covers it.

Sorry, dear reader. I am sure you think I am exaggerating. You probably also think I must have some personal vendetta against this eldest daughter. Actually, I really don't. I don't know if it was entirely in the genes or the upbringing, but that young lady thought she was a gift to mankind. She certainly considered herself superior to most, if not all. Again, this is no exaggeration. I immediately didn't like her, so I just stayed clear of her as much as possible.

But then poor Phil had to live with her and her husband. To describe the husband, I would have to say he either already had a goodly amount of self-importance himself or acquired it from linking up with Caryn Sue. I am fairly discerning and, I later learned, quite intuitive, but I can't give an exact measurement when sizing up Ben Weber. Somewhere beneath that tough exterior, he seemed to have a heart, but his demeanor was somewhat similar to his wife's—serious and unyielding. Reportedly, most of the young people did not like him and were afraid of him.

Mind you, Ben and Caryn Sue were about twenty-four years old, recently had graduated from the Pentecostal church college, and had a small baby. Ben was a teacher. Caryn Sue had not applied her college degree—I am not certain what it was in—but was an at-home mom devoted to applying her wisdom and many so-called gifts to the fellowship at hand.

Again, I know I sound sarcastic, but this is verified by those who escaped the cult but were close to her during the cult years. You've likely seen movies in which certain individuals in an antagonist group are so arrogant that they don't realize their effect on those around them, or if they do, they don't care. I suppose you could call this narcissism, but I'm not sure the label completely applied to Caryn Sue because on occasion, she was able to show caring and concern for others, whereas the true narcissist is incapable of any kind of empathy.

In her case, however, she seemed to believe that others' weaknesses and maladies were largely caused by their own faults, and she delighted in pointing out possible remedies. Ben was the strong arm to back her up. He could apply a no-nonsense stare-down and keep a classroom of any age group in line. Again, whether his deportment was inherent, learned, or acquired, I'm not sure. He didn't bother me so much. Again, I always believed he had a heart ticking beneath his rough exterior.

Phil was quiet and uncomplaining, so it was some time before he shared what it was like living with the Webers. He was pretty upset one day because Ben borrowed his new van to transport some kind of pig food—or slop, as he called it. The Webers were raising a couple of hogs in their backyard to eventually butcher. Borrowing from each other in the fellowship was becoming a more common occurrence since we were sharing everything and learning not to look on our property as our own. That was more difficult for some of us than for others. I was careful with my home and belongings, and so was Phil.

As it turned out, the pig slop spilled all over in the back of Phil's van. Phil said Ben was somewhat apologetic, but there was an underlying tone that carried the message of "Don't be so materialistic. It is only mammon. Relationships are more important than mammon."

Two other young, single men were living in the Webers' household as well. Phil got along well with them, and somewhat later, both fellows communicated to Phil that Ben was gruff and expecting in his demeanor toward them as well. I can only imagine, years later as I write about this arrangement, that Bud was grooming his son-in-law to be a leader in the church. The profile of the leader in that fellowship evolved into one who was unyielding and capable of inflicting strong punishment. There were several such leaders by the time the fellowship dissolved.

Caryn Sue cooked evening meals for everyone and left a disastrous kitchen cleanup for the fellows. Phil told me much later, after we were married, that it appeared she left all dishes from cooking throughout the day for them and was not much of a housekeeper. He did say that she was fairly pleasant, and they had no issues between them.

Phil worked at his construction job from early morning to late afternoon, came home to the Webers' household, did his chores, and attended all of the special evening meetings and all-day Sunday worship sessions. He became integrated into the fellowship. Since he was basically easygoing and friendly, everyone in the fellowship liked and accepted him.

The boys and I still had our Saturdays to get more acquainted with Phil, and generally, we did things together as a family. Phil became one of the children when he rode motorcycles with them on our property and played competitive video games on our television.

The children adapted to him well, though even after our marriage, they never called him Dad, probably because he got down on their level. I was happy to have a healthy family unit and again figured that staying in the fellowship must be part of God's plan for us.

Second Marriage and an Untimely Tragedy

Phil and I married in the summer of 1981, almost exactly a year after we met and started dating. The fellowship helped put together a small, inexpensive wedding in Bud and Sandra Sue's backyard.

I might mention that this home was different from the one they'd built on the denominational church property. I recall them making some kind of trade to acquire that larger home in a more central location. It was located on a street named Treetop Lane and was near the high school as well as several rentals occupied by some of the young couples. The rentals were large enough to house extended households, such as the Webers', where Phil had resided for the past year.

There were also several duplex rentals just off Treetop Lane that eventually housed more young people in the fellowship. The community lifestyle was evolving, and it was becoming increasingly more evident that Bud intended to create a place of commonality where we were integral in each other's lives on a daily day-in and day-out basis. The neighborhood hub on and near Treetop Lane became known as "living in proximity" and encompassed the equivalent of a couple city blocks.

A week and a few days before Phil's and my wedding, I got news that my brother Ethan was killed by a drunk driver weaving in and out of the traffic on a busy freeway overpass. He was heading home from work to his wife and two young sons, who were four years old and eighteen months old. He rarely had taken the street bike out since starting his family, but the car was in the shop that day. He was coming home with good news for his wife and family: his father-in-law had landed a big electrical contract, and celebration was in order. Ethan was an electrician and worked for his wife's father, who owned his own company. Construction work was difficult to come by, so the breakthrough was a welcome relief for their financial status at that time.

Ethan survived four years of active service as a Navy SEAL on the Underwater Demolition Team (UDT) during the Vietnam War only to return home, marry, start his family, and then get killed by an irresponsible, reckless driver. I was devastated. Our entire family was overwhelmed with shock and grief. Ethan was pivotal in our extended family. Both the young and old could relate to him, and he was loved dearly by all of us.

Though he was tough enough to become a Navy SEAL and most likely participated in many dangerous missions, which he kept to

Seeking Oz

himself, he was a kind and thoughtful man of thirty-one years—way too young to leave us all.

I thought, *This just can't be real! This has to be a bad dream. Ethan was so very alive, so vital, and so bigger-than-life. No! Please! No!*

I was in a fog. *Surely I can't get married in a week. I will have to postpone the wedding. This wedding just includes our fellowship and Phil's and my parents and siblings. Not a lot of preparation went into the wedding. It shouldn't be too difficult to postpone it. I can't possibly go through with a wedding right now.*

I went to Sandra Sue, Bud's wife, and asked her if we couldn't postpone the wedding. She said, "No! Too many people have helped to put this together. We need to move on with it." Her tone and demeanor were emotionless and emphatic and left no room for discussion.

I turned and left with my foggy thoughts, which were something like *The wedding is in her backyard. They probably went to a lot of trouble to make sure it is ready for the wedding.*

Looking back, I realize the backyard was a simple, uneventful venue for sure. We had the small reception in the detached garage in the rear of the house, next to the backyard. The preparations included cake and decorations provided by a few of the ladies in the fellowship.

Before I continue further, I need to describe Sandra Sue. From the first day I met her, my immediate reaction was that she was a hard, cold woman. She rarely smiled and seemed to me to have some hidden, sad past that festered just below the surface of her unyielding manner. Her father was a retired minister in the same denominational church of my upbringing and the church where I first met Bud. Sometime later, after I met her father, it bore out that this former pastor had a serious deportment, and I imagine she might have suffered as a young person under his harsh rule.

Whenever Bud spoke glowingly of his wife in her presence—and he frequently did so—she never smiled. My intuition told me that either he'd cheated on her sometime in the past and was trying to compensate with flattery, or there was some disappointment between them in their marriage, of which she couldn't relinquish. I saw her softness on occasion, but mostly, I saw her stiffness and distance to accepting those she didn't want to get close to. I felt I was one of those people and always had an inner struggle to try to gain her approval, when I really felt no warmth from her.

I was innately a people pleaser and lacked confidence when I was confronted by someone like her. I have since learned that I have no reason to win others' favor when they have given me no reason. I will come halfway if they make an effort, but no more do I lower myself to gain their acceptance. It's like approaching an angry, snapping animal and, when reaching out, expecting to get a warm reception. Sometimes they bite. It's foolish to expect differently.

It was a Thursday when I got the news of Ethan's death; on Sunday, I was expected to attend the fellowship's Sunday potluck picnic at a nearby park in my honor as the upcoming bride, and I was to be part of a humorous skit. My part was to get on all fours and act like a table. I remember looking at the grassy ground beneath me and hazily asking myself, *Why am I here?*

On Monday, I attended the funeral. Sometime that week, I bought gifts for Bud's three daughters, who were to sing in a trio at the wedding. I remember being in shock and saying repeatedly while driving to take care of wedding details, "I love you, Ethan. I love you, Ethan. I love you, Ethan."

I couldn't cry much because I had a feeling I was expected to be stoic for everyone.

Upon seeing Phil shortly after getting the news, I went up to him and hugged him, crying. His response was "I wish we were on another planet." That was it. That reaction was all I was going to get in the way of sympathy. I knew I had an emotional makeup, and evidently, no one would be able to handle it. I cried to myself at night and repeated, "I love you, Ethan." That was all I could think.

As mentioned, the wedding took place that following Saturday, a week and a few days after my brother left this world so tragically and suddenly. The wedding photos show the shock in my eyes as well as my family's as we stood together with the wedding party—my new husband, Monica, my maid of honor, my two sons, Bud, and both of our sets of parents. My family graciously attended, and we all smiled, shook hands, and behaved normally for everyone's sake. All the while, we were all dying inside.

I regret putting my parents, sons, and family through that when we were all grieving. I should have said no to Sandra Sue. But I didn't. I put the church first before family. I was following the dictates of Bud's interpretation of Christian living.

My First Paranormal Visitation

Immediately after the wedding, Phil and I followed through with the honeymoon. His idea of a honeymoon was to go to a mountain cabin near a lake or stream, hike, and go fishing. I was raised on summer camping trips with the family, so the idea was appealing enough, though I had no desire to fish. I just enjoyed the outdoors. Phil never brought up my brother's death after that initial hug, so again, I felt it was my responsibility to keep any grieving from his sight.

The day following the wedding, I found myself on a steeply sloping mountainside, walking briskly and sometimes stumbling, next to a fast-moving stream making its way to the river below. I was thankful that Phil generally walked way ahead of me so I could try to feel my body and see the trees and my environment, because I felt numb, and the world was gray. At that time, while watching the creek bubble down the hillside next to me, I had my first paranormal experience from the Other Side. I didn't see anything, but my mind's eye simultaneously projected imagery and sound while I experienced a sudden rush of exhilaration.

How do you describe exhilaration like no exhilaration you have ever experienced before? The imagery was a bright white spiritual being, winglike, within inches of the surface of the stream. It was traveling at an incredible speed with a whooshing sound, as if to say, "Wahoo!" If I were to try to make a movie of the imagery, sound, and feeling, there would have to be a thunderous "Wahoo!" I knew immediately that it was Ethan. Ethan always loved the water and swam like a fish when he was just four years old. He was adventurous and a bit of a daredevil, extracting every bit of life from performing on unicycles and motorcycles, jumping out of planes—you name it. Nothing could stop him from living life to the fullest.

When he decided to join the military service for his country, he aimed high—Underwater Demolition Team, Frogman, Navy SEAL. Ethan was one of more than a couple hundred servicemen who entered the training program. He shared with us after the fact that during the initial training period, sometimes after the extremely rigorous physical requirements—running miles in the sand while carrying navy boats, swimming for hours in the rough ocean waves far out at sea—the fellows who couldn't take the physical and mental stress would go to the center of camp and ring a huge bell, pulling the rope repeatedly, indicating, "I quit! I quit! I fucking quit!" He was one of thirty or so who remained standing and officially passed to become a Navy SEAL. He was highly respected in his unit and was one of three to be included in the backup helicopter to retrieve the astronauts in the *Apollo 17* splashdown.

I had no doubt that was my brother skimming the surface of the stream I walked next to. He was not only letting me know he was okay. He was more than okay. He was experiencing some kind of exhilaration in another realm outside this three-dimensional plane, and somehow, with imagery and strong feeling, he was able to reach through the veil and communicate with me. That experience helped me tremendously. I still grieved his passing, of course, and missing his presence at family gatherings and his occasional visits was beyond painful. But I kept that beautiful paranormal experience tucked away in my heart.

I couldn't share the experience with anyone—not my family, not my church members. They would have said that anything other than what we can see and hear on this plane is more than likely a trick of Satan. I remember my mom quoting that the devil was a trickster and that the scriptures revealed he could appear as an angel of light. We could not trust anything of that nature to be other than an evil trick. But that time, I didn't let go of what I knew in my heart was true. I kept it hidden within the accessible recesses of my mind and thanked God and Ethan for bringing me such beautiful, loving peace when my heart was breaking.

Several times since that first experience, I've thought about how foolish we are to ignore our hearts and our own experiences, when all organized religions speak of countless miracles of angel visitations, ascended masters, and prophets—all paranormal activity. We are to believe ancient texts set down by man as infallible, yet anything related to our own relationship with the entities on the Other Side is to be questioned as evil and from the devil. This reflects fear, not love. Fear is the antagonist. Love is the protagonist. Fear keeps us in subjection so we don't realize we are part of the divine, as Jesus tried to tell us. Love sets us free. We need to love ourselves and others. We need to know that we have the divine Creator within us and need fear only fear itself.

Decisions and Choices Unapproved

When Phil and I married, Phil moved into my home. Monica was placed in another home with another couple. A short time later, Phil expressed a desire to move elsewhere since he felt odd living in the home I had shared with Steve. Phil had always wanted to build a home, so we decided to put the existing home on the market and, in the meantime, use the commercial property money to purchase a plot of land. We purchased a small two-acre parcel on the other side of the freeway, on Dogwood Lane, about four or five miles removed from the Treetop Lane hub. We looked for property for a long time and fell in love with that plot of ground, with its natural landscaping of oak trees and shrubbery.

Within six months, we sold my house and moved temporarily into a rental about three miles from Treetop Lane so we could start drawing up our house design and planning our project. We were in the rental for a little more than a year, when I became pregnant, so we put some of our plans on hold until our son Jacob was born in 1983. Joe was seventeen, and Matt was thirteen. A couple weeks prior to Jacob's birth, I quit my job at the engineering firm. I didn't go back to work for the remainder of the time I was in the fellowship.

During that time, it somehow got back to us that Bud had plans for Phil and me and was just leaving us alone for a time to let us adjust to marriage and have the additional child. I wasn't sure what that meant, but I figured it probably had something to do with others living with us in our home.

As mentioned earlier, I was not in favor of community living and didn't want to think about it. Wasn't it enough that we contributed to the fellowship in so many ways? By then, I was helping with many of our special events, having Bible studies in the home, attending women's meetings, and having some of the younger teens come to my house to learn how to cook. Phil was helping out as well to troubleshoot any mechanical issues that arose within the fellowship, such as vehicles not running properly.

Also during that time, Phil built several little infant cribs to store in the building where we fellowshipped. By then, several of the young people were marrying and having babies, and we needed a place for the babies to sleep during our all-day worship time. Phil and I purchased the materials on our own, and Phil worked on the little cribs in his spare time. I believe there were about six or seven cribs, and we purchased and outfitted them with mattresses and fitted sheets. We painted them white, and they were sturdy, well-built little cribs. I was impressed with Phil's handiwork, but he was matter-of-fact and humble about the project. He enjoyed making them.

Bud expressed disapproval when Phil presented him with the cribs. Bud thought the project was overkill and said Phil should never do a project on his own. It was self-serving not to include others in the project. The thought never had occurred to either of us. We saw a need and were delighted to fill it. It was disturbing to leave our babies on open blankets on the dirty, carpeted floor in the other room with the door closed. I remember thinking how odd it was that none of the young parents thanked Phil for building the cribs. I also found it odd that a couple years later, when we had to move the fellowship again, nothing was said about bringing the cribs to our next location. They were discarded.

Looking back, I know exactly why the young parents did not express thanks, and our gift of the cribs went unrecognized. Bud had a way of getting his point across, and he used such happenings as teaching moments. Sometimes he would share his thoughts and opinions with just a few members and sometimes before the entire group. By that time, we were becoming more cloned and learning to march to the same beat, so his mere mention to a few members could ensure a group consensus. What Bud said was becoming law and somehow synonymous with what God wanted. Bud's disapproval was equated with God's disapproval. Bud made it clear what was right and what was wrong. Right was doing everything together as a group and not making any individual decisions, such as building cribs without including the group's weigh-in and possible participation. We were to submit even some of the smallest of decisions to the group, particularly the elders, who were becoming closer and closer to resembling Bud. (Please note that we now had elders—they were not necessarily senior or experienced, just well tutored by Bud.)

One of those decisions that really wasn't so small was Phil and I choosing to build our home on the plot of ground we had acquired on Dogwood Lane. When Bud found out we had purchased a property a distance from Treetop Lane, he was visibly angry with us. When he spoke to us about it, he revealed his livid, reddened "Shame on you" face. "What were you thinking? You need to take these decisions before the group." That really was the beginning of the strong control building in Bud's mind to create community.

Though I certainly had expressed a dislike for forced community living, Bud had already been working on my conscience, as well as the others', in his sermons. We were called to follow God's admonition, as the young church in the book of Acts had. They displayed to the world how much they loved each other by sharing everything they had, thus behaving as true Christians. They were beacons to the lost as to what true Christianity was all about. That lifestyle was imperative to be true Christians. We needed to do the same. Anything short of that lifestyle was wrong, self-serving, and ungodly. Both Phil and I stood guilty as charged.

Bud came up with a plan that would get us off the hook. We would be absolved from such selfish action if we sold the property we'd purchased and participated in buying five acres just around the corner from Treetop Lane—on Horseshoe Court. He just so happened to have all of the facts on the property. Since the property was zoned for splitting into five one-acre parcels, three other adults in the fellowship were willing to contribute to the cost of two and a half acres, and we could purchase the other two and a half acres and build on it.

Again, I was of two minds—the mind that came from my logical, analytical side and the mind that was influenced by unnecessary guilt and shame. My logical mind told me, *This proposal equates to messy dealings. I am not completely sold on this community way of not owning property and sharing everything. How, legally, does this turn out should the fellowship dissolve? I am jeopardizing my family's financial future. This scares me.*

My increasingly brainwashed side said, *I am selfish and self-centered not to agree to Bud's proposal.*

Phil looked at me, and I looked at him. We mirrored the shame in each other's eyes from having absorbed Bud's angry accusations.

Shame on us.

We agreed to the proposal.

✝ Years Six and Seven

A Difficult Move to Horseshoe Court

Shortly after Jacob's birth and Joe's graduation from high school, Phil and I worked to get our banking in order to start building the house on Horseshoe Court, near Treetop Lane. Primarily, we planned to use the equity from the sale of my house. Though we sold the Dogwood Lane property, at that time, we were compensated in monthly payments, not a lump sum.

We thought we would have enough to pay for everything outright, but since a portion of our money was tied up in the Dogwood Lane property we hadn't built on, we had to take out a small loan. We decided to use Phil's Veterans Affairs mortgage—a VA loan—he had coming from serving in the armed services during the Vietnam War in the late 1960s. The next step was to get our house plans drawn up and calculate costs from there to determine how much we would need to finance through the VA loan.

Though it was the dead of winter, we had to move to the undeveloped property on Horseshoe Court in order to avoid capital gains from the sale of my home since, at that point, we had been in the house rental for just under two years. We arranged to borrow my brother-in-law's little travel trailer and put everything but the bare necessities in storage. At that time, Jacob was eight months old.

I have to say, the move was no small feat. The travel trailer was only about fourteen feet long, used mostly for short camping trips.

How we all fit in that trailer escapes me, but we did it. We put up a small baby crib at night for Jacob, and Phil, Matt, Joe, and I slept in small bench-type beds. When the weather improved in late spring and summer, Matt slept in a tent outside. Mind you, this property was next to established homes near the high school. We had no electricity or plumbing. We moved to undeveloped property thick with brush, along with some scrub oak trees, which managed to provide us some privacy from the neighboring homes. We did everything the hard way until that spring, when we could move the trailer close to the framed house and hook up to the septic and water.

In the interim, for a total of about three months, we brought water in and dug holes in the earth outside to go to the bathroom. One evening shortly after we moved, we all got the flu—the kind that had no mercy. It induced both vomiting and diarrhea, unrelenting for twenty-four hours. It went through the trailer inhabitants like the Tasmanian devil! About every hour or so, another family member would groan and run outside. At one point, Matt, my highly pragmatic son, got up in the night and went outside. When he came back in, I asked, "Sweetheart, are you sick also?"

He said, "Not yet, but I dug two holes for both ends, so I'm ready when it hits." My sons were amazing throughout the ordeal.

About two months after we moved, Joe moved in with his father in the city. Steve, by then, had bought another home. Though we hated to see Joe leave, it did relieve some pressure for close-quarters living. While living with his dad, Joe worked full-time, gaining some income to start college the following year at the local state college. He continued faithfully to come up the hill every Sunday to participate in the fellowship and helped out with the house building whenever he could. Joe loved his father and absorbed a lot of the pain, as is typical for the eldest child of an alcoholic.

Joe undertook undue responsibility for his father after the divorce. That burden for a young eighteen-year-old added to both of our suffering because I didn't want Joe to feel that unfounded guilt

Seeking Oz

and responsibility. No amount of talking would help. He just quietly, without complaint, helped his dad with the sideline of auto bodywork and eventually helped him build another house. There were many occasions when Joe bailed his dad out of difficult situations and helped get his huge six-foot-four-inch frame to bed when Steve passed out from drinking too much.

I didn't know about the incidents related to Steve's drinking, of course. Joe kept the painful ordeals to himself. A close cousin who adored and respected Joe told me sometime later. As it turned out, Joe stayed his entire four-year college career with his dad until he had to go away to Birmingham, Alabama, for his master's degree. His curriculum was premedical, and he achieved excellent grades throughout, making the dean's list.

After Joe went to Alabama, that same cousin also confided in me that Joe had been up all night bailing his dad out of jail the night before Joe's finals, just prior to graduation. Joe would spend eight-hour shifts studying. He was exceptionally bright, but getting high grades in his college courses didn't necessarily come easily for him. He required his study time. The news made my mother heart ache. Joe had a strong constitution and a beautiful, loving spirit throughout that time, and he continues to do so as a fifty-year-old husband and father of two.

He continues to work hard as he owns and manages a successful clinic. He paid for his college on his own, paying off student loans within the first ten years after graduating. I bring all this up so you can understand the caliber of man Joe is, because he suffered considerably from the dictates of the cult—but that part of the story is further down the Yellow Brick Road.

Again, the winter of 1984 found us living in the travel trailer and preparing to build the house. Phil, my sons, and I did all of the physical labor of clearing the land ourselves. Phil whacked down the scrub brush, and the boys and I dragged all of the prickly branches to burn piles. In many instances, Phil had to use his three-quarter-ton military-surplus rig with the winch to pull out the stumps. We worked, untiring, for hours at a time, dragging, clearing, and burning.

We all got poison oak, particularly from the burning, but we had to keep up a steady pace because we had a time limit in which to finish building the house. The VA loan, at that time, provided a voucher system for us, with multiple timeframes for the various stages, such as framing, septic, rough plumbing, electrical, and the finish work, interior and exterior. All totaled, once the funding commenced, we had six months to finish the house.

Once again, Bud approached us and told us we needed to include the fellowship in the building of our house. Bud's son Curtis would do the framing, and we would use construction expertise available from within the fellowship. Those helpers who did not have the expertise would learn from those who were experienced. Unbeknownst to us, the idea was to develop that expertise for future community projects. Once again, we were taken aback.

We had no problem with the prospect of hiring out the work we couldn't do ourselves, but Bud insisted we would form crews to help out. My initial inner reaction was *Yes, we agree that synergistic effort is a beautiful thing—but our house? It's one thing to help others with their groceries, mow lawns, prepare meals when sick, and gather together for events and potlucks, but everyone working on our house?*

My privacy and logic were challenged again. Less than ten years ago, I'd been able to help my ex-husband build our house, hiring out the work we couldn't do ourselves. My inner struggle was *Why do we need everyone interfering with the building of this house? Phil and the boys are more than capable of building the house, and what they can't do, we can afford to hire subcontractors with the hard-earned money gained from the previous house. I will, as before, paint, stain, and handle the contractors and voucher system; help with construction cleanup; keep the home fires burning with cooking in the little trailer; and take care of the baby.*

My dad taught me to owe no man anything. Daddy enjoyed helping others, but he became indebted to no one. I certainly do not want to feel indebted to anyone.

The sense of dread and undue entanglement showed up again.

We are already in partnership on this five-acre parcel with three other contributors. We are traveling down this road of community living at a little quicker pace now. We are building a home that is strategically placed in the fellowship, and it feels like it is slipping away and becoming the property of the others as well.

I felt invaded. Now community was more than a mention; it was fast becoming a reality, and we were in the vortex. We were rapidly being swept along.

I always feel compelled, dear reader, to pause and explain why I kept going when I felt I was being invaded and my choices were diminishing. Why did I go past the logic talk, the feelings of dread, and the desire to take my family and flee? To provide the list, I was

- raised in a fear-based religion by credible parents;
- educated from an early age not to question the Bible;
- tutored by experience in a difficult marriage to be submissive, long-suffering, and sacrificial;
- brainwashed by a convincing, charismatic pastor to believe the highest calling of a true Christian was to give up everything for the sake of the whole and not trust one's individual relationship with a higher power;
- self-taught to hang on to the positives and endure the negatives as a coping skill; and
- of the mind-set that I was inherently selfish and guilty, and anything short of perfection to please an exacting God was dangerous, particularly because I was called to that lifestyle. It had to be no coincidence that the snowstorm had brought me to that group of believers. Likewise, it was certainly timely

that Phil had come on the scene when I was ready to leave. I was given a lot; a lot would be required of me.

You might have to refer to this list more than once, dear reader, to understand why I would press on when I was struggling with the dictates of the fellowship. Unfortunately, it took a great deal of needless inner pain and suffering before I could challenge the list.

To continue with the narrative of forging ahead with the house-project scenario, the inner conflict was there, but I pushed it aside for fear of not pleasing God and the church. I guess that sums it up: fear. I continued to travel through the Dark Forest.

Though our family still did the bulk of the work, including my dad, who did the electrical, several others were in and out, either providing skills they already had or helping out to gain those skills—basically some painting of the outside of the home and eaves and some of the rough plumbing and rough electrical. There were a few who could help with finish work, such as tile and sheetrock. Everything else was either done by our family or hired out with the proceeds from the previous home equity or VA loan money. Our family participated in most aspects of the work and did all of the cleanup work, carrying truckload after truckload to the dump and constantly sweeping and cleaning up. It was exhausting—and all the while, we were living in the small travel trailer as a family, including a small baby.

I would like to say it was gratifying to have people in the fellowship helping out, but the underlying feelings I had during the project were not appreciation, not feelings of being supported by loving friends. I felt that deep down, they really didn't want to do the work. My intuition was validated several years later by a fellow who participated but was not in the core group. He recalled some participants "jokingly" referring to our home project as "the house from hell." I wish I had heard those comments outright and not just felt them. Perhaps I would have acted, but then again, I would probably have been

Seeking Oz

admonished and pulled back into the vortex of the community-lifestyle belief system.

Again, I felt a deep sense of fear that I was being invaded, and my property, home, sanctity, and ability to make my own decisions were being usurped. I was beginning to feel entrapment. Ironic, isn't it? I was afraid of entrapment, but my fear of God kept me there. Fear can really do a number!

During that same time period, Bud was proposing we start our own school and was holding meetings to work on developing a church school for all grades, first grade through high school, starting with high school only. Eventually, middle school would be added and then on down through grade school. I attended those meetings because I was designated to teach the high schoolers grammar, writing, and English literature. I have to say, that was one proposition to which I had no opposition. A positive came into view.

I'd had plans early in high school that I would get my college degree and teach elementary school—preferably first or second graders. I loved children, and that particular age, to me, was delightful. I taught that age group in Sunday school, starting when I was fifteen years old. They were innocent and impressionable yet refreshingly honest and bold in their expression.

Well, I never got my teaching degree; hence, I did not have the proper education to pursue the career I'd dreamed of as a young child. As my story goes, I married at age nineteen, and the rest is history, since my children were my priority above trying to attend college. I was satisfied with teaching Sunday school, which actually ended up spanning a period of twenty years. Now Bud was proposing that I teach my favorite subject, English, to the high-school-age young people in the fellowship.

Here is where I will give Bud credit. He knew each of us—our strengths and our weaknesses. True, he used them to his best advantage to carry out his plan of building a community of believers with him as the leader, and unfortunately, he carried that too far, which was his undoing—but that comes later in the story. He knew my weaknesses clearly, which I have mentioned innumerable times. I was unnecessarily guilty and easily shamed. However, he also knew my strengths. I was a strong role model for young people. I was cheerful, nonjudgmental, and encouraging. Teaching came naturally to me. I was a teacher at heart.

Though high school was not my chosen target age group to teach, because I remembered how difficult my junior high and high school years were socially, my heart went out to those young people in our fellowship. They were walking a narrow path, as I had during that time period, and sometimes that path felt alienating and sad.

The positive side to our close-knit fellowship was that the young people were being taught an excellent work ethic and good sportsmanship, both by example and by participation. They were surrounded by supportive, loving people. That was all good, no doubt. However, as you will learn, the parameters became more closed in. In some instances, the young people were severely limited. The strong interference and potential for developing what I would call "crippling factors" increased, as was the case with my middle son, Matt, who was caught in that escalation of separation and alienation, as you will learn sometime later in the story.

The proposition for me to teach was within reach, in spite of my lack of education. I was excited about the possibility, and it was a positive distraction to my concerns about the house building. Bud and a small committee put together a charter that would designate our church school as not accredited but legal. I could teach in the school. I was delighted!

The principal of the school would be Ben Weber. I would teach English literature and typing, Bud would teach social studies, and Harris Jensen would teach math and science.

Harris Jensen was a young, single man about five years my junior. He joined our fellowship sometime after we moved from the campground barn. He stayed close to Bud and seemed to enjoy learning from him. He was studying to be a doctor, but Bud encouraged him to get his real estate license instead. Real estate provided flexible scheduling, so Harris was able to teach in the mornings and devote afternoons to his work. Ben would be on a salary paid for by the fellowship monetary contributions and tithing. My contribution to teach, of course, was voluntary. The same applied to Bud and Harris.

So simultaneous to our family living in the travel trailer with a young baby and building a house, not to mention business as usual with Phil working full-time in construction and the all-day Sunday meetings and fellowship events continuing, I was now involved in discussions to plan a school.

Terrible News

About three months into the construction on our house, we got news of a terrible accidental death. One of the single women in the fellowship, Marilyn, whom I'd worked with in the engineering firm when I was dating Phil, learned that her seventeen-year-old daughter, Candy, had been killed in a car accident. The young daughter had run away from home when she was sixteen and become pregnant with a young fellow, Blake, who was about seven years older than she was. At the time of Candy's death, she left a five-month-old infant with Blake, whom she'd never married. I will provide a little background information here, dear reader, because I would be approached to raise that little girl shortly after we completed the building of the house.

When I worked in the engineering firm with Marilyn back in 1979, she approached me about going to the church I attended. At that time, our fellowship was in the honeymoon phase. We were worshipping in the barn, and the environment was upbeat and loving, as mentioned earlier. Marilyn was a few years older than I. She was a single mother with a young teenage daughter. I never learned much about Marilyn's background, as she kept it private. My intuition told me there was probably some drinking and possibly multiple partners. She was a chain smoker and had a little edge to her, but she was always soft and kind when she spoke to me. She was a beautiful woman and outwardly confident, and her career seemed to be highly important to her.

Just prior to Marilyn joining our fellowship, I took notice that she worked late hours most workdays and was known to work weekends as well. Her wage was probably double mine, but my priority was my children. I always compressed my workday in order to get home to my children since I also was a single mom at that time.

On one occasion, I stopped by Marilyn's desk as I was leaving and asked her if her daughter, Candy, was home alone, and if so, would Marilyn object if I stopped by and took her daughter home to have dinner with me and my sons? My eldest son, Joe, was the same age and attended school with Candy, so we were acquainted. Marilyn's response was that her daughter was home alone and didn't mind. "Candy knows to fix herself something to eat and do her homework," Marilyn said, politely but firmly refusing the invitation.

Sometime later, I had to drop something off for Candy at their small duplex, and I was disappointed to see Marilyn's home was devoid of any warmth. There was little furniture. The small area was dark and depressing, with cold linoleum floors stained with age and neglect. There were no signs of hominess whatsoever, and Candy herself was less than welcoming.

Candy had developed a somewhat masculine and flip demeanor for someone so young that seemed to say, "I'm fine, and I don't need anybody!" I checked myself and thought I was probably transparent, and my empathy was showing. I would have to speak straight with that young lady because she was obviously street smart and had no intention of being coddled. I had to respect that.

After Marilyn joined the fellowship, when I was still single and working outside the home, Bud suggested Candy spend time with me in the evenings; I could teach her to cook. I tried to get Candy to come into the kitchen with me on two or three occasions, but she would always sit on the couch with her arms folded across her chest and pout until her mother picked her up or I took her home.

I wasn't one to push or cajole, and frankly, I didn't have the energy or the inclination to make that happen for Candy. She was obviously against spending time with me in the kitchen, and I didn't blame her. She had no interest in an activity that was unknown in her own home. She had other things on her mind, and learning to cook was not something she aspired to by any stretch of the imagination. I communicated the outcome to Bud, and he agreed that plan was not working for either of us. I knew in my heart that Candy knew I didn't dislike her, and I knew that she really didn't dislike me. It was just too late to try to turn the rudder on a boat that had been going in a single direction for a long time.

The next step proposed by Bud several months later was for both Marilyn and Candy to live with his eldest son, Curtis, and his wife, Linda, who did not work outside the home. At that point in time, Linda had twins—a girl and a boy born a year prior to my son Jacob—and as were the rest of the women in the fellowship, she was very busy. The idea of moving Marilyn and Candy to Curtis and Linda's home was to familiarize both the mother and wayward daughter with a godly home life in which the objective was to help prepare the meals and sit down together at the family dinner table, as well as participate in all aspects of the church life.

Marilyn, who wanted to change her life and become a devout Christian, was amenable to Bud's suggestion. She revealed an inner softness at the time, a contrite spirit, and I could tell she was tutored by Bud as to the right thing to do. Obviously, her rough exterior was a cover to hide a great deal of pain and fear, because for her to follow through with the proposal was quite a change for both her and her daughter.

No doubt turning to the church was Marilyn's solution to try to undo the damage to her daughter, who by then was found to be hanging out with the firemen at the fire station next door to the duplex. As it turned out, Candy did not adapt to the newly presented home life, and at age sixteen, she ran away from home—the home with Curtis, Linda, and her mother. Shortly thereafter, Candy contacted her mother, Marilyn, and told her she was pregnant with a young man seven years her senior and planned to live with him and have the baby.

Linda felt terrible that Candy had run away, and I could tell she felt guilty for not providing the help Candy needed to keep her out of trouble. The unfounded guilt was visible, and it started to take its toll on young Linda. That was only the beginning of the changes I noted in Linda. Now, to get caught up where we left off in the story, we received the news of Candy's tragic death. Evidently, Candy left her baby, Melissa, who was five months old, with the young father and departed in a rage. Her self-destructive behavior found her traveling at reckless speeds, and she ended up crashing into a concrete wall, killing herself and a young friend. Marilyn, of course, was frantic, and young Curtis and Linda were left to console her.

Looking back, I realize how sad it was for that young girl, Linda, to have taken on raising a teenage girl who was already set in her ways. Linda was not a trained counselor, nor was it within her scope to raise a child close to her own age. The task was not necessarily something she aspired to, nor was it necessarily part of her life's purpose. That happened because someone equated community living with serving God, and God would be happy with nothing less than our sacrificial love. No questions were asked. No negative response was accepted.

Move into House on Horseshoe Court

The summer of 1984 wrapped up the completion of the house. Jacob was about fourteen months old. Phil and I were weary from the past year of living in the small trailer and working on finishing the home in every spare minute and, often, late at night under lamps. Our son Matt, who'd helped untiringly with the building of the house in every aspect, could finally abandon the tent he'd lived in throughout the summer. Matt never complained about the hard work or the discomfort in the living circumstances. He also helped out by caring lovingly for his baby brother.

We were all thankful to be in our home, and we were thankful for the help we'd received, though throughout that phase, I continued to feel that we would have been happier to have paid for the labor rather than feeling indebted in some way. Even though over the course of our entire stay in the fellowship, Phil and I contributed more in labor than most everyone, that phase of receiving help on our home came with a price—a price well planned by Bud. Entanglement of that sort eventuates in entrapment. I knew better from the start, but I continued to doubt my logical side every step of the way, particularly whenever shame or guilt was introduced.

We gathered our belongings from storage, moved into the house, and experienced a few months to ourselves—Phil, Matt, Jacob, and me. Jacob was a delightful young toddler and seemed to be very astute, almost prodigy-like, in his speech and interests. On tiptoe, he played the piano, barely able to reach the keys, and would complete an entire tune, such as "Twinkle, Twinkle, Little Star," which later we discovered was the musical gift of playing by ear.

He sat and listened to story after children's story every evening, and if I paused in reading, he recited verbatim the remainder. By age three, he was asking me to read from the encyclopedia about airplanes and how they were powered. After the first paragraph, written for grade school students, he would tell me to keep reading.

Back in the day, encyclopedias were designed to provide increasingly detailed and highly sophisticated reading for precollege and, ultimately, college students and professionals. On his insistence, I read Jacob the information intended for adults, of which I had no comprehension myself, continually prodded by him to keep reading. Though the reading level was way beyond anything he should have been able to understand, we found out later that he was absorbing and comprehending, even at such a young age.

Our family missed having Joe in our household, but by then, Joe was attending the local state college in the city, and he continued to pay room and board to his alcoholic father by doing auto bodywork—sanding, spraying, and detailing cars and trucks. He continued to attend Sunday worship all day, so we did get to see him once a week.

Sometime during that period, Bud's youngest son, Cory, and a few young people in the fellowship went on a joy ride with Cory at the wheel. Cory and Joe were close in age and had attended middle school and high school together. They weren't particularly close growing up, as they were different academically and in temperament, but on occasion, Cory would spend a little time at our house. Cory, who was not as bright as his siblings, tended to be less than careful with his body and other people's possessions in general. You might say he was reckless. Unlike his brother, who was intense, Cory was laid back in his temperament, so whatever he tended to destroy was out of thoughtlessness and carelessness, not necessarily intentionally.

I always liked Cory because he was somewhat innocent in his behavior. However, he always made me nervous when, while over at our house, he asked to ride Joe's motorcycle. Joe had worked hard as a janitor at the engineering firm to earn the money to buy it, and Joe was always exceptionally careful with his possessions as well as with others' belongings. Of course, Cory would end up dropping the bike or slamming into something. Since neither Joe nor I would be able to replace it if it were damaged, we would both wince when watching him behave recklessly. However, we felt as if we had no say in the matter since we both had absorbed the brainwashing and teachings from Bud that everything we owned belonged to all of us.

At any rate, that particular joy ride eventuated in Cory taking out several yards of fencing along the busy country road leading to the high school. The fence divided goat property from the well-trafficked road and was owned by an elderly gentleman who had lived there for a long time—long before the high school and houses were built. I felt bad for the old gentleman. I was embarrassed for Cory, but as it turned out, Bud said to me, without shame or regret, "Joe should have been in the car with the young people. He should be a part of the group."

I was confused and had no comment for such a statement, which lacked any apologies for Cory's reckless behavior. That was not the way I was raised. Bud always seemed to put our church group above everything and everyone—even if we were remiss. His statement made no sense to me and didn't seem Christian. He showed no indication of any remorse on his son's part for the damages Cory had done to the elderly gentleman's property, not to mention the fact that Cory had put the young passengers in jeopardy with his reckless driving. Fortunately, no one was hurt.

Though I still spent another five years in the fellowship, I was starting to register some things that seemed wrong to me, and they had nothing to do with my feeling guilty or ashamed.

I thought, *I am proud of my son, who lives his life responsibly. Cory should be admonished for his irresponsible behavior, not my son for not being part of Cory's reckless actions.*

Deep down, though I travailed for Joe living with and caring for his alcoholic father, some part of me was thankful there was some distance between him and the fellowship. In time, I paid more attention to those feelings.

As it turned out, further down the Yellow Brick Road, my children played a big part in bringing me out of the imprisoning cult.

Ultimately, the injustice I felt regarding my children could not be ignored, regardless of any self-doubt, false guilt, or needless shame. Unconditional love eventually took precedence. Thank God!

Church School and Expanding, Expanding Household

Speeding along with Bud's masterminding our lives, we were starting up the church school. We held the school in the basement of our new house. We started out with just high schoolers, three boys and four girls. Those young people, within the year, became some of the strongest and most enduring little workhorses anyone could imagine for that age group, which included my son Matt.

As mentioned earlier, the principal of the school was Ben Weber—fitting. Though in his midtwenties, he was intimidating to the young people—an unyielding person who rarely smiled and was all business. Again, Harris Jensen, part-time real estate agent, taught math and science. Harris was affable and well liked by the students. Matt appreciated Harris and enjoyed his sense of humor. I taught English literature and typing.

Bud taught social studies and tutored the young people in what it meant to live in community and love each other through sharing. He discussed philosophical ideologies and applied psychology. He encouraged them to think—to not be sheep and to consider the best ways to help people overcome their shortcomings—or, more accurately, as I found out much later, to strongly persuade people toward positive behavior for the highest good.

My son described to me much later, while attending college, what those daily lessons included. Matt, an impressionable but intelligent young man, appreciated Bud's instructions to do the right thing. However, in his junior year of high school, he began to doubt some of Bud's teachings, when Bud seemed to be stating, "The end justifies

Seeking Oz

the means." That way of thinking did not sit well with Matt. That was not something he was comfortable with—coercing people to do the right thing.

All seven high schoolers were wonderful young men and women. Their fathers and mothers were intelligent, conscientious people. I have to mention here that all of the people who joined the fellowship as sincere followers of their faith were amazing people. They were hardworking, creative, caring people. I'm sure, dear reader, you have figured out that the only people I had issue with were the Royal Family—Bud, his wife, and their family. They placed themselves over us in all aspects of the community life—from start to finish.

Each and every one of them, to one degree or another, was unyielding, arrogant, and full of pride. I emphasize this for a reason. Proverbs 16:18 bears out, as you will see down the Yellow Brick Road: "Pride goes before destruction, a haughty spirit before a fall" (NIV).

Simultaneous to my family opening our basement for the school, the following circumstance emerged. Andon, a young, single man and brilliant engineer about ten years my junior, joined our household. Bud believed Andon would be a good role model for Matt. Matt's teachers, Bud and Harris, readily recognized that Matt was an exceptionally intelligent young man and had the same high aptitudes as Andon in math and science. Matt had tested as gifted in grade school, so that observation was nothing new to me. He was excellent in my English literature class as well. Matt eventually graduated from public school as a 4.0 valedictorian and senior varsity first-string athlete.

I make no apologies for recognizing that all three of my children are gifted. The reason I emphasize this in this narrative, dear reader, is to further point out the arrogance of the Royal Family. They put me down if I said anything to uphold or protect my children. Another label I had was "overprotective." I was not. I could give examples to the contrary, but I'll forego the self-defense at this time.

I think it will be sufficient for you to know the caliber of my children and then see how, one by one, the Royal Family was exposed as being inferior in their thinking and their conduct while they worked to control me and my family. With that being said, however, the emphasis here is not to find fault with the Royal Family. That will be self-evident. The exposure to folly is my own foolishness for following that less-than-worthy family and not listening to my God-given inner guidance. There lies the problem; there lies the blame; and there lies the eventual liberation, for which I am eternally grateful. But there is much more to the story to unravel.

Andon moved in and was indeed a wonderful role model for Matt. Matt bonded with him to some degree. I say "to some degree" because Andon was not easy on Matt. Andon was tutored by Bud. One of Bud's biggest platforms was to be tough on children and maintain high expectations. But Matt was a strong young man, so he handled the heavy-handedness from Andon well. Andon was good, and I had no problem with him, other than my cooking volume was considerably amped up because that six-foot-three-inch young man worked hard in the field, surveying, and ate as if there were no tomorrow. He became my greatest supporter as I cooked for a growing household, and he continued to do so as we added more to our dinner table, often bellowing, "Everyone out of Makena's kitchen while she is trying to cook for us!" Soon we did add more to our dinner table.

About that same time, Bud approached me to raise little Melissa along with Jacob. The father, Blake, wanted to join the fellowship and was struggling in trying to raise Melissa on his own. The grandmother, Marilyn, for obvious reasons, was not equipped to help out much other than occasionally on a weekend. In his serious "I don't take no for an answer" mode, Bud presented his case: "Jacob is like an only child, Makena. His siblings are adults—high school and college now. We don't want Jacob spoiled. He is already a bit too independent for his age."

Seeking Oz

Melissa was eighteen months old, just six months younger than Jacob, who was two. It worried me to take on another toddler along with teaching school and doing the extra cooking. I readily confess that this wasn't something I would have volunteered to do. However, I found that conscientiously, I couldn't refuse to take her in. She had been tossed around among babysitters. I appeared to be the likely candidate to help out.

The biggest problem I had with taking on the young child was that Phil and I would also be taking on the father, Blake, who was twenty-five going on nineteen.

I thought, *Here we go, raising adults again. That can be as wearing as raising little ones.*

However, I don't remember putting up too much inner resistance to the proposition. There was a legitimate need there.

A young toddler lost her mother. The father is not adequate for the job. The toddler is the granddaughter of my friend Marilyn. Candy's little girl. Poor little thing.

I said yes.

I probably need to add that raising a baby, a toddler, a child, and an adolescent in the fellowship came with the Royal Family's rule book. Again, expectations ran high. As a fellowship, we did everything the same. Therefore, we supported and reinforced those expectations for all of the children at all times. For example, little ones, before they could talk, were trained to stay on a blanket for quiet time. There was no need for a playpen. They stayed on the blanket with just a few toys. That took discipline. I have to say, it came in handy when I was cooking or when we participated in meetings where babies were present. They stayed on the blanket—no ifs, ands, or buts!

Young children were never to cry out in defiance for their own way. If they did, we administered the wooden spoon to their backsides. That punishment needed to be consistent and harsh enough to ensure the children did not repeat the poor behavior.

I thought it was oftentimes a cruel treatment, but it would not go well for my ability to control my children if I allowed excessive out-of-control behavior. Though I didn't always agree with the discipline, I did it because I was expected to. To not discipline the children in the home would have been evident in group gatherings. I have no excuse. I do stand justifiably guilty for not following my own instincts as to when to punish and how much. Any infraction got the wooden spoon, and it could be administered by any of the adults in the home should the child require it. However, in our household, primarily Phil, Blake, and I were the disciplinarians.

Melissa and Jacob got along well, which was amazing since they were both strong characters. They were highly intelligent little beings and added a great deal to the household. I was so busy cooking and preparing for and teaching school that I would often jot down something humorous they would say to each other and put it aside. Later, I compiled those anecdotes and enjoyed reliving their childish witticisms at a time when I could relax and enjoy them more. I never once neglected to read to them at night after bath time, and though Melissa challenged that activity at first, she soon sat next to me on one side while Jacob sat on the other side, and she readily and happily contributed, just as Jacob did.

In time, Melissa called me Mamia, something she came up with on her own, and eventually, it was Mama or Mom, with all that came with the full understanding that I was really her mother. We didn't try to stop her from recognizing me as her mother, because it seemed a natural progression. Little ones are so accepting. It didn't confuse either Melissa or Jacob that Melissa had two fathers, Jacob had one father, and they both had me as a mother.

Phil and I took Melissa with us everywhere if Blake was unavailable, such as when he participated in the young singles' group. Before we became restricted on separate family vacations, it was only proper to take Melissa with us on our family vacations. She and Jacob were brother and sister. Matt was always helpful

Seeking Oz

also. Caring for Melissa and Jacob was like having twins, and he was an extra hand.

Matt also went with me once a month to shop for our huge household. He would put Jacob in his oversize shopping cart, and I would put Melissa in mine. We bought everything in bulk, and I cooked everything from scratch. I then had Andon, Matt, Blake, Phil, Jacob, and Melissa to cook for, so it took extra planning to keep costs down. Andon didn't pay for rent since the extra monies coming from joint households were going toward the church school. That arrangement became a rule of thumb in the fellowship as we continued to grow into communal living. However, food costs in the extended households were divided accordingly.

Blake was an exception. He paid for food and also a small amount for rent since not only was he boarding, but I was a full-time babysitter for Melissa, even to the extent that I got up in the night whenever she was restless or cried. I tended to her 24-7, just as if she were my child. Blake helped out, of course, and would often play with Jacob and Melissa while I was cooking. Bud encouraged us to apply Blake's rent money to the VA mortgage, which we did faithfully for the full six years that Blake and Melissa lived with us.

The activity in our household, needless to say, increased considerably. Yes, I was not working outside the home, so I believed I should be more open to having less solitude and be willing to take other young people into the home. However, the scenario at our house went something like this for me: I got up at four o'clock in the morning every work day and fixed a full home-cooked breakfast of bacon, eggs, and toast for Phil, who was out the door early for the usual construction work day. While he was eating, I packed him his lunch, which I'd prepared the previous evening. Next, at about five o'clock, I cooked breakfast for Andon, who also needed a hearty breakfast for his engineering work in the field. Again, I packed his lunch. Next were Blake at six o'clock and Matt at six thirty. They got the usual—home-cooked breakfast and packed lunches. At seven o'clock, little Jacob and Melissa would wake up, and there would be the diaper-and-dress routine as well as their morning breakfast, at which time I would eat as well. By nine o'clock, I took both little ones to Lilith James's house. She would watch the children while I taught school. Lilith James and her husband, Sam, lived in proximity, about a fifteen-minute walk from my house.

Lilith was an especially warm-hearted person and had three girls of her own; the youngest was just a year older than Jacob and Melissa. I feel bad saying this, but as much as I felt comfortable with that sweet lady providing my children loving care, I also felt extremely uncomfortable with the degree of safety she provided them. Whenever we heard a loud thump and a squealing baby during worship, it was usually Lilith's youngest, who had slipped from Lilith's arms and landed on her head on the hard wooden floor. Lilith would giggle and say, "Oh dear," and worship resumed while she consoled her somewhat battered baby. I had no say, of course, as to who would take care of my children while I taught school.

Continuing the daily schedule, I taught typing for forty-five minutes and English literature for an hour and fifteen minutes. As soon as my teaching time was complete, I would scurry to pick up my two toddlers from Lilith and get back home to try to feed them before they fell asleep in their high chairs. I would work quickly to prepare their food, because they would get sleepy, and sometimes I would turn to feed them only to find two little bobbing heads. They were adorable. I'd have to keep encouraging them to stay awake to eat. Then off to their naps they would go.

While they were napping, I grabbed a bite and prepared my lesson for the following day. There was always a great deal of reading to do for the English literature class, and I remember chewing on ice cubes to stay awake and in order to comprehend the material sufficiently. I tried to review any homework or assignments at that time and during blanket time; otherwise, it would happen at about eleven o'clock that night.

Seeking Oz

By two o'clock, Jacob and Melissa would awaken, and I would spend time diapering or, eventually, potty-training; setting them up for playtime in the attached bonus room; and then tending to domestic chores, such as laundry and cleaning. By four o'clock, I needed to start dinner because it always took almost exactly two hours to fix the meal and have it on the table by six o'clock.

My pots and pans were huge, and I cooked a full meal every night, seven days a week. We never went out, because we were supposed to conserve as a fellowship. Home-cooked meals were considered an important daily must. That ideal was not foreign to me; however, I'd never dreamed I would be cooking for so many adults! I always served an entrée, a vegetable, salad, and bread. Most often, my hungry, growing family would consume an entire French loaf of bread in a dinner meal. If I got away with a hearty soup and bread, two loaves were needed. Always, home-cooked dessert was provided at the end of the meal. The beverage was sun tea or water.

After dinner, I did the dishes. After a while, I enlisted help with the dishes from the extended household but not for the first two years in the Horseshoe Court house. Dishes took me over an hour. After dishes, I bathed the children, put them in their pajamas, and read to them—which was my favorite time of the day besides teaching. I would then go back to the kitchen and prepare all of the lunches for the men in the household. If necessary, I continued with my classroom work. My time with the children and the teaching were what kept me interested in the fellowship. Everything else was ramping up so fast. I got to a point where I didn't enjoy the cooking, any of the domestic chores, or the constant interruptions—and there were constant interruptions.

Most of the interruptions were added on without our consent. The single adult ladies in the fellowship used the basement every Friday night for meetings. They were not a quiet group, and they helped themselves also to the main part of our home, making trips to the bathroom and kitchen toward the front of the house. We had no privacy. People came and went.

Since I was a respected woman in the fellowship, often, people would come to my house for counsel. I was asked questions about everything from how to cook nutritious meals to how to sew and garden. Sometimes they would come to confide something in me, and I listened and counseled as mercifully as possible, trying to keep in mind the strict rules of our fellowship. Those sessions, in time, increased as our fellowship evolved into following a narrower and more restrictive belief system. The visits were often late in the evening.

I need to mention here that around that time, everyone in the fellowship was assigned a one-on-one mentor. I would be a mentor, and I would be assigned a mentor. I found it strange that my mentor was Bud and Sandra Sue's youngest daughter, Colette.

Let me describe Colette. She was, of the three girls, the most alluring and the most voluptuous. She dressed tastefully and was well covered, but somehow, her clothing always revealed her full form. She carried herself with the same disdainful posture as her sisters. She had a beautiful singing voice on par with her sisters'. She was one of those people who weighed everything you said, and it took her a little while to decide whether your comment deserved a smile or a frown. Either way, you would get her opinion. As with the other Collins girls, because I never detected any warmth from her, I avoided her. She seemed to get along well with her peers and laughed freely, so on occasion, I would doubt myself, but then I would ask myself the same question: "Are you jealous of this girl?" My answer would come readily. No. Otherwise, I would be equally, if not more, jealous of the other beautiful girls in the fellowship, who had sweet spirits and were open to engaging conversation without judgment or guile. I just didn't like her—I felt similar to how I'd felt about her father and mother when I first met them.

Surprisingly, on the few occasions we met for the mentoring sessions, I noticed a little humility in Colette, and she actually seemed to have genuine, caring questions for me, as if she wanted to know me better. I remained guarded, however, because I always felt that Bud wanted to use me as an example for the younger girls in the fellowship of what to avoid. After all, I'd made the mistake of marrying a non-Christian and suffered the life of an unequally yoked wife. I also had gotten pregnant before marriage—double the sin.

During those mentoring sessions, I had no intention of talking about my past, especially not with a haughty girl who would treat me with even more disdain if I were to show inferiority of any kind. I also was becoming more distrustful of Bud at the time because he was getting more narrow and heavy-handed in his push for communal living. It made no sense for a young, inexperienced girl to be my mentor.

I thought, *Why did Bud assign his daughter to me? What does she know of life, other than the Royal Family rule book?*

Well, there was a reason for the humility I sensed in the young girl, of which I was oblivious at the time. But of course, I would never have been privy to the hidden secrets taking place in the Royal Family. The Royal Family was keeping a lid on several cans of worms at the time, unbeknownst to the entire fellowship, as we were becoming busier and more entangled.

Our communal life, in general, was escalating and becoming increasingly more task- and project-oriented. We had more events, more elaborate Sunday all-day worship times, more midweek meetings, and frequent potlucks. Since we had to provide the same amount of food at potlucks that our family would eat, my portion would be two or three large casserole dishes or something on that order in terms of volume. Cooking was never easy, and there was never a break. I cooked seven days a week always.

Whereas I had enjoyed cooking for my family, I was beginning to hate cooking in volume day in and day out to feed the extended household. Plus, I had to cook to the level of a variety of their dislikes, such as avoiding raisins, mushrooms, avocados, coconut, and certain dairy products when considering recipes. True, I didn't have to cater to all of those dislikes, but then I wouldn't expect to be any different with them than with my own family. I didn't cook anything that Phil or Matt didn't like; I couldn't show favoritism and disregard the dislikes of the others.

A situation that took place with Andon somewhat exemplified the state of affairs and where my mind-set was concerning the responsibilities surrounding my large household. As mentioned, my parade of morning breakfasts and evening lunch preparations was demanding, to say the least.

One evening, on arriving home from work, Andon approached me in a somewhat genial manner and said he had a confession to make. As usual, I was in the kitchen, preparing the evening meal. I stopped with the food preparation and gave him my full attention.

He said that day at work, he'd taken one of his sandwiches from his prepared lunch—which always included fruit and possibly homemade cookies—and taken a big bite. He'd immediately spit out the mouthful and pulled the bread covering back from the exposed lunchmeat to find that I had included the packaging label in the sandwich.

He said, "I threw the sandwich across the field and said aloud, 'Doggone you, Makena!'" With a chuckle, this six-foot-three-inch fellow of wholesome, ruddy countenance and big smile continued. "Sorry, Makena. I guess I am getting spoiled."

I pride myself on being a good sport and having a sense of humor. However, I distinctly remember standing there staring at that man, speechless. In my mind, that was not funny. In fact, that act of disgust and lack of appreciation for me was deplorable. There standing before me was one of my most appreciative household fans other than my own son. Even my own husband was not one to express appreciation for me or provide me any protection.

My body was locked in place. My face must have shown some confusion. My inner thoughts, as if in slow motion, were *Andon doesn't really understand my plight, or he wouldn't have shared his anecdote. He isn't necessarily malicious in his insensitivity. He is just clueless. Totally clueless. Doesn't he realize how exhausting it is for me to feed a huge household day after day and actually spend evenings long after he and the others have all gone to bed to prepare the lunches for the next day?*

I realized in that moment that as a matriarchal head of household, I was all alone in that prison. Though there were other extended households, no one else had as much as I did—no one had as many adults to feed and interact with and children to care for in addition to teaching school and managing a household. No one could really understand how I was feeling, not even Phil. Matt was the only one who seemed to understand, and that was why he was always so helpful with Jacob and Melissa.

I was getting tired. I was becoming disillusioned as more and more assumptions were being made and more freedoms were diminishing. Appreciation was replaced with expectation. The activities, the expanding household, and the communal demands continued to ramp up. It got worse—much worse.

✝ Years Eight and Nine

More Leave the Fellowship

There were small groups, big groups, and special groups—all designed to make sure we pushed on in the community lifestyle and had no time to think or challenge. Push on! Busy became busier, and there was less time to spend with outside family or on any personal hobbies or objectives. Everything was focused on our group, and nothing was decided without the approval of the group—hence, small, specially formed groups often convened to make decisions for an individual.

I was frequently the token mercy person included in many of the groups. However, as time went on, it became obvious to me that my input was not taken seriously. Either Bud or one of the Royal Family would assert his or her strong opinion, and that swayed the group in his or her direction. Usually, that decision resulted in the individual not being allowed a request, or a restriction was imposed on an individual who was not in line with Bud's teachings.

An indicator that the fire of discontent was building was that four couples with families withdrew from the fellowship. The couples were not necessarily deeply entrenched in the community lifestyle but were amiable, kind people. They no doubt were pressured by Bud to become more committed, and they chose to leave.

Some of those remaining passed judgment that the deserters were not committed enough and not able to withstand the fiery darts of Satan. A few of us felt the loss and became concerned that the balance was slipping away—that those of us remaining were like sheep to the slaughter, so to speak. We were the sacrificial lambs carrying the banner for community, when we were not fully convinced that sacrifice was the answer. However, we members who were of that mind-set, unknown to each other at the time, kept that thought to ourselves because any opposition was met with heavy confrontation; and we, the peacemakers, avoided confrontation.

I believe I need to pause here to describe the sway that Bud and Sandra Sue gained over the group and why people left or stayed.

As mentioned earlier, Bud was indeed a charismatic individual. Equal to his disapproving frown and angry demeanor that said, "Shame on you," his smile and twinkle could light up a room and certainly say, "I love you, doggone it!" With the twinkle, his eyes would narrow down in merriment, and even though you couldn't see them, they were laughing in approval—or so it seemed. The twinkle was just as manipulative, if not more so, than the judgmental frown. You were either right or wrong in his estimation. If you were wrong, you were told. He used his powers of manipulation and, of course, whatever labels he could apply. The victim either felt so bad that he or she complied, or the victim left—period.

Somehow the twinkle also seemed to coincide with God's approval of us.

I thought, *Bud's teachings are of the highest calling, are they not? If we are in line with his teachings and receive his approval, surely God is passing favor as well.*

In contrast to Bud's seemingly good-natured side, we were confronted with his wife, whose demeanor shrieked disdain and disapproval most of the time. In my estimation, she couldn't even conceal her disapproval of her husband. However, due to his frequent references to her goodness, we felt we had to respect her. Somehow, she was a constant reminder to us that we were capable of failing and were unequal to the task. She was the epitome of discipline and self-control. She had her own shaming mechanism. She was like an old school marm who always had a ruler in hand, ready to smack the child who committed the slightest infraction of the rules. I guess she represented the heavier side of God, who was capable of drowning an entire group of people in a flood because they weren't obedient.

Dear reader, I would like to be able to convince you that those two people were capable during that twelve-year period to corral and control an entire group of intelligent, loving people. Yes, some people left, but the ones who stayed were deeply caring, committed people. Did those of us who stayed doubt during that twelve-year period? I can only answer for myself and my family: a definite yes. However, I know there were some who went to other cults after ours dissolved. I also know that some did not necessarily get targeted as much as my family and me. (Property holders received the greatest pressure.) I observed at the time of dissolution that some were ashamed but unable to admit they'd been used and manipulated, similar to a young child who is molested but unable to come forward to place the blame.

Focus on the Positives

Before going down the slippery slope of total disillusionment, I need to provide some of the positives I experienced in the fellowship. Had we experienced more of these positives without the constant pushing and bullying from the cowardly lion, we might have continued down the Yellow Brick Road with much less heartache and weariness caused from lack of choice. Yes, our choices were narrowed considerably. However, the positives kept us hanging on.

Though I doubted Bud's and Sandra Sue's extreme personalities, at that point in time, I still equated that sacrificial lifestyle to obedience to God and rightfully doing what he expected of me. I had a difficult time justifying that the early Christians in the book of Acts were on a wrong path. My inner conflict had to be due to my selfish nature, I thought. I pushed aside my doubting mind and tried to focus on the positives.

Among the positives, as mentioned earlier, were Jacob and Melissa. The dynamic they provided to our household was enjoyable and entertaining. Phil was great at creating a fun environment. He could take a simple activity, such as hide-and-seek, and, with a few moderations here and there, create a fun time for everyone. Whatever the activity was, oftentimes, everyone in our household joined in, adults included.

Before our finances were totally controlled and restricted, Phil and I bought some little pygmy goats, and Phil built a small pen for them. On occasion, Phil would pile some scraps of lumber in the center of our lawn, and we all enjoyed watching the little goats jump and cavort over and on top of the obstacles we provided for them. Sometimes they would run beside the children from one side of the lawn to the other and then run over to the pile of lumber to show off with a few somersaults.

Bear in mind, dear reader, there was no television in our home. No one in the fellowship watched television, which, in some regards, really was not a negative, because our family was more interactive and creative without it. Most outsiders looking in deemed that an extreme, and they were correct. The adage "moderation in all things" is pure wisdom, in my estimation. Extremes were imposed, and we dealt with them as positively as possible. However, in that case, our household activities were fun and enjoyable, and the children didn't suffer without the television.

One Christmas, when Jacob and Melissa were three years old, our household visited Blake's father, who lived about forty miles distant at a higher elevation. His property, populated with innumerable large pine trees, covered two or three acres. He generously gave us permission to cut down any tree desired for our Christmas tree that year. Since our house was a two-story with a living room open to a high ceiling, we could accommodate a tall tree. By that time, we'd added another young single fellow to our household, Gary, and a young single girl, Edith. Gary, Andon, and Edith were all the same age—about ten years younger than I. We would use Gary's pickup truck to haul the tree. We all loaded into the truck and a couple of cars. Phil, Matt, Blake, Andon, Gary, Edith, the two three-year-olds, and I all headed up the hill to cut down a tree.

When we got there, we discovered that all of the trees were huge—most were around thirty or forty feet tall. The guys decided there was only one thing to do: top one of the trees. Gary, with chainsaw in hand, climbed up a tree several feet, and the fellows coordinated a feat to cut the top of the tree and lower it with ropes. With much maneuvering and wrangling, they bound up the tree and attached it to the top of the pickup because it was too big for the pickup bed—about fourteen feet tall, with a base circumference of about eight feet. It was huge—far bigger than we'd anticipated! We were all a little overwhelmed by the whole prospect, but we had to follow through since the big tree had given up its top for us.

When we got the tree home, the fellows made a base for it, and we set it up in the small living room. The tree base took up a large part of the room, and we had to climb the stairs and reach over the open balcony to decorate the upper portion. I didn't have enough ornaments, so I made what must have been a hundred ten-inch sugar-cookie gingerbread men to hang with red ribbons from the tree branches. We had to string about eight strands of lights, and everyone helped out. I watched Matt take turns with the little ones, holding them out over the balcony so they could reach the tree toward the top.

When others in the fellowship came over, they were aghast at the size of our tree. I loved it! We'd spent no money, so no one could say we'd been extravagant in that regard. It felt good to do something unconventional since we were all becoming so cloned in how we did things in our homes. I guess at that point, we were starting to exhibit signs of rebellion.

Something else our family did that was unique to the fellowship was to have what our household called "red meat night" on Saturday night. Though each adult person in our household contributed to the food budget, it was still limited. The extended households were encouraged to be moderate with their cooking budget and refrain from indulgences. Red meat was considered one of those indulgences. When I say "red meat," I don't necessarily mean ground beef but, rather, a good beef steak.

Typically, Blake took pride in preparing the steaks and barbecuing them while I provided the remainder of the meal for that night. When word got out among the fellowship that we had a weekly red meat night, it was frowned on, but thankfully, that was one activity that was not curtailed during the time when we had some control of our household budgets. The truth of the matter is that I worked at it to make the budget accommodate buying the steaks.

I spent three or four hours once a month planning a monthly menu and food budget for my large household of six adults and two children. I planned the meals so they were varied but resourceful. Fresh ingredients were not wasted. If there were leftovers, they were incorporated in a subsequent meal. Because I planned an entire month of menus, I was able to shop resourcefully as well. I bought all bread from the day-old bakery and purchased all other food and nonfood items from a large warehouse-type store that provided a savings to customers by not providing customer-service baggers.

I did that shopping once a month and then made twice-monthly visits for other items, such as fresh produce and milk. Needless to say, I stored much of the food in the freezer until the menu required it. The monthly shopping eventually became my only outing as an individual. After shopping, I took Matt and the two children to meet Phil at a local fast-food place before heading back home to my expecting household. It was our immediate family's monthly night out. I cherished that day. I felt free and autonomous.

Our household worked together as a family—one unit in the total unit, the fellowship—when participating in special events. We had one Fourth of July parade event for which each household created a decorated means of travel for the small children. There were bicycles, tricycles, and wagons, some simply decorated and some elaborate but all in red, white, and blue. We met at the beginning of Treetop Lane and paraded up and down the street, and as was often the case, it was actually pretty impressive. Again, the group included people who were creative and resourceful, and it was always entertaining and often amusing to see what the different households would come up with.

Some of the children were dressed in costumes, such as Uncle Sam or Betsy Ross with the flag. The combinations of wagons pulled by tricycles or old, discarded baby buggies—painted and draped with red, white, and blue streamers—were proudly pushed, dragged, pedaled, or wheeled while happy-faced children seriously took their places in the lineup. In a few cases, a family pet would comply with patriotic adornment and participate.

Our fellowship also hosted a huge project one year: a Christmas play performed by our members in a neighboring rural community theater about ten miles away. The director of the play was Caryn Sue, Bud's eldest daughter. She had taken several college drama courses; therefore, she took on the project seriously. She was perfectionistic, and the play needed to be nothing short of first class. I have to say, it was! The lady was talented and did a great job. Again, I never appreciated her superior attitude, but I have to give her credit for her abilities. Everyone in the fellowship participated in the project in one way or another, except, of course, the young children, unless they were cast in the play.

The play was a period play, a typical late-1800s Charles Dickens– type presentation. The story had a plot and a significant Christian message. There were props made, backdrops painted, and costumes sewn by various members. Since all rehearsals were at the community theater, it was necessary for participants to make repeated trips. Along with the usual household obligations, making the twenty-mile round-trip put a strain on everyone, but the synergy for that particular activity was good, and the spirits ran high and happy.

After three or four months of our intense preparation and advertising the event locally and in the surrounding communities, the play received a good audience and was well acknowledged. However, there were rumors overheard about our fellowship becoming cultish, which by that time didn't surprise me because I was beginning to think the same. I thought that privately to myself. That event was one of the last events my son Joe was allowed to participate in. But that part of the story is a little further down our weary Yellow Brick Road.

Legalism to the Max

Dear reader, let me further consult my memory of what took place during that time period. Around that time, Sandra Sue was having more influence on the fellowship in terms of what was okay and what was not okay. Whereas Bud, the visionary, had an agenda to lead us to a total community-based, common-purse lifestyle, Sandra Sue had legalism in mind. She was a hard-core black-and-white legalist—a product of her religious upbringing.

Sandra Sue was brought up in the same denominational church I was. The difference in our upbringings, from what I observed and learned, was our parents. Her father was a hypocritical, exacting, and not-so-nice pastor. In earlier years, he'd ended up having an affair with a younger woman in the congregation. A child several years younger than Sandra Sue and an ensuing scandal had been the outcomes. Sandra Sue's mother, a sophisticated but somewhat edgy lady like Sandra Sue, had divorced her father sometime around Sandra Sue's early college years.

My parents, though marching to the beat of the church's drum—or legalistic doctrine—walked their talk and were loving, kindly people. Consequently, as a result of the two different upbringings, Sandra Sue was hard and unyielding, while I was the token mercy person.

In one of the small groups, Sandra Sue's eldest daughter, Caryn Sue, said to me with a furrowed brow, "You just want everybody to be happy." I didn't respond to her because she made it sound like that was a bad thing. I was familiar with tough love—being strong and unyielding for the sake of the loved one—but I often felt the fellowship decisions went considerably past tough love and were harsh and unnecessary. The Royal Family was all about tough love, though their definition of *love* proved to be different from mine.

Sandra Sue inserted her legalistic doctrine into the group. She did have a large influence on Bud, and the way I have viewed this in retrospect is that Bud probably figured the additional restrictions applied to the members was a good thing—just another means to militarize them into thinking alike. We needed to think like Bud. If we were cloned into submission, we would indeed think like Bud.

Hence, through the weekly women's meetings led by Sandra Sue, we women, for starters, were told to dress a certain way. I will never forget Sandra Sue pushing her forefinger into my collarbone and saying, "And you will wear your clothing up to here!" Mind you, dear reader, I was a far cry from an exhibitionist. My clothing never showed cleavage, which I didn't even have. Even now, the act outrages me, and then I laugh at how silly I was to take such an admonition. Now I would say, "What the hell? Back off, lady!" Back then, I just stood there and cowered from reading her snappy, darkly cold eyes.

The clothing restrictions carried over to the men's meetings, where men were admonished to never wear knee-length shorts—always long pants. Swimwear became so outrageous that I remember thinking, *Even if I had time to go swimming somewhere, I would never wear what the young people are required to wear.* The swimwear for women was ridiculous—as high as the collarbone and as low as the knees, as was the case in the 1920s.

My son Joe, who still was in college while living with his dad and attended the fellowship meetings on Sunday, made a statement in his quiet, contemplative way: "You know, Mom, if the objective is to downplay sexuality, the call to cover up is putting more emphasis on sex than if left alone." Well said, my wise, kind, soft-spoken Joe. But of course, no one listened to Joe. Again, after all, per the Royal Family and, by then, some of the cloning supporters, Joe didn't attend all of the meetings, just Sundays, and wasn't fitting into the community lifestyle.

Furthermore, the legalistic, stiff-backed Sandra Sue eliminated folk dancing, which was something the fellowship members thoroughly enjoyed for a few years. She thought the male-and-female contact presented temptation toward familiarity, and the elimination of folk dancing altogether was the best solution.

I thought, *Wow! The sin of dancing is back to haunt me!*

Then came the introduction to the old Christian hymns. Sandra Sue not only introduced us to the hymns, but we were required to memorize all four or five verses of an assigned hymn every couple of weeks. They were the same hymns I'd been raised on, which I'd never liked. They reminded me of those morbid altar calls. How fitting for Sandra Sue to introduce an attack on our self-esteem under the guise of returning to the sacred. The lady was incredibly insecure and miserable. She would of course be in favor of contributing to the brainwashing under the cloak of good old Christian hymns.

Eventually, we needed no hymnals and could sing over and over the memorized words that reminded us of God's view of us and his conditional love for us. How could God love "a wretch like me" or "such a worm as I" unless I accepted his requirements by faith?

Yes, dear reader, if you are familiar with the hymns associated with those phrases, as in most of the Christian hymns, there is mention of the love of God by sacrifice of his son, which is our only hope for salvation—our only hope to escape eternal damnation. At the expense of sounding sacrilegious to Christians, I must admit that understanding was one of the areas I presented to God as a challenge once I got to the point that I had the courage to question God himself. I had feared questioning my father's religion, so it took a further trip down the Yellow Brick Road to gain the courage to ask all of the hard questions of God himself—even if it meant angering a God who could send me straight to the hell of my religion.

I eventually learned that the Source of Love is far greater than our narrow belief systems. However, in order to gain that courage, it was necessary for me to travel further down the Yellow Brick Road.

Synergy and Projects

Our fellowship group was now accustomed to the expression "Many hands make light work," and we used the word *synergy* frequently. Being Busy with a capital *B* continued for all fellowship members as we embarked on a major group project: building a church. The property was within close proximity to the community households along Treetop Lane and Horseshoe Court, in a commercially zoned location near the high school.

The property was purchased by another member, Sam James, husband to Lilith. Sam was an outwardly stern but inwardly kindhearted man, and at that point in time, he was a relatively new Christian of about ten years. He was a tall, strapping fellow with a tenacious work ethic. He was raised, from my understanding, in a dysfunctional family. He had to grow up fast and help out by contributing hard labor. In addition to three young daughters with Lilith, he had two teenage daughters from a previous failed marriage.

Perhaps a good description of Sam could be summed up in

an account Matt provided me on his return from one of the many fellowship wood-gathering trips. The trips included adults, teens, and children, and the purpose was to gather wood at no cost by taking advantage of clear-cut government land in the higher elevations above the foothills. A few of the stronger men would chainsaw the larger logs; remaining adults and teens would split the wood with axes; and little children would gather, haul, and stack the wood near the flatbed truck to be loaded and eventually transported back home.

On one such occasion, Sam, dressed in suspendered black jeans and no shirt, inadvertently chainsawed near what soon was discovered as a wasp nest. Matt, who was working nearby, described the instantaneous eruption of bees as a sight and sound he never would have believed if he hadn't experienced it firsthand. The sound was a deafening drone that drowned out even the high-pitched whir of the chain saws at work. The air was filled with a black mass that immediately blanketed Sam. Everyone, without further thought, dropped what he was doing and ran for cover inside the vehicles parked nearby, except Sam.

Sam, planted in place, just went to task, swatting the bees that were stinging his upper body. Kevin, one of the high schoolers and Matt's friend, was about to run for it as well, when Sam bellowed out, "Kevin, get those bees on my back! I can't reach 'em!" Kevin, wide-eyed but accustomed to obeying, slapped at the bees on Sam's back until he knew he had to run as well. Sam continued for what seemed an interminably long time—until the swarm diminished and the bees seemed to just give up.

Matt said he didn't know what to think of the situation. He summed it up recently as "It sure seemed like a stupid thing to do. But I have to say, Sam sure was a badass!"

As it turned out, Sam picked up his chain saw and, without further ado, went back to work. Matt said that slowly and cautiously, everyone eventually came out of the vehicles and joined in without a word. That was Sam. He had unrealistic expectations of himself and, most often, for those around him.

With all that being said, I never viewed Sam as being unnecessarily harsh, as did many in the fellowship, because I believed his motivations were pure, actually, as were those of most followers in the group. Whereas Bud seemed to be expanding in his ego-person with notions of control and power, Sam genuinely believed Bud's teachings were right in the eyes of God, and he followed Bud explicitly. I think there was something about Sam that reminded me of my ex-husband, Steve, and as with Steve, I excused Sam of his stern, serious demeanor due to his upbringing.

I also, in time, excused his misguided devotion to Bud, attributing it to the fact that he was a new Christian and wanted to please and do the right thing. At that point in time, I myself was not at a place where I had made any clear determinations as to right or wrong in terms of the fellowship's direction. I just knew that I personally was becoming increasingly more uncomfortable and unhappy. I wavered between questioning my own lack of faith and commitment and questioning the belief system that seemed increasingly harsher and more limiting.

Thus, with Sam's generous property purchase, plans commenced to construct a church in phases, starting with a basement with a ceiling, where we could worship and expand our school to include elementary and middle school grades. Eventually, with contributions from fellowship members, subsequent phases would include a first-floor building above the basement.

Within our fellowship, there were several men in the construction trades who could oversee construction and lend their expertise to teach other members to contribute their labor to the project—the same principle implemented in building our home applied. The primary contributors in that category were Curtis, who was a carpenter, primarily a framing contractor; Andon, an engineer and surveyor; and Phil, who was a concrete and forms specialist.

Although most of the work would be done by hand, such as mixing and wheelbarrowing concrete, there were equipment and tools to buy.

Unbeknownst to us, the project was the forerunner to what we referred to eventually as "common purse," where our money was no longer our money. Everyone contributed some of his or her money to the project. Eventually, everyone contributed all of his or her money to the church—period.

How, you say? Well, that happened a little later and became the goal I'd secretly feared all along. Control continued to slip away as the mastermind carried out his plan to entangle all of us for the sake of the whole. He would say, "We will show others how much we love each other by giving up all of our earthly goods, and that will win others over to Christianity." In the meantime, neighboring church groups were questioning our extreme notions and were concerned. Of course, we were too busy to notice what anyone else thought or did.

However, prior to our building the church, another project took place. Bud and Sandra Sue set up a temporary home by having Curtis, their eldest son, and a few men in the fellowship put up a small dwelling on another plot of land purchased by our group, just below Phil's and my home. Bud and Sandra Sue moved out of the large home on Treetop Lane, and Curtis and his wife, Linda, moved out of their previous home a few miles' distance and into Bud's large home, centrally located in the community. The temporary dwelling was actually a small barn structure from Curtis's home, which was moved to the newly acquired plot of land and converted and embellished as a small house.

The proposed plan was that the small fellowship would eventually finance and build Bud and Sandra Sue a new permanent home on the property, still in proximity to the church's growing community. In addition, I believe the idea behind the temporary move was for Bud and Sandra Sue to downsize and allow Curtis and Linda to take over more leadership responsibility, providing another extended household centrally.

I always got the impression that Sandra Sue chafed under Bud's ideas for communal living, but she staunchly supported his efforts—legalistically so. She always carried a too-serious countenance and was visibly unhappy and angry in her demeanor more often than not. The move would relieve Sandra Sue from extended household living. I could certainly understand that. It was exhausting! However, it might be interesting to note that the only extended family Bud and Sandra Sue had included in their home to that date were a single mother and her son, who was Matt's best friend in the fellowship. They, of course, were relocated elsewhere at that time.

The plan for Curtis and Linda to take more of a leadership position in the community proved to be a disappointment, as Linda began to show signs of resistance that we all eventually started to notice. For one thing, Linda was pregnant again, and she refused to include Marilyn in the household any longer. "Marilyn is not a help. She is a liability. She doesn't cook or clean or help out in the home," she said. Marilyn was placed in another fellowship home with a couple of single adult ladies.

I have to say here, dear reader, that Linda had fortitude, something I didn't have yet. Unfortunately, that strong young lady paid a price for it down the road.

To set up the temporary home, Bud rented a serviceable outdoor porta-potty and used the electricity and water from our home. Sandra Sue used our washing machine and dryer to do their laundry. I found it disturbing that she never knocked first before coming into the main part of our home. I guess she figured that since our back door was used for the school, as it gave direct access to the basement, there was no need to announce her entry. However, that part of the house was separated from our living quarters by an additional door. The laundry room was square in the middle of our living quarters. Without knocking or giving warning, she would open the dividing door, walk right in and down the hall adjacent to our living room near the kitchen, and do her laundry.

Again, I felt the dread of increased invasion and entanglement. The arrangement was not comfortable for me. The home I'd grown up in had been a sanctuary for the immediate family. We'd entertained a lot—both family and church members—but no one in the church I'd grown up in had managed extended households. However, the growing belief was that our church was special because we loved each other so much that we shared everything. Anything less was pure selfishness.

Again, my conflicted mind reflected, *I am too private. I am selfish in my thinking to question anything otherwise. I am afraid to make any changes because God has brought me to this way of life through his Word, and I need to obey, or else I'll disappoint God and suffer punishment.*

I continued down the Yellow Brick Road, not realizing that God had nothing to do with that sacrificial life imposed on me. I was just not awake enough to see the Danger signs along the way, until all hell broke loose—but not for a couple more years.

Changes and More Changes

Also during that time, changes were made to our household to accommodate more young people to join us: Gary and Edith, as mentioned earlier. The high school was moved to the finished garage behind the Treetop Lane house now occupied by Curtis and Linda, which freed up our basement for more bedroom space.

The young people added to our home were all kind and polite. Andon continued to be my strong supporter and appointed role model for my son Matt. Gary was a dear with a great sense of humor, and he would make little Jacob laugh when he described how he was treated as a young boy. "My dad would scowl at me when I did

Seeking Oz

wrong and said, 'Watch out, young man, or I'll smack you, and you're gonna fly!'" Gary made me laugh too. I loved it when Jacob would ask him, "What did your daddy tell you?" I would interrupt my task at hand to watch Gary gather up the meanest face he could and deliver the snarling one-liner that prompted giggles from Jacob.

Edith was a bit of a heartbreaker for me. She did everything she was told and did so without emotion, though I sensed a lot of fear and trepidation in her. I know Bud and some of the elders were unhappy with Edith. For one thing, she seemed to be in love with Bud's right-hand man and faithful follower Harris Jensen. Harris was a do-gooder, and from rumor, Edith had a promiscuous past and wasn't always honest. Harris was obviously in love with Edith.

I probably should mention here that any romantic interests were now completely under inspection by the elders, and no one dated singly, only in groups. No one took a mate for marriage without the sanction of the church—meaning the elders, Bud and company. I took all of that into consideration as I watched Edith take part in our household, but I couldn't really find any fault with the girl. She did everything she was told to do and then some.

I was supposed to teach her to cook and have her fix a meal once a week. At first, I helped her, but in time, she drew on her own creativity, found great recipes, and did an awesome job of preparing a meal for the large family. She worked full-time in a dental office as a hygienist, so it was quite an undertaking to cook for our large extended family, especially for a young single girl who would rather have grabbed a bite at a fast-food establishment on her way home.

Edith was in our home for approximately a year before her fatal accident. I'm stating this now because, dear reader, you will see how a loving God helped me, in spite of my wavering about the rights and wrongs in our fellowship, to love this girl before she met a violent death. In fact, I was inspired to apply grace more than once before someone crossed over, and for that, I am eternally grateful.

I was part of a group that was heading in a wrong direction, which made me an accomplice. I appreciate not having certain regrets, though there were some major and painful ones, mainly associated with my own children. But here I deviate, so let me continue to describe Edith, because on some level, she was unique and special. She was one of those people who ended up getting negatively labeled to a large degree. Though some aspects of the labeling might have been true, beneath the exterior, there was something that, if allowed, would elevate the soul of any person willing to pay attention.

First of all, Edith was a physically beautiful girl. She had the most amazing clear white skin I have ever seen—translucent-like. She didn't smile a lot, but when she did, she briefly transmitted without speech "I like you." She was also intelligent, often winning the household strategy board games. Plus, I felt she was highly intuitive—a label not considered in the fellowship at all. We were discouraged from listening to our own hearts and minds. We always needed to check in with the group for any important decisions—and increasingly more often for even trivial decisions.

I didn't know her background, but I suspect either there had been some family home-life dysfunction, or possibly she carried some type of guilt from her past. Again, I never heard any specifics, and I really didn't want to know. I wanted to accept her at face value because she seemed to do everything out of fear. Normally, I would have found it off-putting to have someone help around the house because she was motivated by fear, but I knew she was not afraid of me. She was afraid of being punished by Bud. How did I know that? Because she confided in me one day that Bud had threatened to send her to another fellowship a good eleven-hour trip south of our location.

I suspected the proposal to move her was to help Harris avoid making the mistake of taking Edith as a future mate. Sending Edith a goodly distance from Harris would make her or break her. Edith didn't say much about the threat, but I remember having an immediate strong reaction and telling her, "You are not going to be sent away.

Seeking Oz

I don't believe in correcting the fear of the dark by putting someone in a dark closet. Edith, I won't allow it."

Don't ask me where that came from, because up to that point, my mercy contribution hadn't been worth a darn, but I always thank God that I gave her that sense of protection in the few remaining months of her life—or, rather, God, or the Source of Love, gave her that protection through me.

Back to the school moving to the garage. The move was seamless for a group of bright young high schoolers who were open to the constant changes taking place in their young lives. I have to mention here that all of the high schoolers were unique and special young people, and I continued to enjoy teaching them English literature and grammar. They were all gifted in various ways, and the two boys—Matt and Kevin—had a great sense of humor. Occasionally, they would play a harmless but creative prank on the teachers—at least me and Harris.

One time, they temporarily moved back the ceiling tiles to run a nearly invisible twine from behind the teacher's lectern to a spot near their desks. At the end near our teaching post, they would lower a tied carrot and control the up and down action from their desks, dangling the carrot when we were unsuspecting and jerking it back up into the ceiling crack before we turned around to see why the students were laughing.

On another occasion, they filled the garage with wadded-up newspapers about two feet deep. They had to do that prank late at night. You probably wonder how they got away with that behavior, since everything I've relayed about Bud has been about discipline. To Bud, the young people were the future of the fellowship and would eventually prove to be the backbone. He didn't mind that they were a little mischievous as long as they didn't disobey anything he was teaching. As mentioned previously, they were, in fact, tutored regularly during his teaching sessions, not only in the social sciences but also, eventually, in being upstanding contributions to the church.

To further their schooling in what it meant to work hard in the community, they became the core workers in Bud's latest brainstorm to pool all extraneous household work projects, such as lawn mowing, window washing, chimney cleaning, and any miscellaneous house projects. Thus, on a regular basis, the young people spent their Saturdays going from home to home and performing those tasks and more, lending a hand to each household. Of course, those same young people also were to become laborers in the upcoming church building, which came to be known as the Meeting Place, as well as the eventual Timber House, a permanent home to be built for Bud and his wife.

Ben Weber was the overseer of that weekly Saturday project. Ben was quite the taskmaster, so that position, in addition to his role as school principal, suited him well.

I might comment here that teaching young people the value of working hard and helping others is certainly a positive endeavor. I have always been a proponent of encouraging children to contribute to the household and community by having regular chores and lending a hand when needed. Prior to the more invasive fellowship years, my sons Joe and Matt helped in our huge family garden and with all of the household chores. They were not spoiled, and they were not idle, but they had time to be young and enjoy riding their dirt bikes on the country roads and participating in creative outdoor projects, such as building obstacle courses and motorcycle ramps.

With the increased workloads handed to the young people, there was no time for any such activities.

At face value, Bud's objective was a good one no doubt. Not everything was wrong about our fellowship. There were many positives, as stated earlier. However, as everyone knows, if a cult leader has an objective in mind—a singular goal—that leader must create a common agenda to keep everyone busy. In fact, he or she must keep people so busy that they lose objectivity and are less able to think on their own, make individual choices, or express preferences.

Hence, dear reader, I need to convey to you that we all—both young and old—were becoming busier and busier. We were living in the middle of a normal, well-populated rural city just outside a large, major metropolis. We were doing everything the hard way to conserve money, and most of the adults had two jobs: the money-making job and the community-living job. Our obligations and commitments to the fellowship isolated us from former friends and even close family. They were welcome to visit us, but they had to abide by our rules and schedules, and we always honored our church members and associated commitments above everyone else. Were we extreme? Yes, we were, emphatically, and becoming more extreme. You might even say exponentially so.

Phil and I have said many times since that had death and destruction not intervened, Bud more than likely would have set up his kingdom in some remote area and proclaimed himself as king of that kingdom. How that would have looked or eventuated, I don't know. I'm fairly confident there would have been no Jim Jones Kool-Aid or sex orgies, but it wouldn't have been *Little House on the Prairie* either.

Negatives and Hidden Negatives

With the fellowship getting more closely knit (another term for *entangled*), it became increasingly apparent to some of the more legalistic members, starting with Bud and his eldest daughter, Caryn Sue, the leader of the young people's group, that my son Joe was not fitting into the mold. In other words, just attending what Joe deemed as Sunday church was not enough—not nearly enough. It didn't matter that he lived in the city, a near fifty-mile round-trip from the church. It didn't matter that he was taking premed classes in the city and working part-time for his father.

The message was made clear to Joe. Joe didn't tell me; I saw his face one Sunday after his young people's small group dismissed and before the main meeting. Unfortunately, Joe was like me. He was conscientious and self-doubting in many instances. Being rebuked for not being a full-fledged member of our group would cause Joe to doubt his faith and his integrity. Mind you, this was a straight-A student who won best-citizenship awards in school. As described earlier, my son has a huge, loving heart and responsibly put himself through college while attending to his alcoholic father, and he respected the God of the religion I taught him by taking one full day of the weekend to attend church.

    I wish I had been stronger at that point in time. I wish I would have followed my aching heart and approached Joe to ask him what was troubling him. The problem is, I was afraid to ask because I knew it most likely had to do with some members passing judgment on him for not being a more involved participant in the group. I knew I was unhappy in the group, but I hadn't yet asked the hard question for myself: "Is this really what God requires of me?" How could I tell my son he was right to be somewhat distant, when I didn't know for certain whether or not I was wrong for doubting my desire to stay committed?

    Even as I write these few words here, dear reader, it still causes me much heartache and shame. Nothing is worse than abandoning your child when he or she needs you and trusts you. Joe was always stoic, but he was transparent—at least to me. Joe always kept his pain—both mental and physical—to himself and internalized it, but I could always tell when he was hurting. I knew even when he was a small boy that he was a strong man who wanted to bear his pain on his own and figure things out on his own. But in that case, though he was a young man of nineteen, we were talking about God—the God I'd introduced to him and the God that I, the mother he trusted, followed. We happened to be in that certain group with specific and strict requirements. It was a group that required full commitment to the group, or you were not following God.

    I learned later from someone in the fellowship that Joe's peers put pressure on Joe, telling him he needed to either commit completely or stay away. Again, this topic is painful, but though I am going to incriminate some foolish people, I point the finger mainly at myself for not standing up for Joe.

The story goes that the main persecutors were Bud's youngest son, Cory, and his girlfriend, Tiffany. Of course, I am sure Bud and Caryn Sue fostered the confrontation in order to ensure that the other young people in the fellowship did not trifle with what they deemed as half-hearted allegiance to the fellowship. You can imagine that Joe was used in the peer arena as a poor example. The ultimatum was issued by his own peers.

As a side note here, lest I forget to insert this later, within a few months after that incident, Tiffany disappeared from the fellowship and did not return for another year. Reliable rumor that proved out much later was that Cory and Tiffany were intimate regularly, and though they eventually married, their intimacy was kept secret from the rest of the fellowship. Not only does this point to hypocrisy where Joe was concerned, but you will see later in the story that there was also a double standard where Matt was concerned.

And, dear reader, there was so much more hypocrisy in the Royal Family that was not fully uncovered until beyond dissolution. The scripture stating that your sin will find you out certainly applied to those people who were supposed to be our examples to keep us from sinning. Ironically, the Royal Family's hidden sins were not what dissolved the fellowship. Death and destruction further down the road did. Had it not been for the extreme events leading up to dissolution, many of the secret sins might never have been discovered.

Since that part of my life journey in the cult was one of the most painful, I am going to purposefully jump the timeline here and complete what happened with Joe prior to my deliverance in 1990, at which time I had opportunity to speak openly with Joe and work through this transgression. However, bear in mind that Joe never blamed me, and he bore the brunt of his excommunication from our fellowship on his own. Like his mother, he needlessly took guilt on himself.

About a year after that first incident, Joe approached me and said he would like to move back into our home and become a part of the fellowship. By that time, he had helped his dad build another home in the rural area another twenty minutes beyond the fellowship location and a good forty-five miles from the college he attended in the city. His father's behavior was worsening from alcoholism, and he was belligerent with Joe. It was becoming more difficult for Joe to complete his schooling. Plus, I knew that Joe's conscience was bothering him due to his being barred from the church. He was equating following God with being part of the fellowship.

When I approached Bud with Joe's request, I was shocked when he said, "No, Joe needs to stay with his dad to ride it out and learn from his mistake of neglecting the fellowship." I cried silently to myself at night over that, but by then, I was really questioning the validity of staying. Had I known of the secret sins infesting the Royal Family, I would have shot out of the group like a cannonball on fire!

The only good thing that came of the awful treatment of Joe was that it was the beginning of my overwhelming desire to get out of the fellowship. Prior to all hell breaking loose, more incidents eventually took place that involved my other two sons, Matt and Jacob.

The Source of Love knew my vulnerable points. If I couldn't trust my own heart to help myself, surely I would listen to my mother heart, the heart that loves unconditionally—the heart that comes the closest to understanding the love of God, the Source of all love. This is the God I love. This is the God I adore because he doesn't want my sacrifice; he wants me to love myself first, and all love follows—love for mankind, love for all of God's creations, and love of the earth. Amazing concept! But I did not yet comprehend that.

Phil's Labor Contributions and the Church Building Project

Work ensued on the church building project, the Meeting Place. I can't do justice to explaining the amount of work that was then placed on all members of the fellowship. During that period, all other expectations continued—meetings and gatherings; potlucks and special celebrations; school; synergistic household projects; and so forth. I continued to teach school, cooked large meals seven days a week, raised little ones, and raised adults by counseling and teaching domestic household skills.

Also, there was always household movement. If a rental became available that was closer to the community, families and singles were encouraged to vacate their current homes and move closer to the proximity hub. Everyone helped. Men and boys physically moved all belongings. Women and girls cleaned the relinquished home as well as the new home. Sometimes members were called on to paint the new dwelling. Now we were adding a new project: building the church building.

Regarding cleanup of the homes, I developed a resentment that I had to conceal when participating in those projects. I have mentioned that one of my values, based on my upbringing, is to keep a clean, organized home. The old adage "Cleanliness is next to godliness" was never spoken in my childhood home; however, example said it all. The home of my youth was simple but tastefully decorated and always clean and well kept. My mom was a wonderful homemaker, and every one of her children naturally followed suit. We all worked hard at maintaining a clean and welcoming home for our husbands and children. I never sat down to relax as long as my housework was unfinished for the day. Of course, in the fellowship, unless I was doing work for the school or reading to the children, I pretty much didn't sit down at all. Relaxing was nonexistent unless I was asleep for the night.

At any rate, on many occasions, I felt overwhelmed with the amount of cleaning and organizing required to help members of our fellowship facilitate their move into communal proximity. Not all members maintained clean homes. Up until then, I had never been judgmental about how others kept up their homes. I knew the level of cleanliness I was comfortable with, but I didn't have expectations of others to do as I did. In fact, I often wished I could be more relaxed. That is, I didn't have a problem until I had to help others in the fellowship clean their homes. Again, we were constantly moving. Even after families and singles were in proximity, there were often changes and repositioning that required a move, which required more cleaning.

One occasion in particular, I found myself cleaning someone's stove and oven. Never before or since have I seen such a mess! The stovetop and oven must never have been cleaned during the entire course of that woman's stay in the home she was renting. I must have scrubbed for a good three hours on the stove. I used steel wool and harsh cleaning supplies in an effort to pry loose layers of caked-on, melted-on food. It was always important to get a returned cleaning deposit, so the job had to be done.

My resentment built because I worked hard at keeping up with my busy household and maintaining a level of cleanliness only to have to help someone else who was neglectful and lazy. I often felt that the few female workhorses in the fellowship were often held to the lowest denominator when it came to pitching in to help with that type of activity. I do have to add that Sandra Sue was in that category as well. As much as I disliked the lady's attitude, she was exemplary as well in maintaining a well-run household in both cooking and cleaning. She was one of the hardworking matriarchs, and though she never said anything, it was obvious that she too struggled with those activities.

At that time, Phil got more involved in the physical labor. Bud referred to Phil as a "mechanical genius." As it turned out, though

Phil was quiet and unassuming about his work, he not only was an excellent carpenter and concrete foreman but also was especially talented with anything mechanical. As Bud discovered from observing, you might say Phil really was a mechanical genius. Phil came from a family of doctors and concert musicians talented in both left-brain and right-brain aptitudes. Phil was definitely true to his genetics.

Since Phil was basically a passive, humble person, he didn't realize he was talented. After all, upon finishing his military obligations of four years during the Vietnam War, instead of continuing a college education, he chose to do hard labor, working for a concrete contractor. Originally, he started with laying forms for residential pours. Eventually, the company moved to commercial contracts for high-rise building projects of significant size and scope. Phil earned the reputation in his company for being extremely accurate—within a small fraction of an inch—in his measurements for laying out foundations for skyscrapers and large commercial buildings.

On our honeymoon, the old Volkswagen bus Phil had purchased after selling his new van broke down alongside the road on the way home. Phil didn't say a word. He reached into the glove box and rummaged for something to fix the mechanical problem. I recall a rubber band being one of the makeshift items he used. We made it all the way home without a problem. Anything that might break down around the house, inside or outside, Phil could fix it.

He thought everyone knew what he knew. He used to accuse me of having no sense of basic physics. Mechanics were definitely not in my range of aptitudes. In retaliation, I couldn't really accuse him of not being able to spell, write, or create through art, because he could do all of that also! Since I sewed from scratch everything from my clothing to the children's clothing to curtains, I would retort, "I bet you can't hem a dress." He never answered; he just smiled.

When Bud noticed Phil's skills, he put them to work. A used John Deere 440 bulldozer and a large secondhand rototiller were purchased for the church project and would also be used eventually for the Timber House project. Of course, they were old and in need of repair. Phil worked laboriously on them with little to no options to purchase parts. He worked until they were running and useful. Also, Phil was asked to work on a flatbed truck to be used for work projects and for hauling wood to heat our homes—another conservation effort to limit utility bills.

In addition to the strong, pervading attitude that no one owned anything but, rather, we all shared, the overriding principle was also to be as resourceful as possible. Resourcefulness can mean different things to different people. To Bud and his band of male followers, or elders, mainly Curtis, Harris, Sam, and Ben, the idea was to spend as little as possible on anything that could be repaired or built by the fellowship—period.

Phil often was troubled by the fact that safety, ethics, and good common sense were sometimes cast aside when making determinations in favor of frugality. For example, when Bud's temporary home was being built and the elders decided to use the shell of an old barn, makeshift equipment and leveraging were applied, and in the process, one of the young single men was suddenly and violently knocked off the roof. Fortunately, he didn't suffer any life-threatening or permanent damage, just some scrapes and bruises, but Phil had a difficult time with such unnecessary accidents. He worked around large cranes and commercial equipment, and he had a healthy respect for proper tools and the correct way to work with equipment and vehicles to best protect the workers involved.

He expressed some of those concerns to the elders on occasion to no avail. Phil was considered too particular and perfectionistic. He was told that his job was to repair and troubleshoot with whatever resources were available, since he had the knowledge to do so. He didn't need expensive tools or parts. We would make do to get the job done.

That slipshod mentality encompassed other areas of our community life, with the lowest denominator of common sense often taking the lead, and I felt it many times where my children were concerned, such as the time we all vacationed at the ocean, and a strenuous hike was imposed on all families, including little ones.

Against my better judgment, we let Jacob walk on his own, as was encouraged, though he was only four years old. The trail was narrow, steep, precarious, and, at one point, elevated seventy or eighty feet above the sandy beach below. At that point, Jacob stumbled and tumbled about ten feet down the rocky cliff, fortunately landing in a clump of brush. Though no one in the fellowship ever uttered cuss words, I let out a resounding "Shit!" which was delivered with righteous indignation. That utterance attracted the attention of a young married woman, Ellie, who approached me several months later as a possible ally—an important part of the story that takes place further down the Yellow Brick Road.

I always reflect fondly on that incident where Ellie was concerned, though the incident was deeply disturbing and proved my greatest fears—that we were following someone who was not safety-conscious. Thankfully, Jacob was safe, but my mother heart and brain were fully activated. It was another tally mark on the wake-up side of the equation.

Unfortunately, another label that Bud and Sandra Sue assigned me was "overprotective," as mentioned earlier. There were many times when I had to look the other way when they would insist on having a situation their way, regardless of possible danger to adults or children. Looking back, I don't know why I would accept that label.

Previous to joining the fellowship, I allowed my children to ride motorcycle dirt bikes down country roads, and sometimes they would be out all day. They constructed ramps and ditches, working several days to create obstacles and hurdles. Joe and Matt were strong, courageous young men who were adventurous, imaginative, and daring yet not outrageous or ridiculously out of control. They always strategized and calculated before leaping—something I always appreciated about them. Though he wasn't their natural father, Phil was like that also and often commented on the intelligence and sensibility of the boys.

In our first year of dating, Phil and the boys rode dirt bikes regularly, often creating tag games and competitive games of skill. I never worried because I trusted all three to have common sense.

Bud's ideas of manliness sometimes just seemed plain foolish and half-assed to me. I didn't use that word then. I use it now. His disregard for common safety was asinine—and I followed. That made me foolish at the time. I am abundantly thankful that the Source of Love delivered me from that bondage. However, I needed to pay attention to my higher guidance, which, at that point, was becoming more and more of a possibility.

The work frenzy to build the church the hard way was under way. No, there were no accidents during that time. The half-assed mentality took its toll a little further down the road. But what did happen during that period was absolute commitment for all hands on deck, including, as mentioned before, no time for family, friends, questioning, or thinking, just working.

Everyone was becoming sufficiently cloned. Any deviation, no matter how simple or innocent, would be attacked not just by the Royal Family or the elders; any single member had the right and duty to call his or her brother or sister to the righteous path described and underscored by Bud during his ongoing and relentless teaching about community living.

We were called to follow God and his son, Jesus, by devoting ourselves entirely to the church and its teachings—to love each other by owning no property, sharing everything, and relinquishing individualism. We could never trust our own thinking but needed to turn everything over to the church, and collectively, we would decide what was best. *Collectively*, again, meant meetings made up of the fellowship members. Now that all members were becoming brainwashed, it wasn't just the Royal Family or the elders who would come up with restrictive, punishing decisions; the entire group was in unison. We were all marching to the beat of the same drum.

Some of us were silently suffering under it and questioning, but we didn't dare let on—not yet.

✝ Years Ten and Eleven

A Community Sharing Company

During that period, my worst fears concerning living in community were realized. We were diving into what we referred to as "common purse," a term commonly used in Bud's teaching for the past several years. To follow God's leading and to put our faith into practice, we were repeatedly admonished to share everything we had, as the early Christians in the book of Acts had. Now we were taking that next step to give up all of our money and our homes to the church, our fellowship group.

I don't know the legalities Bud and the elders enacted to launch that final phase of our giving up all of our material goods, but launch they did. They formed a community sharing company. All of us in the fellowship who were committed believers were encouraged to join the company and sign the membership document.

The elders gathered four or five individuals, some single and some married, expert in the emerging technologies of that time to create a software system that kept track of all of the monies collected and all of the bills to be paid by each individual or family. Our salaries were turned over to the church.

The finance group took our entire paychecks and paid our monthly bills. Every month, depending on how many were in our family, we were given a little green cloth pouch sewn by Sandra Sue, which contained cash for groceries and all incidentals. The monthly amount my family—Phil, Matt, Jacob, and I—were allowed above the grocery allowance was sixty-five dollars. The remainder of our paychecks, which was significantly more than what we were handed back in the pouch, went toward the Meeting Place and Timber House.

The allowance we received in the green pouch was to cover clothing, shoes, and any extras that might come up during the month. Since we had been practicing frugality by sewing our own clothes or purchasing them from thrift stores, that was not supposed to be a problem. Most miscellaneous purchases could be bought from secondhand ads or thrift stores. We were not buying anything but the bare necessities by that time.

Needless to say, the sixty-five dollars didn't go far, and we had to make many sacrifices to ensure that amount worked for us. Once, when one of our pygmy goats fell ill, we asked for a little extra to take her to the veterinarian, but we were denied. Thankfully, with extra care provided on our part and much prayer, the little goat survived.

Christmas shopping was difficult. The gifts we bought for our immediate family—Joe, Matt, and Jacob—were ridiculously cheap. Pitiful, you might say. Christmas shopping for extended family was a tradition with Phil's family, and we felt we needed to continue to honor the tradition, or they would be offended. However, we certainly couldn't tell them we were signing over our paychecks to our church and living on a pittance for miscellaneous purchases. They would never understand. It was difficult enough for them to accept our increasing isolation from family. Since my family was more in number, we'd stopped exchanging years earlier and focused on our immediate families only; hence, we were able to avoid any such issues on my side of the family.

During the Christmas of 1987, at which time we were participating in common purse, I had to be resourceful for my mother-in-law's gift. I put together a photo album of Jacob and Melissa, including the comical and witty things they had said throughout the year. I padded the album cover and creatively crafted with material, lace, and ribbon an attractive presentation. I was proud of the result and figured a labor of love would cover the fact that we weren't giving our usual, more expensive gifts. I recall my mother-in-law's look of disappointment after opening the gift. She said, "Honey, don't you like to buy gifts for people?"

Now I had another label. I was a tightwad. Ugh!

Additional to common purse, each family owning a home was to sign their home over to the fellowship as part of their membership in the community company. Many in the fellowship, of course, particularly the singles, did not own homes. But those of us who did were approached solemnly, as if our very salvation and potential to escape from the fires of hell were dependent on yielding to the call.

As mentioned earlier, Phil and I had taken out a small loan to build our home four years prior, and the balance was low, as we were encouraged to pay down the balance as soon as possible. That was considered to be the responsible thing to do as wise and faithful stewards of our money. Thankfully, we had not paid off our home when came the latter days of the time of death and destruction, as you will learn later in my narrative. Dear reader, in looking back, I see that the Source of Love started answering my prayers to be free long before I was released from the cult prison.

We also had to turn over to common purse a payoff balance from the sale of Dogwood Lane. We originally contracted with the buyers to make monthly payments to us, but a few years following the original transaction, the new owners took out another loan and paid us the lump-sum balance. That lump sum was several thousand dollars that went to the community sharing company as well. Remember, we were to own no property and were to give over everything to the whole, to the church.

Moving to common purse, signing over our home, and turning over the additional real estate money was like a death sentence to me. Shortly after Phil and I signed the membership document, my thoughts, reinforced by unusually extreme frugal practices, were *I will never have freedom of choice again. No matter our wages or what we are actually capable of purchasing, our choices are limited to the small amount of money in the green pouches delivered by Sandra Sue.*

This feels like dying of thirst within reach of cool, fresh water. I am absolutely miserable and frustrated. Am I the only one who feels this way?

The choices weren't just related to giving up all of our material possessions. Even more difficult than relinquishing our hard-earned revenue source was surrendering our decision-making where our children were concerned, as you will learn a little later in the narrative.

My joy considerably ebbed away at that time. The world became a little grayer. The dulling of my surroundings was similar to what I'd experienced when my brother died.

Only this time, I was dying.

Though I was experiencing a form of depression and anxiety, because I was a tenacious person, all of my suppressed emotions were building like a smoldering volcano about to erupt. I was raised by my father to never say die. So what did I do? I became angry— very angry. This all seemed so wrong to me.

I thought, *I am so angry! I need answers! Can this be right? It feels so wrong!*

Dorothy's indignation stepped forward.

Final Straws and the Big Questions

In May 1988, I became angry and miserable enough that I challenged God.

Without confiding in anyone, including my husband, I expressed explosive and unrepressed anger in the secret place of my own heart and mind. I was angry with God!

I spoke clearly and directly to what I knew as the highest authority imaginable and said, I hate community living. I resent not being able to make choices for myself and my family. I doubt the authenticity of the leader of the group, and I doubt his interpretation of the Word of God. In fact, the Word, in many cases, leads me to believe that you are a mean, vindictive, exacting, and expecting God. You expect sacrifice from me, and I feel no joy of living. I don't feel "life abundantly," as Jesus expressed in the scriptures. I doubt the scriptures. Some of the scriptures make me feel less than loved and in jeopardy of the fires of an eternal hell.

Where is my joy? Where is the pleasure of discovery and choice? I need answers. I need them for me and for my family, whom I love unconditionally. Surely you love me as much or more than I love my children if you are indeed the creator God, the Source of Love. Why then do I want to run away from you, when I grew up loving you and depending on you? I believe these teachings are wrong. I believe the leader of this group is wrong. But I want answers from you and you only.

I will give you two years to answer my questions. During that time period, my promise to you is that I will listen, but I will listen only to you. I will be aware of everything you bring to me.

My questions are the following:

(1) *Is there something wrong with me for wanting to leave this fellowship? If so, let me know, and I will decide whether to stay per your insistence or leave and take whatever punishment you may inflict on me for doing so.*
(2) *Is there something wrong with the group's teachings? If so, please make this abundantly clear to me, and I will leave.*

Understand, dear reader, that the brainwashing of the group was such at that point that should anyone in the core group decide to leave and his or her household was divided, the dissenter would leave with the possibility of a spouse and children not coming with him or her. Believe it or not, at that juncture, in the core group of individuals most dedicated, no one openly challenged the possibility of leaving.

The more vested the member was, the more entrenched the member was, and the more difficult it would be to leave. The possibility of leaving part of your family was a strong reality. I was in that core group. I didn't know if Phil would insist on staying with Jacob should I decide to leave, though my mother heart was prepared to fight because the fighting spirit was rising to a fever pitch within me.

There were several final straws that contributed to resolving that challenge. The courage it took to challenge was sheer desperation, and I have told many friends and acquaintances since that time that the Source of Love honors such courage. Remember Dorothy. The desire to protect her dog, Toto, and her newfound friends from the bullying lion incited her to challenge the fear that bound them all.

The goal is to acquire a brain that thinks and makes clear, positive decisions and choices; a heart that feels, loves, expands, and grows; and a sense of going home to the inner guidance given us as a rightful inheritance. We have it all, but it often takes many miles or experiences and many detours to find out that Oz has no answers. We already have them inside us. But the first step is to cast aside fear.

My first step after putting forth questions to God himself was to confront Bud—alone and without talking to anyone else about it. I believe that the grace of God covered me more than sufficiently in those moments, because up until that point, Bud had had a great deal of influence over me, as with all of the members of the group. But I was prepared to stand my ground. I remember thinking, *This will be a statement to Bud, not a question. Not for discussion. Not for his input. I will deliver and not wait for his rebuttal.*

I made arrangements to speak to him alone, and as always, Bud was available, because we were important to him. He had sway over us, and I am sure such requests were received happily. He was a master of manipulation, and his ego was fed on a regular basis by those of us who relinquished our God-given choices to him. This exchange made him important and powerful. After all, whatever he determined was law. There would be no discussion, unless, of course, we needed to go before the entire group or create a small group, which was by then the same as getting direction from Bud. This time, there would be no large group, no small group, no Bud, no Sandra Sue, and no Royal Family member to answer my questions or make decisions for me. I would consult God and God alone.

In spite of the fact that twenty-eight years have lapsed since that time, I can clearly recall what I said to Bud that day in May 1988. Prior to that brief meeting, I documented a short handwritten note in the margin of my Bible, opposite 1 John 5:15: "And if we know that he hears us—whatever we ask—we know that we have what we asked of him" (NIV).

The scribbled note was "May 1988. 2 yrs. Expect answers!"

My brief message to Bud was "I am questioning leaving the group, but I have given God a sufficient amount of time to let me know if this is the direction I should take. I will watch and listen. I expect God to let me know. In the meantime, I do not want you to confront me, check on me, or send anyone to talk to me about this. You will have no influence in my decision. In the meantime, I will continue, of course, to be a part of the fellowship. I will carry on with my household responsibilities, attend all meetings, teach school, and do everything I normally do."

Bud's response was "Don't you think, Makena, that you should deliver this to the group at large?"

I looked him straight in the eye and said, "No, I do not. God is able to answer me directly, not through the group." And I left.

Dear reader, I sound bold and confident. The fact of the matter is, at that time, I was extremely angry—angry with God and angry with Bud, his wife, and their haughty family.

I thought, *Call me selfish, call me private, or call me overprotective!*

I don't care! I want out, but I am trapped by a punishing God and a controlling belief system. What are my choices? Follow the belief system and be miserable? Or run away and possibly forfeit my husband and child and, ultimately, an eternity in heaven? I need answers! The only way I can go forward with any peace is to have answers—from God!

Dear reader, I don't know how my confrontation with Bud affected him, but he did, for the most part, leave me alone. Since I gave God a two-year period to answer my question, Bud had sufficient time to influence me, but unbeknownst to me and everyone in the group, Bud had his hands full with trying to hide the sins of his own family, as you will eventually learn. As long as I was still doing what I needed to do and one of the main households in the community was still operating full speed ahead, there was no need to worry about my jumping ship.

Allow me to enumerate in this section, dear reader, some of the signs God presented in the way of straw after straw that would and did indeed break the camel's back. Sometimes I reflect and marvel at the Source of Love, who delivers exactly what our hearts desire.

The responsibility in expressing such definitive, demanding questions is that we need to be still and know that the Source of Love is indeed capable of delivering answers and will do so. It is our part to be aware and be patient with the unfolding, because unfold it will. Somehow, that was conveyed to me when I came up with the two-year deadline. I have often reflected on that.

Where did that timeframe come from?

Dear reader, it was exactly two years later that Phil and our family walked out safely.

May of 1988 looked like an impossible mess—a crazy and unnecessary imprisonment. May of 1990 ushered in glorious freedom on all levels!

Experience after experience—as many as we need—will punctuate, accentuate, and highlight until we get it. What we want or need is there for the asking. I wanted answers, and answers I would get. This is a God I can love with all of my heart and all of my might and to whom I will always and forever be thankful. My heart fully praises and adores this God!

Straw Number One

As mentioned previously, the situations that most impacted my desire to leave the church fellowship were related to unjust treatment of my children. I included in an earlier account that around 1988, Joe requested to come back to live with Phil and me and take part in the fellowship.

Bud's denial of Joe's request was heartbreaking to me. I knew how difficult life was for Joe in going to college and living with a hard-core alcoholic. Joe loved his dad, but it was getting increasingly more difficult for him to endure the belligerent treatment when Steve was in a drunken stupor. How did I know that? Not from Joe. I lived it.

Joe was not only maintaining an academic status of being on the dean's list at the state college several miles from his father's home but also doing auto bodywork on the side, and he had recently helped his dad build a home.

Joe was a quiet, stoic soul who never complained. When he was still in high school, about seventeen years old, he once fell off an elevated log at a church social—the old-fashioned Victorian picnic. I saw him fall, and then he disappeared from view in the large crowd. Sometime later, I was aware that he tapped me on the leg from behind. He had broken his femur—an injury that eventuated in a full-body cast—and crawled around the outside perimeter of the crowd to get to me. He didn't want to draw attention to himself. That was Joe.

When Bud said that Joe needed to work it out with his dad, he was trying to send a message to Joe that he had made an easier choice to live with his dad than to sacrifice his life for the church and join our group.

Bud couldn't have been more wrong.

Joe had been sacrificing his four college years for a father he loved, but he found he was enabling his father to get worse. Joe felt it better to get back to the church and pray for his dad. He was going to have to leave soon to get his master's degree in another location, and his dad was far too dependent on him.

Bud's unwavering pronouncement was more than difficult to justify. My thoughts, driven by an ever-growing anger, were *I married an alcoholic, and my son is paying for it. Steve is even worse than when I lived with him. He verbally abuses his son, the son who takes care of him. How unfair and unjust that I am denied the choice to take my son into my home during a critical time in his life—to break free from his abusive father and complete his education.*

Yes, I kept it to myself, but my self-talk was building in fury.

How crazy—utterly crazy—is it to deny my eldest son a place in my home, when I am housing several young adults even older than Joe to whom I owe nothing and from whom I receive very little? Yet I lavish all of my mother nurturing on them in order to provide equality in the home where I still raise my own remaining children.

This is an insane imbalance! Joe deserves my love and support more than anyone in my household other than my own children. This can't be right! This is insane!

I could endure the refusal of Joe's request only because at that time, I was looking for answers directly from God to determine whether I stayed or left the fellowship. Bud's negative response to Joe's request was a resounding push in the direction of leaving, which would prove beneficial to Joe not to join our group. I kept that in my heart and registered it as one of many a tally in favor of leaving.

Straw Number Two

Earlier, dear reader, I told you I shopped once a month, and it required traveling downhill from our home about twenty miles to the main city. I looked forward to that monthly trip because I felt such independence. I could take my immediate family—Jacob, Melissa, and Matt—and be gone for about five hours with no expectations from our extended household to fix their dinner. After shopping, I could meet Phil at a local fast-food establishment and have a meal that I didn't have to fix. Temporarily escaping from heavy responsibilities in my home and spending time with just my immediate family was heaven.

I loved that Matt would take half of the long grocery list and take charge of one of the extra-large shopping carts with Jacob in tow. He would head one way in the large warehouse marketplace, and I would go the opposite direction with Melissa. We would then meet at checkout. Matt always gave me such a sense of support and protection, though he was only in his teens.

As a side note, in 1988, Matt was back in the public neighborhood high school. Due to some families leaving the fellowship, the high school group was down to only four in number. The four remaining high schoolers included Matt, Kevin, April's daughter, and one other young lady. The young people petitioned the elders to attend public school for their senior year, and Bud and the elders conceded. I thought the elders probably determined that it would be good for the high schoolers to integrate prior to going to college. That way, the fellowship could guide them with dealing with the outside worldly ways before they were sent out into the college arena. At that time, the elders integrated middle school, which numbered about seven young twelve- to fourteen-year-olds. The same teachers taught the same subjects with the age-appropriate curricula. I taught English.

To resume, I started noticing that after shopping, when I headed back up the hill, I would get chest pains. I was only forty-one years old and healthy. I thought, *Why am I having chest pains? Why is the pain especially pronounced the closer I get to home?*

I felt as if something were sitting on my chest—something heavy. I made a doctor's appointment. The doctor applied the usual test for possible heart issues, an electrocardiogram (EKG).

I remember thinking how unconventional the doctor appeared to me. After the tests, he took me into his study and asked me if I was under any stress. Data gathered from the applied treadmill test revealed normal heart activity. However, what I'd described to him as symptoms could be related to stress, he said.

Dear reader, it is amazing what brainwashing can do. Of course I was under stress! After I was free from the cult, neighboring churchgoers in our community said to me, "We are amazed you didn't blow a fuse!"

Did I tell the doctor anything at all about my daily regime and for how long I had been at it? No. Why? Brainwashing. I would not be spiritual if I claimed stress, I thought. I should be able to withstand any pressures if I was doing the right thing. Yes, I was questioning at that point, but I was still not operating with all of the awareness that trusts my own thoughts and rationale. I was looking for answers from God himself. Regarding that particular situation, God did deliver, but the solution didn't come through the doctor. A little later, it came from Bud himself.

The doctor prescribed a pill but didn't tell me what it was—just that it might help with the chest pains. I am sure, looking back, that he could read my body language. I refused to admit stress. He didn't press me for any answers. I could have been in an abusive spousal situation or any number of stressful situations I was unwilling to admit.

I went home and took the pill. Again, I never asked what it was, but I was sure it had to be what we called "tranquilizers" in that day, now called antianxiety or antidepressant medication.

From that one pill, all I felt was the ability to cope better, which

Seeking Oz

actually was really nice, but when I felt the difference, I immediately threw the medication in the garbage.

I thought, *I will not rely on medications. I need to keep my wits about me and find out what is truth without the support of any type of medicinal, mind-altering escape aids. God will get through.*

However, I did go to Bud and tell him I needed to have less responsibility from teaching for a time because I was having chest pains.

Late at night, I made my way the short distance down to Bud and Sandra Sue's temporary home, making sure not to trip over the electrical umbilical cord to our home and dodging any poison oak, with little to no moonlight to light my way. It was a downhill grade and a little difficult to navigate among the scrub oak and woody brush, so I had to watch my step. Phil agreed to watch the children and asked no questions when I said I needed to speak with Bud. I had forewarned Bud that I needed to talk to him, and he was waiting for me when I arrived.

I briefly explained that I was having chest pain and would like some relief from teaching for a time. Without any dialogue, Bud motioned for me to sit in a chair near him while he pulled a book from his small bookshelf. He quietly and solemnly reached for his reading glasses, and under the dim light of a lamp, he read me a short story.

The story was about a widow who was raising her small child alone, when she contracted a fatal disease. She was concerned about leaving the earth and her young dependent child. Though she was worried, as fate had it, someone came forward and offered to raise the child when she died. As it turned out, it was for the best, because that person was better equipped than even the mother to do the job.

When Bud finished the story, I felt mortification. Bud removed his glasses, set them on a nearby desk with the book, leaned back in his chair, folded his hands across his chest, and offered no further explanation for reading me such a story. He didn't address my request to get relief from teaching. It was clear: his message was that if I died, someone else would fill my shoes, take over my job of raising Jacob and Melissa, and probably do a better job in the long run.

I said nothing further. I saw the expression on his face. It was set. He was somber and serious. His penetrating gaze was hard and fixed. He wanted me to understand that I was dispensable, even to my own family and children. I knew in that moment that he knew I was becoming increasingly unhappy with my situation. I knew that he knew I possessed an important piece of property in relation to the community. I also had a credible standing in the community. However, I was becoming a little more expressive in the groups. Remember, I was the token mercy person who generally went opposite the direction of his leadership and teachings, and I had already expressed to him that I was asking God for answers as to whether I should leave. I was becoming a threat. I saw it in his face.

Furthermore, there was no need to discuss whether I would teach. He knew me. I wouldn't abandon the children if there was to be no replacement for me. I would conscientiously carry on—and on and on until …

I stumbled home in the dark night, responsibly wiping aside an outpouring of unstoppable tears to clearly and safely make my way uphill. My self-talk was *Nothing is more important to me than my children. I need to be sane and healthy for my children. This is a message, a warning. I will record this in my heart and brain. I can't tell Phil or anyone else because I can't trust them. It could get back to Bud. I can't let on to Bud that I am afraid.*

Help me, God. Help me to find my way. This scares me! Surely this has to be wrong. Very, very wrong! This man is evil!

Was that a reason to leave? Emphatically, yes.

Straw Number Three

As I said, Matt, Kevin, and the other high schoolers attended the nearby high school in their senior year. They had been out of the public school system for a couple of years, so there were adjustments to be made in going back. Both Matt and Kevin were athletic, so they tried out and were accepted to the senior varsity basketball team.

Getting up to speed with public school athletics at that level was no easy feat, but the two boys did well. In fact, though both started on the bench, they worked diligently and eventually became starters. The boys accomplished that milestone with a group of athletes who had been playing together consistently while Matt and Kevin were in the church school.

Dear reader, if you know anything about high school athletic politics, coaching, and athletic peer pecking order, making the team and excelling in senior year of high school was not the norm, and there were many trials for both of them in the process.

Also, there were social pressures to contend with as they reentered the public school system. Bear in mind that these high schoolers had been taught daily by Bud himself, so they were sufficiently brainwashed to follow all of the rules set forth in our community. To reiterate, one of the rules of our community was that there would be no dating. All single male-and-female interaction took place within the group. There were sufficient group activities, of course, so there was ample time for adolescents and young adults to interact appropriately and without any temptations. When old enough to marry, the male would approach the elders for them to determine if the match was acceptable.

The next situation that provided a tally mark in favor of leaving included Matt and happened simultaneous to Cory, Bud's youngest son, and Tiffany secretly having intercourse well in advance of marriage. Cory and Tiffany were only four or five years senior to

Matt. Of course, no one knew why Tiffany left the fellowship for a year or so, and we didn't know about any of the details regarding her one-year disappearance until the cult was completely disbanded.

Matt was about halfway through his senior year, when a girl in his English class took a liking to him. Matt was not quite his full height of six feet five inches but was well on his way at about six feet four inches. He was handsome. Matt inherited his father's good looks and regal posture—shoulders back and head erect. His father used to complain about male strangers taking an immediate dislike to him and wanting to fight. On hearing that, even at my young age of eighteen, I knew exactly why. Steve carried himself with confidence. He had no fear and, actually, was prepared to fight anyone who challenged him.

Matt had the same deportment as his father without the underlying anger to fuel a spontaneous fight. Matt carried himself with confidence but in a quiet and polite manner. It was no surprise that a student in his English class would be attracted to him. Matt was not only good looking, on the senior varsity basketball team, and a polite and thoughtful young man but also a straight-A student and the chosen candidate for valedictorian. To summarize, he was a catch.

Matt came home one day and told us that a nice, somewhat shy student in his English class had invited him to a school Sadie Hawkins dance by way of slipping him a note after class. We knew, of course, that Matt would have to get permission to attend. Though the fellowship rules were stringent, I figured that since the dance was chaperoned, there would be no problem. After all, these young people would soon be attending college.

I was wrong. Bud and the elders not only told him he couldn't go to the dance but also held a special meeting to let him know how dangerous it was to be alone with a young woman at that age and particularly to have physical contact with her while dancing.

I'll never forget how awful that meeting was for Matt—and not just because he was told no—though he made no indication that he was upset. He sat quietly and without rebuttal throughout. We met on the deck of Bud's temporary home. Attending were Bud, Andon, Harris, Ben, and Curtis. It was odd that I was invited, but in retrospect, I believe it was only because Bud knew I was challenging the system, and he probably thought I would be flattered that they included me with something that could and should be handled by just the men. They did not invite Phil. To be honest, Phil was passive and would not have cared to attend. In many respects, at that time, Andon had more influence in molding Matt than Phil.

The men went too far in letting Matt know he couldn't trust his hormones. They portrayed him, the male, as being out of control and wrong to even consider getting near the girl in something as intimate as a dance. Having no idea who the young lady was, they portrayed the girl as most likely a wayward, worldly, ungodly woman who undoubtedly could lead him into the temptation to have sex. Mind you, Matt was a late bloomer at that stage and hadn't considered such possibilities. His focus was merely to go to a high school dance with a shy female schoolmate, and the entire meeting was about men and women having sexual relationships.

Again, to jump the timeframe, Matt carried their words with him well into college, when he told me much later that the visual he'd been left with was something Andon said during the meeting: "Whenever you are with a young woman, just picture me in between the two of you." They managed to instill fear in him—that he was incapable of managing himself when in the company of someone he might be attracted to. He also couldn't trust the advances of a woman. A forward woman was not to be trusted. Unknown to me at the time, Matt had to go to counseling to assist him with the resultant damage. He recalls that the counselor couldn't believe Matt actually experienced such guilt and fear related to a natural act. The counselor's reaction only served to make Matt feel further isolated in his struggle to overcome his needless but real-to-him fear. Matt experienced the pain that comes from living through an extreme—a fear-based, shame-based religion.

Isn't it always that way? The conscientious one who wants to do right suffers the most under such insidious indoctrination.

Up until he approached the deck of Bud's house that night, Matt was an innocent young man who wanted to go to a dance with a shy schoolmate who'd worked up the courage to invite him to a chaperoned dance. When he left, he was sad, ashamed, and confused. He was going to have to tell the girl no, when he knew it had taken courage for her to ask him. He liked the fact that she'd chosen him. He felt good about that. Now he had to tell her no and probably hurt her feelings. Worse, he had to tell her why. He couldn't tell her what the men had told him. He had to say that his church forbid it—period. He could give no further explanation as to why the church forbid it and no further explanation to soften the rejection.

His heart and head were in conflict. I got the picture loud and clear. The conflict I had been working with was now a real one for my son. I knew the elders' decision had to be wrong, but I couldn't coach him otherwise. I wish I had. I believed at that time that I had to wait until I knew for sure if I was wrong; otherwise, I could confuse my child even more. The right-or-wrong scales, however, indeed tipped considerably again because another of my children was suffering needlessly. What could have been a normal, happy situation had turned into an ugly nightmare for my undeserving son.

Unnecessarily, my son was hurting, and my heart was aching for him. My thoughts churned within.

How can this be right? If I were in control of my parenting, Matt would go to the dance, and I would be delighted for him.

Matt is so good. He works hard helping others in the fellowship, and he supports his home and family untiringly and unselfishly. He never asks for favors or complains about anything. He has made innumerable sacrifices, he has unnecessarily endured financial deprivation, and he has traded his youthful activities willingly to

Seeking Oz

serve others. He simply wants to honor a young girl's request to attend a chaperoned dance. Instead, he is told he should keep his hormones under control and avoid wanton women. He is delivered an ugly and cruel message.

He doesn't deserve this! Dear God. This has got to be wrong!

Shortly after that incident, we learned that in another private men's meeting, another young member about Cory's age had been berated by the men because another member had found a popular worldly magazine depicting nude female models in his possession. I can't remember all that was included in that young man's punishment, but it was more than just an admonishment. I believe he was not allowed to drive for several weeks, and other privileges were taken from him. He was shamed significantly before all of the men in attendance.

Someone told me that twenty-one-year-old was spanked mercilessly like a young toddler with brute force before all of the men. I found that harsh, ugly, and degrading.

I thought, *I am so angry. All this can't be right. Another tally mark for leaving. Leave! Leave! Leave!*

As Joe had so astutely pointed out previously, they placed the emphasis more on sex than what would have been typically normal, thereby drawing attention to it. Also, sex was made to be a bad thing. It is no wonder every one of Bud and Sandra Sue's five children were transgressors, not only by their own skewed standards but also by society at large. It seemed that Bud and Sandra Sue bludgeoned the innocent members with thou-shalt-nots and disciplines to provide examples to their own wayward children, all the while holding them out as our role models.

I thought, *Isn't this a typical bully trademark?* "Do as I say, not as I do, and if you don't, you shall pay."

That double standard hit home even heavier with their daughter Colette, who got caught in a hidden deception. The deception took place a little further down the Yellow Brick Road—actually, not far at all. But the Royal Family did not meet with elders or any fellowship members when dealing with their children's transgressions. Bud and Sandra Sue took matters into their own hands and hid their sins, and none of us were the wiser—not yet anyway.

Straw Number Four

By now, dear reader, it is redundant for me to tell you that our small fellowship group did everything together—worship, work projects, building projects, school for our children, picnics, events, and on and on. Everything! We were so close that we determined what books we would read, what types of clothing we would wear, what limitations were needed in regard to secular entertainment, and how we spent our money. At one point, we were even told what type of car to buy.

A few of the men got together and researched economy cars that could last a good while and that were easily maintained well into the future. We would be able to swap out parts for a distant time, so we would be frugal and responsible in the area of transportation. The car turned out to be a small, foreign-made economy SUV. It was certainly not everybody's cup of tea where cars were concerned, but at that point, having been sufficiently brainwashed to be nonmaterialistic and more concerned with the group than the individual, we were in no position to argue. We were again being cloned in order to march in unison with Bud as our leader.

It should be no surprise that in one of our group meetings, we were also told that we would henceforward all take our vacations at the same time and spend two weeks camping on the ocean coast, which happened to be the Royal Family's favorite vacation spot.

Considerably before the time of death and destruction, which I now refer to formally and ominously, the entire membership went on two such vacations. For some, it was a great time of communing together in a beautiful, natural environment—sharing our entire days; enjoying the ocean-side; and spending late evenings around the campfire, singing and fellowshipping together. I was not one of those people. I believe I can safely say that most, if not all, of the women responsible for extended households were definitely not happy campers (pun intended). To provide an explanation, I will try to describe the insanity that went into those extensive, strenuous vacations.

The first ocean camping trip was preceded by several months of group discussion and planning. The second trip didn't require as much discussion since we were sufficiently experienced to repeat the entire plan for what was supposed to be a yearly event.

I do need to mention that there was one male head of household who challenged the ocean camping trip in favor of a camping trip to mountainous lake regions with which he was well acquainted. That particular man, Jim, was a well-educated and intelligent but quiet man who ran a successful arborist business known throughout several counties. Neither Jim nor his wife, Louise, was the first to challenge a group proposal. Several couples with families had preceded him in venturing to express opinions on various proposals. At that time, most of those strong souls had left the fellowship, as I mentioned earlier. Individuals who exhibited inflexibility in their own opinions were often confronted by either Bud or one of the elders. Oftentimes, they were made to appear small and troublesome in a group meeting. I feel compelled to digress in my narrative to describe that particular man in more detail because of the change I saw him undergo.

When Jim and his wife, Louise, joined the fellowship in the early years, they were newlyweds without children. Afterward, they had four children born in rapid succession. Eight years previous, the couple was happily located in a lovely home in the upper foothills, among majestic pines and oaks—a likely haven for one such as Jim, who had an affinity for nature and, particularly, trees. Louise was the perfect nurturing mother and homemaker.

With pressure from Bud and the elders, Jim was coaxed to

relocate in proximity to our community to a home that was considerably substandard but available at the time. By comparison to his previous home in the pines, the natural environment was also far inferior, but Jim and his wife made the sacrifice for the sake of the whole and joined our community in proximity. They could not argue with Bud's teachings that underscored what it was to be a true Christian. As with my situation, Jim had the finances to make the move happen, and he and his wife gave up their own ideas of happiness to accommodate what they believed God expected of them, according to Bud's teachings.

I watched Jim try to hold his head up and express himself throughout the years only to be intimidated by predominately Bud and Curtis. That intelligent man was another soft-spoken soul like my son Joe. He had a strong heart and mind but wasn't one to fight a bully. At least he wasn't willing to use the same tactics. He tried to challenge through logic and expression. Like Joe, his expression was clear and articulate.

This type of person eventually has one of two choices: capitulate to the bully or leave. The eventual outcome for Jim was that he became worn down by trying to stay. He seemed to grow old overnight. His shoulders drooped, and the happy smile lines on his face were drawn down, indicating an expression of defeat and hopelessness. He wasn't bitter or angry, just tired and worn down. The pressures from Bud and the elders worked negatively on his and Louise's marriage, as was the case with many of the marriages in the fellowship. Eventually, after they'd had six children, Jim and Louise's once happy marriage ended in divorce. Needless to say, Jim made no ground in changing the venue from ocean to mountains as a variable in the vacation planning.

Returning to topic, mainly the first ocean vacation trip, I think it fitting to bullet-point the agenda derived from the Royal Family's vacation experiences of their past. I might add that I found it particularly arrogant on their part to think they had a monopoly on what constitutes a happy vacation, but narcissistic people rarely overcome the ability to see others' perspectives. As a sidenote observation, unfortunately, people who are not narcissistic often fall prey to such seemingly confident people.

Following is the list the Royal Family provided for the two-week ocean vacation trip. (Please bear with the parentheticals, which are solely my own contribution.)

- Each family will provide their own food for the entire two-week trip. No eating out is allowed. (Needless to say, it was quite a chore for me to provide for several adults and two small children. I had to pack five large ice chests and several boxes of food for the trip. In addition, I was the sole person to serve up the food for my extended family—all three meals. Women did women chores; men did men chores. By the time I fed everyone and cleaned up, there was little time to enjoy the environment.)
- Each family will provide certain snacks that we will have nightly around the campfire, such as marshmallows and ingredients to make s'mores.
- Each family will provide a bicycle for each member of the family. These bicycles can be picked up at disposal sites and thrift stores. All bicycles will be transported in the community flatbed truck. (Caravanning down the freeway six hours to our destination, we could see the mountainous heap of bicycles bobbing up and down in the flatbed truck. All I could think of was the old theater comedy of Ma and Pa Kettle traveling in hillbilly style. It was somewhat humorous but also a little embarrassing.)
- Bring appropriate clothing for the beach and beach buckets and utensils for a sand-carving event. Everyone will participate.
- Bring hiking shoes. You will hike.

- No money is necessary for when we go to town. We will sightsee in the gift and art stores and look at all of the lovely items but won't purchase them because we have no need. (Pardon the sarcasm, but this is actually what happened repeatedly. We were taken to the special gift and art shops but could never aspire to owning anything for ourselves. I resented these trips tremendously on principle.)
- There will be a woman's day and a man's day. All women will have one all-day activity together (usually shopping—that is, window-shopping), and the men will have one all-day activity together (usually free diving and coastal exploration). The men will watch the children while the women go, and the women will do likewise when the men go. There are no exceptions. (I was sick with menstruation one day and asked to remain back. I was told no by Sandra Sue. When I add these types of comments, it is not a "Poor me" statement. It is more to illustrate what cloning and bullying result in when the victim continues to concede. Looking back, as I have often done in relaying this narrative, I now marvel at this type of behavior—on both sides of the equation. Why the bully? Why the victim? The bully cannot exist without the victim's relinquishing. Freedom from victimization is personal choice. Choice is God-given, and we all have it. It is amazing how many of us give in to the cowardly lion. It's not necessary. Thank you, Dorothy, for teaching us how to eliminate bullying.)

Some might say, "That doesn't sound that bad. After all, how many people get to go on vacations with a large group of like-minded people? The activities sound wonderful—campfires with singing and s'mores, hiking, sand-carving contests, coastal diving, day trips to nearby picturesque ocean towns. So you were a little inconvenienced? That's what camping is about—you trade domestic conveniences for the pleasure of enjoying nature in the great outdoors. Are you a prima donna that you don't like camping or getting a little dirty?"

In answer and in defense, I can tell you, dear reader, that I was raised in a middle-class family who delighted in going camping. Some of my fondest memories are of camping with my mom, dad, and siblings and, often, a few of our friends. We would go to many of the beautiful open-to-the-public mountain lake locations and spend a glorious week hiking, boating, swimming, and doing all of the activities that young families enjoy when outdoors and away from the hustle and bustle of routine.

We camped simply but wonderfully. My mother cooked a variety of food over the campfire. She started our day by cooking us full bacon-and-egg breakfasts. Our day often ended with sitting under a starry night sky while roasting marshmallows over an open fire. So what was the difference? The answer is simple. There was something missing in our community vacations: the element of choice.

I would not choose to camp with very young children. I never took my older children camping when they were very young—not until they were at least five or six years old, when they could enjoy it, and I could enjoy it as well. Jacob and Melissa were still toddlers on the first trip. They also vomited all over the sleeping bags the first night we arrived due to the road twists and turns en route to our destination.

I would never choose to camp when responsible for feeding several adults and two small children. All mealtimes were a strain for me. Plus, remember, I was already exhausted from a 24-7 responsibility that had been going on for years. A vacation for me would have been a relief from all of that responsibility, not making the same responsibility more difficult and burdensome.

I had to walk a distance to the public restroom to clean the children and bed them in the tents. Sleeping was uncomfortable, and I was often awakened by one or both children for a drink of water or reassurance in an unknown nighttime environment. Again, that is part of life when having children, but that vacation was not my idea of a vacation. It was not my choice.

As mentioned earlier, the second trip had its own drawbacks, such as taking still-stumbling four-year-olds on rigorous hikes and all of the required ocean activities. Like the hike during which Jacob fell off the side of the cliff and was saved by a clump of bushes, there were other incidents that were less than safe simply due to keeping up the pace of the vacation pack, because now the young children were considered able to keep up.

That vacation was not a vacation; it was taxing and ridiculous!

If my objective on that twelve-year journey to seek Oz was to gain courage, use my brain to make proper choices and wise decisions, and develop a sense of being at home by relying on my own inner guidance, I was definitely being challenged to reconsider the path I was on. My courage that was lacking was being called forth, my brain was screaming at me to make a different choice, and my inner guidance was a small whisper of sheer common sense. I had put the question to God, and God was getting through.

Leave!

Straw Number Five

Please bear with the repetition, dear reader, when I speak of my Achilles' heel in terms of the biggest challenge for me during the cult years: opposition to my parenting instincts where my children were concerned. Unfortunately, I wasn't the only older parent in the group who suffered interference from Bud and his family in how to raise our children.

Though the fellowship initially was young, with many young people in their twenties, there were also families with parents my age whose children were, at that point in time, in late adolescence or college entrance age. Even though several families had left, about

Seeking Oz

three or four families in that category remained. Our total number, including children, was approximately eighty or ninety. The irony is that many of the younger men and women in the fellowship who were just starting their families were making strict and unyielding decisions for some of our older children.

I can assure you that those same young men and women, in later years and outside the cult, did not raise their children with such strictness when their children reached the ages of my children. But that is another story, and I don't need to tell it, because life does change and evolve. I will repeatedly state that the lesson proposed in this narrative is mine. It is a lesson that finally woke me up to realize that I needed to take personal responsibility to remove myself from being a victim and to take back my God-given rights as an individual and a parent. Unfortunately, my children were the main catalysts that sent me in that direction. A wise and loving God would, of course, use unconditional love to prove that point. How could a loving God love us less than we love our own children?

Straw number five, again, involved my middle son, the most heavily controlled of my children by the cult's teachings: amazing Matt. I won't elaborate much on that particular situation because ultimately, it turned out all right. I might say it turned out positively mainly because at that point, I was gaining more courage and expressing myself more strongly and firmly—not settling for what, by then, was a foregone conclusion based on the direction we were going.

I was blessed with intelligent, honest, and ethical children. I can make such a statement and have it backed up by a host of teachers, family members, and friends. Again, I am fortunate. All of my children were self-motivated to achieve academically, physically, and spiritually. Yes, I held out a high standard, but it wasn't work on my part to gain their obedience as children or their respect as adults. I now deeply respect and honor each one of my children. Now I often defer to their advice and wise counsel.

I have seen my children suffer and survive. I have seen them make difficult but wise decisions. They are all good men, good parents, and good people. With that being said, while raising my children, I felt each child was unique, and I often hoped I was doing the right thing when a teaching moment presented itself, discipline was in order, or major decisions were to be made. Had I not been far enough along in the cult to recognize that Bud's guidance was less than wise where my children were concerned, I might not have argued for Matt's rights for choice of college.

Matt wanted to go to one of the popular state universities to get an engineering degree. He researched colleges and set his sights on a particular college about 350 miles from home. Looking back, I believe Bud and the elders' argument to keep Matt at a local college had more to do with using him as a workhorse or corralling him so as not to run the risk of losing him rather than trying to keep a stringent budget in place.

Due to the fact that Matt was a 4.0 student throughout all four years of high school, was valedictorian of his graduating class, was a senior varsity basketball player, and had donated innumerable community hours to the building of our church, he was eligible for scholarships, which we eventually applied for and gained.

I don't remember how long or how arduous the discussion was regarding Matt's desire to attend his targeted college, but I do remember being adamant in fighting for his request. Matt had lost out on so much of his high school enjoyment by being so tightly held in our cult. I was not going to let that one slide. Matt deserved to go to the school of his choice. He'd earned it—in more ways than one.

Whether Bud felt he was losing ground where I was concerned or he was busy covertly fighting his own personal battles with his wayward family, I don't know, but that particular tug-of-war went in our favor, and I felt that was Dorothy's first breakthrough in delivering the cowardly lion a smack on the nose.

Straw Number Six

Though this next situation might not seem as significant as the others, for me and for young Jacob, it was huge, and it requires me to explain something that exists in children who are prodigy-like and sensitive at an early age. Jacob is what we refer to now as "an old soul." He came into this world as if he had just left a previous life as a college professor and was now back in a young body with full remembrance of his respectable status and place in life.

Even at a young age, he was a leader but never a bully. He didn't need to be. Even as a preschooler, he seemed to command respect. His preschool teacher in our fellowship commented that Jacob seemed to be a natural-born leader. Jacob was stubborn no doubt, but I was often astonished at how he could call me on something, and I would find he was right.

Once, when I was tugging at him and admonishing him to hurry, though I was actually the cause of our being late for a meeting, he looked up at me as I was pulling on his arm, waited for eye contact, and calmly said, "You are blaming me for being late." I never babied my children, lied to them, or played games. I had to ponder for a few seconds whether an apology would lessen my authority as a parent. I needed only a few seconds because I knew my son Jacob, and he was right. I said something like "You are right, Jacob. I am rushing you and have been unnecessarily rough with you. I am the reason we are having to hurry. I owe you an apology. Mom is sorry." That was the end of the situation. Jacob didn't register that he was one up on Mom. He registered justice and fairness.

So you will understand, dear reader, when I describe what happened between Bud and Jacob and tell you that it was painful to Jacob and me and had a lasting negative effect. To precede telling the incident, I must also explain that potty-training in my family was a timely, consistent endeavor. We mothers—myself, my female siblings, my mother—didn't start the training process too early, but once we did, we were consistent. The timing was usually around age two and a half. There was no punishment; there was no baby talk. The process started when the child was ready, and all efforts were made to be sure and provide access to the special potty chair at appropriate times. My job was to recognize patterns, watch for signs, and be consistent. The child's part was to communicate and not wait too long. The reward was a job well done, and both child and mother were pleased with a successful and consistent habit of getting to the potty on time, just like a big person.

I potty-trained Jacob and Melissa at the same time, though Melissa was a little younger. She was ready at two, and Jacob was two and a half. I had discovered with my two older sons that once they were trained, which took no more than a couple months from start to finish, they never had an accident. Once they were trained, the big-boy pants were put on, and they never had accidents during the day and never wet the bed at night—ever. Jacob and Melissa were no exception.

One afternoon, when several in our fellowship were gathered outdoors during a community picnic in our neighborhood, Jacob, who was then five years old and loved climbing trees, often ones several feet high, was climbing on a tall wood pile nearby. I wasn't too far from him, when I heard Bud yell at Jacob to get down while he stormed in Jacob's direction.

Based on comments I heard from Bud, he had been watching Jacob for the past couple of years and was a little taken aback at how Jacob confidently handled himself. I am sure he also had heard about Jacob's reputation in Sunday preschool, which three of his grandchildren attended as well. To this day, I am sure Bud wanted to keep my children in submission to his children and even his grandchildren, and he could see that Jacob would have to be broken down in order for that to happen.

Giving Jacob no time to react, Bud jumped up; angrily grabbed Jacob by one arm; pulled him down hard from the woodpile; and, in a single movement, lifted him far off the ground by that same arm, swung him to his side, and, with his free arm, hurled a powerful blow to Jacob's backside. Bud, having been in law enforcement most of his life, during which time he'd worked with troubled teenagers, was strong and forceful. Jacob was shocked, and so was I. He let out a scream, and I instinctively ran to him. The arm Bud had grabbed was the arm Jacob had broken a year earlier. As I approached, I could tell Jacob had defecated in his pants. I looked up at Bud, who remained standing next to Jacob. He was red-faced and was ready, I'm sure, to deliver an admonition for all to hear. Bud nodded and said in disgust, "Yes. Take him home. He's messed his pants."

Fortunately, we were close to home. I took Jacob's hand, and we ran home. He was crying, and I was in shock at what had just happened. We were always uncomfortable around Bud, his wife, and the Royal Family when it came to keeping our children obedient in every instance, but never had I had a problem with Jacob from the time he was little. Even though Melissa was difficult and was prone to temper fits, we worked diligently with her to ensure there would be no indications we were slacking in our parental duty to keep our children in line.

Though I tried to comfort Jacob and let him know the accident had happened due to the harsh blow, the damage was done. He was humiliated and remembers this incident clearly and painfully to this day.

As I cleaned and soothed my humiliated and confused child, my activated mind pushed aside all doubts and scriptures and doctrines and screamed at me, *Bud's act is out of anger and stemming from some underlying self-serving, sick motivation. Without a doubt, such a harsh overreaction is not coming from a good place. I believe my intuition is accurate. I am not being an overprotective mother. I know this man is not to be trusted. This man is not stable. I have got to leave and take my children with me!*

The overprotective-mother label that had been disintegrating with every crazy, insane, evil, ugly, cruel, and degrading act imposed on me and my children by that so-called godly leader was gone. It was replaced by righteous indignation.

Dorothy was about to be unveiled.

Straw Number Seven

What happened in November 1988 would tip the scales in a profoundly significant way. When I came out of the cult in 1990, I read everything I could get my hands on regarding cults and spiritual abuse. To leave a cult, the individual has to move away from what he or she has been brainwashed to believe, and the subsequent deprogramming can be quite a process. If the cult is linked to religion, it is extremely difficult to choose to leave. The cult victim's allegiance is tied to God. How is it possible to abandon God's directives? I learned after the fact that oftentimes, it is a shocking event that awakens the victim—something shocking enough to cause the victim to question and quick-start the rethinking process.

I thank the Source of Love for drawing attention to the signposts that became more evident as I traveled those last two years along the Yellow Brick Road. By the time all hell broke loose, I was already planning my exit. The time of death and destruction, yet a little further, merely paved a swift and open pathway to freedom.

The straws related to unjust treatment of my children were all equally weighted, and on a personal level, they sufficiently tipped the scales and gave me the answer to the questions I'd presented to God more than a year prior. But to erase any doubt whatsoever, you might say that straw number seven was the last straw and sufficiently gave me all of the confidence I needed to know that I was more than justified to leave for spiritual reasons.

After that particular tragedy, my mind was clear. I needed to leave. Not only was I not wrong to leave, but the second part of my question was answered as well: the fellowship teachings were in error. The fellowship was indeed a cult. I would be wrong *not* to leave.

After that event, I was actually compelled to leave for the sake of my family and anyone remaining who might be feeling the same entrapment as did I. I only needed to work on a strategy and plan to exit. However, it wasn't just me. I had a son and a husband who needed to come with me. I didn't know where my husband was at in terms of leaving. In addition, I was mother to a little five-year-old girl who called me Mom. But I had been guided thus far, and I knew beyond a shadow of a doubt that now I was trusting in the God I loved and adored, the God of my childhood and youth. He would show me the way out. Indeed he did!

So what happened in November 1988? It was not something that happened in the fellowship group. It happened in my extended family—the family I had neglected because of the time I spent serving in my church. I received a call from my mom and dad with shocking news: their grandson, my sister's twenty-one-year-old son, Liam, my nephew, had suddenly and unexpectedly passed away from a seizure. This nephew was the cousin who was close to my eldest son, Joe.

Liam had experienced four or five seizures over a two-year period, and the only link the doctors had discovered thus far was a motorcycle accident that had taken place on his dirt bike while he was riding in a large, open area not far from his home. He had been wearing his helmet at the time, but he'd suffered a mild concussion. In spite of the seizures, no one expected Liam to die during a seizure. The doctor told my sister that the chances of suffering a death from such an attack were one in a million.

My sister and I were not close geographically. She lived two hundred miles from us; however, we were close in temperament and in spirit as siblings, and I immediately felt her pain on receiving the report from my parents. My thoughts were *I wish I could fly. I would fly to her right now. I need to be there for my sister.*

The trip required traveling over the mountains in the early winter—not something to do in the evening. I had to wait until the next morning to be with my sister. I remember standing at the kitchen sink, finishing the food-preparation dishes before the family and household members started to get home. I didn't want to tell anyone about my nephew's death until I'd had a chance to talk to Phil.

Edith was the first to come in the front door. She seemed to sense something in advance, because she came through the entryway quietly and rounded the corner to the kitchen slowly. Before I could turn to face her, she said hesitantly, "Makena, is everything all right?" Her eyes were big and open, and she seemed to sense a tragedy without any indication from me. Even in my grief, I picked up on that, and it was another of those occasions when I felt that Edith had some type of sixth sense. How strange life is, because less than a year later, Edith would leave this earth also.

Once I'd communicated to everyone and packed my suitcase, I left for my sister's home the following morning. It was an excruciatingly long four hours to get there. I cried all the way, having some solitude to express my grief and pray for my poor sister. My sister is one of those tender souls who cares for everyone, putting herself last. She would take in every stray dog or cat that came her way. She couldn't turn down anyone who needed a helping hand or a shoulder to cry on, and she was facing the worst loss anyone could possibly experience—the death of her child.

I stayed with my sister until the funeral, and it was an awful day. The weather was cold, and the clouds ominously promised rain or possibly even snow. As we were standing by the graveside and the pastor was delivering the closing words of comfort to family and friends, he read something that Liam had written and given to his mother. She'd saved his writing because it was a lovely, heartfelt expression of his appreciation for God's love in his life. The writing was like beautiful prose—something that an orator or poet would write.

Liam was one of those impulsive, live-life-to-the-fullest young fellows who had no fear of danger and would even risk his own life to save another. He was bold in his speech and behavior and had a disarming way of expressing himself—communicating always that nothing would stand in his way should he decide to take action.

As I listened to the beautiful words from that young man whom we'd loved dearly, who'd left a mother, father, brother, and sister way too early, two thoughts suddenly hit my brain and heart almost simultaneously. The statement in my head mocked everything my heart was feeling: *By our fellowship's standards, Liam's religion is not as spiritually correct as ours. According to our doctrine, complete giving up of all our earthly goods is the only way to enter the kingdom of heaven.* My heart immediately argued, *Liam lived life to the fullest. His wellspring of energy and joy was fueled by his understanding of a loving God. Of course he entered the kingdom of heaven. His soul is safely home in a realm beyond the confines of our imagination.*

It was as if a tangible, audible blast of reality struck me. I received not only the shock that comes from losing a loved one but also a shocking line of thinking that made it abundantly clear how wrong I was to follow such an insidious, damaging doctrine as was taught by Bud. It was not just in error—it was the total antithesis of what I now understood.

God doesn't want our sacrifice. He wants our love. This wonderful, awesome God took Liam safely home. They had a mutual admiration for each other that could not be argued against by anyone. This God loves all of his creation equally. The agenda is love and only love, pure and simple. Love.

If I had any lingering doubts about my decision to leave the church doctrines of the past ten years, they were once and for all eradicated in that one shocking moment by love. Love melted away all of the thou-shalts and thou-shalt-nots. Love erased all concerns of sacrifice. Love made all mankind one—connected by the Source of Love. Love gave everyone equal status. Love smiled, laughed, and encouraged. It showed no favorites; it wasn't arrogant or prideful. It wasn't demanding or belittling. Love had no limits—it was all-encompassing. Love left no room for fear or narrow, exclusive doctrines.

When I arrived home, quiet and alone, I sought validation by looking up *sacrifice* in the concordance at the back of my Bible. The Bible, particularly the Old Testament, speaks often of sacrifice. However, the guidance I readily received from asking for confirmation was a scripture in Hosea: "I don't want your sacrifices—I want your love; I don't want your offerings—I want you to know me" (Hosea 6:6 TLB).

Two-Year Countdown

I had my answers to my two-pronged question within the first year of the two-year countdown—the amount of time I'd promised God I would stay until I had complete clarity.

> **Question 1:** Is there something wrong with me for wanting to leave this fellowship? If so, let me know, and I will decide whether to stay per your insistence or leave and take whatever punishment you may inflict on me for doing so.
>
> **Answer:** There is nothing wrong with me for wanting to leave. No punishment is necessary!
>
> **Question 2:** Is there something wrong with the group's teachings? If so, please make this abundantly clear to me, and I will leave.
>
> **Answer:** There is definitely something wrong with the group's teachings. My choice—I am free to leave.

Now that I had my answers from God, the Source of Love, I was free to leave. I was not bound by a doctrine that rendered me without choice. God gave me choice in a world of both light and dark in order to choose light and live my life abundantly.

Fear, shame, and guilt did not belong in the light. They could bring me out of darkness to the light, but light was peace, joy, love, and the blessed freedom to choose. Bud's constricting teachings did not allow for individual thought or freedom to make personal choices. Instead, we were held by fear of a punishing God who confined us to a strict and narrow way of thinking. If we did otherwise, we were shamed and made to feel guilty. How much better to love a God who allows his creation to grow, learn, and make choices that bring peace and joy?

That clarity of thought was a huge breakthrough for me and elevated my sense of security; I knew that God had led me that far and would surely guide me safely out of the fellowship I now believed was a cult. Up until that time, I'd ignored outsiders, including my own extended family and friends, who referred to our group as a cult.

It was not unusual for me to stand staunch in the face of ridicule about my belief system. During my upbringing in what would be considered mainstream Christianity, I was restricted from dancing and going to the theater. I was accustomed to puzzled looks when I declined invitations to take part in those activities. How different was it to justify a narrow belief system based on the Bible's teaching? Our fellowship's belief system made it clear that we must be like the believers in the book of Acts—period. My conflicted heart and brainwashed head fought the notion until I could no longer ignore my heart.

That last straw was the final one to break open my heart and activate my brain.

Makena McChesney

My Secret Ally

At this time, I need to reintroduce, dear reader, a person in the fellowship who aligned with me in coming to the conclusion that we were held captive to a charismatic leader and his wife and family, and the progression the church group had taken indeed looked like a cult. Ellie had been watching me closely since the incident a few years back when I'd used profanity when Jacob fell off the cliff during one of our group ocean vacations.

As mentioned, we members never divulged our unhappiness or feelings of entrapment to each other for fear of being reported. Ellie could see that I was experiencing frustration under the direction of our church leadership. I was becoming more vocal in the group in attempting to project another point of view and was always known for being the token mercy person.

Yet I was not on the fringes of our fellowship, as were those who had left. I was deeply entrenched. Phil and I were among those who subscribed to common purse. Those of us who had the most material goods—owned homes and had good salaries—were approached first, as well as the singles. Ellie and her husband, Brian, were a much younger couple and had not yet made the decision to give up all of their earthly goods.

One evening, sitting in lawn chairs behind Ellie's house, we reasoned together in the quiet of the night. We talked for several hours in secret until the sun made its way from descending in the west to rising in the east.

Without aid of research or seeking outside help, we agreed that our church was on a wrong path. We discussed the extremes that existed in Bud's teachings, and though my memory does not serve the exact details of that discussion, I am sure it came close to matching the following defining list that I read about after leaving the cult.

A cult does the following:

- **Claims to have a new and better way of worshipping, often taught by a charismatic leader.** Bud, definitely persuasive and charismatic, claimed repeatedly that the way to prove to the world that our Christian faith was real was to model after the early Christians in the Bible's book of Acts. He believed that most churches were missing the point of Christianity should they live otherwise.
- **Emphasizes certain scriptures and holds them as undeniable doctrine to be obeyed.** Bud frequently repeated several scriptures out of context that served to define our church doctrines. Those scriptures were held out to us as indisputable law to be adhered to by the group. One scripture he quoted that held us to a doctrine of community living was Acts 4:32: "All the believers were one in heart and mind. No one claimed that any of their possessions was their own, but they shared everything they had" (NIV).
- **Separates members from their families and accepts no outside influences.** The scripture Bud quoted frequently to relegate our friends and relatives secondary to the members of our church was Matthew 12:48–50: "He [Jesus] replied to him, 'Who is my mother, and who are my brothers?' Pointing to his disciples, he said, 'Here are my mother and my brothers. For whoever does the will of my Father in heaven is my brother and sister and mother'" (NIV).
- **Promotes the idea that works prove faith and that the works promoted by the group are superior to any other group's works.** Bud controlled and manipulated the church members progressively to do works within the church. We had no time for outside interests or outside friends and family. He often quoted the scripture John 13:35: "By this everyone will know that you are my disciples, if you love one another" (NIV). Of course, Bud's idea of loving one another was to devote all time and energy to the church members. He often

referenced other churches in the vicinity as falling short of expressing their faith by not giving entirely to their church, as we were doing.

- **Allows for no differences.** All members must believe exactly the same. There is no room for disagreement. What started out to be admonitions and militarization from Bud and his family eventually turned out to be the admonitions of most individuals in the group. It was no longer Bud policing. Everyone was watchful and forthright to admonish should anyone dare to deviate from the teachings and practices put forth by Bud. We were becoming clones, molded by the thoughts and ideals of a charismatic leader.

- **Infuses guilt, shame, and lack of self-worth so the individuals can be molded.** The negative labeling started early in the building of the church. Subtly at first, all individuals were made to feel less than and, therefore, incapable of making proper choices. The proposed doctrine was that individuals needed input from the church as a whole—we were never to trust our individual thoughts or decisions. I was made to feel selfish if I would not agree to sharing everything, including signing over my home to the group. I was made to feel too private if I were reluctant to take more and more individuals into my home. Ellie was contributing to all of the shared chores in the fellowship and was feeling weighed down. She had a small infant and was fatigued from the expectations put on her. She looked to me, knowing I had traveled further down the Yellow Brick Road to relinquishment and sacrifice, and she wanted to know how I felt about it. She, like me, had been made to feel ashamed and guilty.

- **Equates salvation, or the assurance of heaven at death, with following the doctrines of the group.** We were made to believe that God would accept nothing short of complete adherence to the doctrines presented in Bud's teachings.

Hence, if we were to leave the fellowship, we forfeited the assurance of salvation. It was understood that the knowledge given us required strict obedience. Otherwise, we were outside of God's protection and assurance of an eternal home.

- **Provides no exit, no option to leave.** Intimidation is applied to those entrenched in the community. Anyone could leave if they wanted to, but the more they were entangled, the more difficult it would be. For example, should I leave, I would leave my husband and young child if Phil decided to remain. I would leave the home that was built with the money I'd acquired in my life to that point. I would be financially destitute. Ellie would have to leave her young son should her husband, Brian, choose to stay. Also, there would be extreme pressure from the other members admonishing us to stay, which did bear out further on.

By the time the first signs of dawn approached, Ellie and I were convinced that we were part of a cult. I confided in her that I had been praying for more than a year and was convinced that God had answered my prayers, and I had peace of mind to leave. Further, I trusted God to lead me out at the right time. I had no clarity on the timing yet, but I knew God would see me through, and he would see her through safely as well.

There were many entanglements. I taught school. I was raising Melissa, a young child not my own who now called me Mama. I was unsure about the signing over of our home. I didn't know where Phil stood in his commitment to stay. Would he be willing to leave as well? I wasn't sure what my other sons would think, particularly Matt, who made frequent visits and was still very much a part of the fellowship, though he was starting to question as well.

You might be thinking, dear reader, that I should have known far in advance of that date that the church I was part of was definitely a cult. I knew what a cult was. Cult followers were extreme in their beliefs. Some mainstream denominations I knew of growing up were often referred to as cults.

I thought, *Wow! They can't celebrate Christmas or birthdays for some crazy reasons. They worship on a different day than other Christians. They can't eat meat. They follow a religion of doctrines built on some man's or woman's isolated vision.*

On and on it went—but that was them. My mind talk would remind me, *They are cults. Surely we aren't a cult. We are just following the scriptures to be the best Christians as exemplified in the Bible.*

It is amazing what brainwashing can do. We come to believe in a doctrine, a system, a creed, and we stay right there. We might suffer under it, and we might even secretly rebel against it, but we don't necessarily question it or remove ourselves from it.

I liken this type of thinking, or lack thereof, to Stockholm syndrome, which is, per *Wikipedia*, "a condition that causes hostages to develop a psychological alliance with their captors as a survival strategy during captivity."

In the case of the cult I was in, I wondered, *Is it possible that during the brainwashing period, my psychological alliance with the cult leader's teaching was linked to the survival of my soul?*

Should I not adhere to the belief system, would my very soul be in danger of hell and damnation?

If that is the case, it might be worth anyone's consideration to clearly examine the religion (man's doctrine) to which he or she pledges allegiance.

Ellie and I were both in a similar situation, and we had only each other in which to confide at that point. We agreed we would be persistent in praying for direction as to when and how to escape the cult. We both knew that was not the time. The timing presented itself over the course of year two of the two-year countdown. I refer to that timing as the time of death and destruction.

Around the time of late 1988 to early 1990, a series of events

Seeking Oz

took place that contributed to that dark (or darker) time period. For clarity's sake, I will group them in the following categories, as I can't necessarily recall them in a chronological order:

- new and more extreme doctrines
- relentless work expectations and imposed restrictions
- secrets kept by the Royal Family
- accidents and fatalities

New and More Extreme Doctrines

I never questioned where or when Bud acquired alliances from other groups. I wondered if the leaders or pastors of those groups were all friends from his law enforcement days. At any rate, there were three groups we associated with during that time period. They were small community-based fellowships like ours. One was several miles south, one was in a large metropolis to our west, and another was in a northern location several miles distant. Frankly, I found the other leaders odd. Though Bud developed our fellowship into something that eventually, from my perspective, was extreme and dangerous, Bud always gave the appearance of credibility. He had, from outside appearances, a proper family, and he himself, with his white hair and mostly friendly and jovial demeanor, or twinkle, exemplified what he believed in and taught.

On occasion, one of the other leaders and sometimes a few of their members would come visit us. The purposes of their visit appeared to be camaraderie and reinforcement of living the community lifestyle as a Christian. The leader from the large city to our west seemed to me a bit like a mad scientist type or an eccentric professor. When speaking, he would wave his arms violently and occasionally jump up onto a chair. He used vernacular that was probably common in the poorer and more corrupt sections of the

Makena McChesney

city. I attributed his style to possibly the need to relate to the group of young people he attracted to his church.

On one visiting occasion, I felt disturbed by his behavior when he and his grown son joined our family for dinner, along with Bud and Sandra Sue. The son openly defied his father and made some angry comment about his father talking to a "head on his desk." The scene was brief but awkward, and no one made any attempts to deal with the situation. I couldn't determine if the son was off, the father was off, or both.

I don't remember much about the leader to our north, but I do recall the leader from the southern location as being serious and direct in his speech to the point of being gruff and rude. He also was not a typical pastor, and we later came to learn that at one time, he had served time in prison for some offense that was not divulged to us. I am not exaggerating when I say that the impression his wife gave me was the complete opposite of Sandra Sue's image of being prim, proper, and just plain uptight. This woman had a careless, almost reckless carefree attitude, and I kept thinking, *She seems like a prostitute to me.*

I may or may not have been correct in that assessment, but after leaving the cult, I never went back to check on the credibility or background of any of the pastors, including Bud. My focus at that point was to try to rid myself of the anger I had at myself for having followed such people. But that is yet another story further down the Yellow Brick Road and, actually, beyond Oz.

I mention these pastors, who actually appeared throughout the twelve-year period, only because it was not out of the ordinary during the last phase of the cult's existence when Bud introduced us to individuals from a group of believers of a relatively small sect that originated in Germany in the early 1900s. Over time and for specific reasons, they'd migrated to various parts of the world, and in the early 1950s, they'd started a settlement in the eastern United States. At one of their eastern locations, Bud contacted some primary members or elders of the group for the purpose of having them visit our fellowship and share their success in living a community lifestyle.

In this narrative, dear reader, I provide you a brief description and my own impressions and viewpoint regarding that group only as it relates to the direction Bud was taking our group.

The members of that Protestant Christian group did not hold private property but shared everything, modeling the practices of the first Church in Jerusalem, as relayed in the Bible's Acts of the Apostles. They quoted the scripture Acts 4:32–37, in which church members were of "one heart and mind, and shared all things in common." Sound familiar?

So which came first—the chicken or the egg? Did Bud start a church fellowship with the same biblical premise in mind and then discover through some type of research a model church that had successfully survived since its inception some sixty-plus years earlier that would prove his ideology as sound and believable? Or did Bud devise a religious appeal from the start, based on the belief system of another sect, such as that particular group, that would militarize a group of people for purposes of creating his own church with himself as leader—a church that would support itself and him and his family?

These questions are a few of many that my family and I asked ourselves much later. I do remember, however, having a conversation on the phone with my son Matt after he had attended college away for a year. He was starting to question, having put some distance between himself and the confines of the cult. I was close to leaving at that time and posed a similar question to him: Do you think Bud is sincere but misguided, or do you think he is a con man? My son's answer was something along the lines of "It would actually be less dangerous if he were a common con man, Mom. It would be worse if he actually believed what he is teaching—a sociopath kind of like Hitler."

Well, no need to settle that question. As I have repeated throughout my narrative, the ultimate purpose is not to place blame.

A bully is a bully. A despot is a despot. In the space and time that the bully is a bully and the despot is a despot, it is my responsibility not to be a victim. If I, the victim, do not give over my power to the bully, the intimidation has no purpose or place.

However, dear reader, you can come to your own conclusions in defining Bud's motives. Perhaps a fact that could assist in your assessment is the following: by reliable sources, it is known that neither Bud nor his wife or any member of his family joined that sect after the collapse of the cult.

Back to our introduction to that particular religious group. On several occasions, we had three or four families worshipping with us and meeting with us. I find it amusing now that Phil and I were not asked to house any of those people during their visits. I have no doubt Bud didn't want to subject any of those people to my household, knowing I was unhappy with his leadership, though almost no one in the church ever suspected, except Ellie.

In all fairness, in describing these individuals, I assume their overly serious, somber demeanor might have been not only because of a restricted lifestyle but also because they were outside their comfort zone. After all, the members were in seclusion for a reason. I have no idea how Bud talked the sect elders into such a collaboration that allowed some of their members to travel to visit our nondenominational church, even though that particular sect encouraged recruitment. But of course, Bud was charismatic and convincing.

Yes, we were beginning to practice similar teachings, such as common purse, but we were certainly not as secluded as that visiting group. We had jobs outside the fellowship, whereas they manufactured goods from within and were solely self-supporting. We wore conventional but modest clothing, whereas they wore old-fashioned clothing. The ladies wore head coverings and long skirts, and the men dressed similar to Mennonites or Quakers.

In all honesty, I don't know if I was somewhat repelled by those people due to wariness about the confining belief system or if they just were not warm and welcoming. They seemed robotic, which is what I was becoming. I wonder even now if the world looks gray to them, as it did to me after being in the cult those last eight or ten years.

On the surface, when considering both groups—that small sect and our own fellowship—I can recognize that the community life definitely had its appealing aspects, especially when observing the young children laughing and playing together. As mentioned several times in my narrative, there were many fun times, particularly where the little children were concerned. But the adult life was one of hard work and confinement, stripped of choice.

I try to remember how many aspects of our life were devoid of choice. They are too numerous to recount. Again, the list includes the following: we shared our homes; watched the same films, limited to *Anne of Green Gables* and a few others; read the same books; drove the same cars; ate the same food (brown rice was touted as a must); took the same vacations; worked inside and outside each other's homes; took care of each other's children; lived in the same neighborhood; sang the same songs; talked the same talk; and lived on the same amount of money.

Was membership in that sect the next step for our church? Not for me. By that time, I was biding my time, watching and waiting for God's direction as to the right time to escape. As mentioned, one of the major differences between the small sect and our fellowship at that time was that we all held different jobs, and the sect had a community business that allowed their group to be self-sustaining.

Phil and I suspicioned that Bud did have a vision and a plan that would allow our group to be self-sufficient. Though the model might have been different from the sect's, it appeared Bud wanted members of our group to conform to jobs that would benefit the church as a whole. By that time, Bud had convinced a premed student, Harris Jensen, to teach school and go into real estate and a father of five, Sam James, to become a lawyer. As mentioned earlier, our group was already equipped with a strong construction base—an engineer and surveyor (Andon Case), a framing carpenter (Curtis Collins), a concrete forms carpenter (Phil), and a machinist (Andon's brother, Will Case).

Additionally, a real estate agent and lawyer might come in handy should we move collectively to some other location and become a commune of our own. Also, we'd already started our own school that had a principal and teachers. The community didn't get that far, thank God, but both Phil and I knew that Bud undoubtedly had a plan and was taking steps to get there.

At some point in time, we were probably going to sell our homes, pack up, and move to a more remote area to build a common kingdom with Bud, his wife, and their eldest son as the dominant leaders. At that point, we would have been entirely entangled, dependent on the community life and living without choice.

I thought, No thank you! And thank you, Source of Love, for delivering me from that eventuality!

Relentless Work Expectations and Imposed Restrictions

The basement of the church was completed, ceilinged, and usable at that point, and the Timber House project was under way. At that time, I would estimate we had about eighty-five people in our fellowship, including children. All of the construction work done to date had been no easy feat. As mentioned earlier, all work was done with consideration to minimal cost and was labor-intensive.

The work was done on weekends and after work, as all men and singles had outside jobs. Before leaving for college, Matt and the other young people had a hand in helping to prepare some of the rough timber for what would become the Timber House, Bud and Sandra Sue's permanent dwelling. With no time to rest between major construction projects, we were to prepare the land and begin work.

In the meantime, the teachings became more and more restrictive, and the punishments became harsher. Bud managed to make it abundantly clear that we were to spend our time and energy more exclusively with our church members—our true brothers and sisters.

Since our doctrine was limiting, it would naturally follow that our choices for a mate would also be a narrow selection. It became increasingly more evident that should the singles wish to marry, they would have to choose from the singles in our church fellowship. To reiterate, there was no dating, only group participation. Should a young man choose to marry a young woman in the group, he would have to seek council and approval from the elders. If a young man or woman became interested in anyone outside the group, he or she would have to introduce the person into the fellowship, as I did when Phil wanted to date me.

However, now, not only did the individual need to commit to the exceptionally exclusive fellowship, but there was no chance to court a potential mate other than in a group setting—and then there was still the approval process. Consequently, the singles and young people started taking a second look at their peers in the group for mate potential. The restrictions were such that taking a mate outside the narrow confines of our group was next to impossible. No one said that out loud, but someone would have to have been pretty oblivious to not put that one together.

I have to say, I was relieved that Matt was away at college and Joe was safely outside the realm of the church, because that additional expectation of the young people was not only ridiculous to me but also sad. All of the singles knew their only chance of marrying and having a family was to pair up with someone from the group. Choice took another nosedive. I know of three couples who would not necessarily have married but did so. Surprisingly, only one of those marriages ended in divorce—but it's less surprising when you understand that the people who got that far into the cult were conscientious and loyal people, including the indoctrinated young people.

Around that same time of interference in the singles' lives, we learned that one of the young single adults, Carson, Ellie's brother, had impregnated his girlfriend, Janelle. After going to the elders with his confession, he was admonished and told that he needed to make a public confession before the entire group. It was heartbreaking to see that young man so humbled before us, when we were all aware that he was deeply in love with his girlfriend, as she was in love with him. They'd met and dated long before the tight restrictions were imposed regarding dating. We all expected a wedding announcement soon, particularly with the heavy expectations being put upon the singles for no dating.

Not only was Carson humiliated, but I could readily tell from his public confession that the elders had applied strong condemnation tactics. Carson berated himself in such a way as to warn all young people that his predicament was a perfect example of why the separation before marriage was so important. The incident was used as a teaching tool, and that young man wore the scarlet letter.

Furthermore, per the elders' decision, the couple would be married not in a beautiful, traditional church but in the ugly building we'd worshipped in prior to finishing the church basement. There would be no frills or lovely decorations—nothing joyful. Folding chairs were placed in even rows over the dirty, worn carpet. The event would be somber to show the group the consequences of having intercourse outside the bounds of marriage.

Unbeknownst to any of us at the time that dismal wedding took place, Bud and Sandra Sue were withholding the secret that they themselves had entered into marriage after Bud impregnated Sandra Sue with their first child. Would it have made any difference to any of us to have known that? Possibly not for some but definitely for others, such as myself and, of course, that young couple.

I wonder if Bud and Sandra Sue had a church wedding. No doubt they did.

Secrets Kept by the Royal Family

I suppose it is no surprise that bullies can also be hypocrites. There is no exception here when I describe to you some of the things we learned about Bud, Sandra Sue, and the Royal Family.

I believe the best way to break this down is to describe the hypocrisies and secret sins that came to light regarding each of the members of the ruling Royal Family, mostly in the last year or two of the twelve-year period. This exposure would not be necessary, except that from day one of the church's inception, Bud's three daughters and eldest son were held up to us as examples. They ruled over us in small groups, as mentors, and even as watchdogs, you might say. The youngest son was not necessarily held up as a role model, but we found he was exempt from the same punishment inflicted on the members, so I will definitely include him as well.

Please bear in mind, dear reader, the emphasis here in this part of my narration is not on the so-called sins. The emphasis is on the hypocrisy of the Royal Family as they chose to hide the errant actions of their own family while punishing and humiliating the other members for much lesser transgressions. This account is not about judging. It is about hypocrisy and provides further examples to underscore the need to follow our own inner guidance.

As for sin, to paraphrase the words of Jesus in John 8:7, "he who is without sin can cast the first stone." We are all entitled to experience life in order to make choices, and we are all entitled to make choices in order to experience life. Making choices includes making mistakes or being less than honorable or loving. Also, as I approach this section, I am reminded by Spirit that all of the members of the Royal Family were victims themselves. They were victimized by parents who were harsh in their expectations. Bud's children were probably manipulated even more than we members who were taught to follow their lead.

Again, the main transgressions are hypocrisy, deception, and concealment.

Eldest daughter, Caryn Sue Collins-Weber: Caryn Sue was the least pretty of the three Collins girls, but she had a certain commanding presence about her with her strawberry-blonde hair and piercing gaze. Sometimes she would look at another person with a certain curiosity, like a scientist conducting research on an animal. It was a harmless look but not necessarily warm and accepting. She had her mother's cold airs, but when she did smile and laugh, she looked more like her dad, who was capable of a joyful demeanor. I didn't dislike Caryn Sue, but her arrogance gave me no reason to draw close to her. I stayed my distance as much as possible.

I believe her most annoying character flaw was that she truly believed she was superior intellectually to most, if not all, of us. She also flaunted her artistic gifts—singing and drama—as well as her intellectual gifts in counseling members. To me, in general, she was Haughty with a capital *H*. Caryn Sue was known to have said on several occasions, "I deserve assistance with my day-to-day chores in order to exercise my gifts that I contribute to the church."

To give an example, there were four or five extended households in the church that required a strong matriarch and patriarch. We who were the matriarchs worked hard at managing our households on our own, and we also had other outside assignments associated with our community living, such as participating in the church school and building projects.

Whereas I did all of my own cooking and caretaking of the household and taught and mentored the young people added to our home, Caryn Sue made sure she had young female singles living with her who were efficient and helpful to her. They participated in cooking, cleaning, and helping her with her children—who grew in number to four. They generally served her and were slaves to the dictates of both Caryn Sue and Ben.

Consequently, I believe her self-importance and indulgence led to her gaining a lot of weight. Caryn Sue, in time, resorted to wearing clothing that was loose and full to hide her increasing girth.

What were her secret sins and her brand of bullying and hypocrisy? This woman concealed her indulgent behavior by enslaving certain members to do her housework, while others in the fellowship did not have such assistance and yet, in some cases, had greater need.

She participated in ostracizing individuals, such as my eldest son, for not living up to God's directives for their lives. In her mind, individuals who did not give their all to the church and live in community did not deserve to be a part of the fellowship of believers, when in actuality, this young lady certainly did not give her all. She made sure all was given to her.

She participated in most of the groups that determined harsh punishments for what came to be known as lesser infractions than those of her own family. Ultimately, she concealed the transgressions of her family. She was a bully and a hypocrite.

Eldest son, Curtis Collins: I actually wince when I bring up this young man. Though I genuinely liked Curtis and believed he had potential to balance out the extremes in his father, Curtis turned out to have committed some of the gravest of sins. Curtis was of average build and height and was good looking and affable like his father, though he seemed to have his moments of moodiness and brooding like his mother.

He evidently was an outstanding quarterback on his high school football team and had a reputation for being tough and ready to fight physically when provoked. The entire family often made references to football being *the* sport, whereas basketball was a mediocre endeavor in the sports arena. Curtis was supposed to be the epitome of a real man—tough like the game of football.

My son Matt, several inches over six feet in height and considerably taller than Curtis, played basketball, and I don't recall any of the Collins family attending any games or providing any encouragement. After all, basketball was, by comparison, a "sissy sport." Matt was anything but sissy, nor was the sport, so it was difficult sometimes to hear the family tout football with the unspoken but obvious emphasis on the sons in the family—Curtis and Cory, football jocks.

Well, I suppose I am a little off topic with the football theme, but I always have to point out the narcissistic and bullying behavior prevalent in the Royal Family. Whatever their preference, whatever their ideal, and whatever their thing, it was held out as gospel. Anything counter to their set of beliefs or preferences was less than and not acceptable.

Back to Curtis. I believe one of the reasons I liked Curtis was because he appeared to like and appreciate both Phil and me. He had a great deal of respect for me, and he genuinely liked Phil, a construction brother in the trades. Whereas no verbal compliments or expressions of appreciation ever came from Sandra Sue, Bud, or any other of the children other than possibly young Cory, Curtis was genuine in his expressions and warm in his delivery. He also was quick to do the opposite when he felt it was needed. He could tear someone down rapidly with his sharp tongue, though Phil, my children, and I never experienced that from Curtis.

Curtis often spoke out in the large group and presided in the small groups. He was obviously being groomed by his father to be a leader. Curtis did have the bearing of a natural leader and was often eloquent and articulate in his speech. He, of course, agreed for the most part with his father's teachings, but as time went on, I noticed he was beginning to express his own opinions, and not all of them agreed with his father's. His individualism was another big reason I appreciated Curtis. He would stand up to his father. However, it was also evident that his father still had the major sway over Curtis, which became Curtis's eventual undoing.

How did Curtis measure up on the bully-and-hypocrite scale? What were Curtis's secret sins? In order to approach this segment

Seeking Oz

of Curtis's unveiling, I need to bring the reader up to date on the changes that had taken place over the last two years in Curtis's wife, Linda.

At first, I thought it was me—that self-doubt thing—and I didn't understand why Linda was pulling away from me. After all, Linda had lived with me prior to my marriage to Phil and been a part of my two sons' lives just prior to her marriage to Curtis. But in time, it became evident that Linda was not only isolating herself from me but also pulling away from everyone in the fellowship. Her behavior was becoming increasingly more abnormal. Linda attended all of the functions, but she didn't go out of her way to speak to anyone. She focused on her three children—the twins were six years old, and the youngest was about two years old. Occasionally, I would see her snap at Curtis and physically pull away from him.

I repeatedly offered to watch her children for her so I could get closer to them, since the twins were only a year older than Jacob and Melissa. She always politely but emphatically refused. I took that personally until I realized something was wrong—very wrong.

I noticed little things, such as the way she would dress her youngest little girl. The clothing was often inappropriate—too warm or too cool for the occasion, such as a heavy jacket in the summer or barefoot in the winter. One time, I saw the young toddler wearing pants at least six inches too long, and she would trip as she walked on a raised concrete porch with no rail. I knew Linda to be strong-willed but not unreasonable or uncaring. She was quite the opposite. Linda had always been thoughtful and congenial. I didn't recognize this person as Linda.

The final decree in my mind that Linda was not mentally right was when I found a cryptic note from her on my front porch. As I was puzzling over it, Bud came up and asked me what was wrong, as he could see I was visibly upset. Before I could think, I handed him the note. I was in tears. The note, addressed to me, made no sense, and somehow, I was equated with Abraham Lincoln. I can't recall the exact words, and that was the last I saw the note. Bud took the note, tucked it in his shirt pocket, and, with pursed lips, muttered, "Thank you, Makena. I will keep this. We may need it." I was mortified when I saw the malevolent look on his face, because by then, I did not trust Bud. I was deeply worried about Linda.

I had to piece things together later as to what was happening with Linda. On one occasion, she good-naturedly said to me, "When are you going to slow down and stop doing so much?" I was startled to hear Curtis's wife say such a thing, when Curtis was pushing the members in the same direction as his dad—toward total commitment to the church, full speed ahead.

I was close to leaving at that point and really had no intention of continuing such an insane pace, but I didn't dare reveal my thoughts to her—particularly with her association to the Royal Family. Her comment made more sense when I found out shortly after her death that Linda was the only person who lived in an owned home but hadn't signed over the community property she and Curtis owned.

I will share more about Linda's unfortunate death a little further down the Yellow Brick Road, but understand for now, dear reader, that Curtis withheld the fact that he and his wife were actually not fully vested, as were the members he and his dad were pushing into submission. They were not vested because Curtis's wife refused to relinquish ownership of their home to the church. Curtis's secret sin was concealing that fact yet continuing to sanction total community sharing.

Some years earlier, Curtis also knew that Phil and I had enough capital to own our home outright but was visibly shocked and highly perturbed when he found out we took out a small VA loan to ensure we had sufficient money to complete the building. Only later did we understand why he was upset. As strange as it sounds, it was Linda, after her death, who revealed to me that the loan saved Phil and me from having to turn over our home. Again, the rest of this story is for a little later in the narrative.

Additionally, Curtis was involved in two violent incidents that were withheld from most of the members. I honestly can't recall who leaked the stories, but they were eventually substantiated, though details were not revealed. To be honest, I didn't want to know details. It was shameful enough to learn that my worst fears were true: not only was the fellowship on a wrong track, but the leadership was unstable and dangerous. I was a part of that fellowship. I naively allowed my participation instead of following my inner promptings early on. To remove oneself from a cult after it has progressed to a later stage is not easy, but the Source of Love is always ready to help us out. However, the lesson becomes increasingly more intense the longer we disregard the warnings.

Back to the violent incidents. They were related to the youngest daughter, Colette. Without my relaying her secret sins as of yet, let it be sufficient to say that big brother Curtis interfered with his sister's male relationships and severely beat up two young men who were outside our fellowship. The beatings also involved the youngest son, Cory, and most likely Bud. Curtis was not alone; I do know that. Oddly enough, both of those young men who were beaten died. They didn't die from the beatings, or at least that was the story we heard after the fact. One young man of about nineteen or twenty years old was jogging, which was his regular practice, and he collapsed and died. The other young man, possibly a little older—maybe twenty-three or twenty-four years old—died of cancer at an advantageous time when Colette's interests were concerned. Again, these were the stories we were told after the fact.

I will move on to the other three siblings, but I need to mention that some of these secret sins did manifest to a pitch all within about a year, during which time I was waiting on God to reveal to me how I was supposed to leave. However, Phil and I knew nothing about additional secrets until well past our agreement to leave together.

Second daughter, Camella Collins: Probably the prettiest of the three daughters, with deep auburn hair, small features, and a beautiful figure, Camella was also the most benign of the Royal

Family. Camella, though soft-spoken and not overly astute, carried out haughtiness pretty well, but she really didn't have any secret sins that we became aware of, though the impact of her family's transgressions became evident in a behavior we learned of much later.

The only compromise I saw in Camella's life as relates to honesty within the group was her agreement to finally marry Andon, who had pursued her for several years. Camella, taking after her mother's cold nature, easily turned away Andon's advances until Bud started teaching about keeping all marital ties within the group. Suddenly, the wedding bells were ringing, even though Camella knew one of her best friends in the fellowship was very much in love with Andon.

However, I can't blame Camella entirely for being an extension of her parents' inflexible control over us. She was devoted to her family and naively trusted her parents' leadership. It is my understanding that after the death-and-destruction period hit, Camella became quiet and remote and took time away. It was also rumored by more than one source that Camella developed agoraphobia. The definition of *agoraphobia*, per *Merriam-Webster,* is "abnormal fear of being helpless in a situation from which escape may be difficult or embarrassing that is characterized initially often by panic or anticipatory anxiety and finally by the avoidance of open or public places."

I have a hunch that as she was the naive and somewhat sensitive one in the family, she was kept in the dark, as were most of us members, until all hell broke loose and there was no way her family could conceal their transgressions. At any rate, I find it interesting that confident Camella actually experienced a similar helplessness and anxiety that I felt. However, the major difference is that she wanted to escape from public view, and I gladly stepped out of the dark confines of her family's entrapment and into the daylight of normal, rational society.

Third daughter, Colette Collins: Colette, the baby girl, was the most voluptuous, flirtatious, and outgoing of all of the female family members. In looks and demeanor, she most matched her father's charismatic nature. With her flaming-red hair and a figure that stopped men in their tracks, Colette was highly confident. Though all three girls had good singing voices, Colette had the most beautiful voice.

Whereas Caryn Sue had a more operatic voice, Camella sang alto and played a more supportive role in the trio. Colette outshined both of them and could surely sing and perform with body and soul.

Colette was also arrogant and was not averse to correcting us adults if she thought we needed it. Once, in earlier years, when in a casual group gathering, I was talking to a young single woman of my same age. We were laughing and reminiscing together, and Colette dramatically sashayed by us closely with head tilted back and said, "Be careful what you say, ladies. Remember, young people here are listening."

I don't recall what we were talking about, but there was nothing inappropriate whatsoever. It appeared to me that she was just exercising her self-appointed position as overseer and erring on the side of making negative assumptions. I would have laughed it off as if she were joking, but she was not. She was tutored by her parents to be exemplary and hold out expectations for all of us to be above reproach in every way. It was common knowledge that Bud set up his family to police us.

Obviously, I did not care for this overconfident little girl and didn't trust her. However, she paid a heavy price later on in learning that life experience is a true teacher and that words and admonishments without understanding have no credence.

With this description of this young lady, it shouldn't be shocking to learn that Colette developed secret boyfriend issues. While my son was told he couldn't go to a supervised high school dance with a shy classmate, Colette was working as a waitress and, of course, wittingly attracting men like bees to honey.

As mentioned earlier, I learned of Colette's problems after the fact from leaked information and, eventually, substantiated facts. Do I have details? No. But I will tell you what I do know for the purpose of further illuminating the old adage "What a web we weave when we practice to deceive." I have since heard that Colette might have been like I was when I became pregnant before marriage—ready to confess her shortcomings but trying to uphold her mother and father's credibility as she saw it at the time.

The first boyfriend or boy who was interested in Colette was evidently a nice young man of about nineteen years who attended a more mainstream local Christian church and questioned our church's belief system when conversing with Colette. He had issue with the control and severe limitations. I never saw that young man. He never attended any of our fellowship meetings. It seemed that just shortly after hearing that a young fellow on the outside was interested in Colette, we heard he'd collapsed while jogging and died from heart failure. Again, I heard only much later that prior to his death, he'd been bullied and beaten up by Curtis, his brother Cory, and possibly Bud.

I never had occasion to meet the second boyfriend, who was probably in his early twenties, but someone pointed him out in a church congregation where Colette was performing a solo. The gathering was a community-at-large gathering, not just our fellowship. I vaguely remember seeing him and observing the adoration in his demeanor as he watched and listened to Colette sing. This man, who was handsome and appeared healthy and of good stature, was not brought up in any open conversation among the church members. We knew little of the relationship until we were told that Colette was going away—some distance from our location—to get away from the influence of this man.

We also learned that again, the men in the Royal Family beat him severely as a warning to stay clear of Colette. However, the going-away story didn't hold for long because we were eventually informed that Colette was coming back with a baby she had conceived with that same young man.

When she returned, she got up in front of our fellowship group and confessed her transgression. She told all of us that the best thing for her to do would be to give up the child to that man.

We all listened intently as she shared the following Old Testament account in 1 Kings 3:16–28 (NIV) as the foundation for her decision:

Now two prostitutes came to the king and stood before him. One of them said, "Pardon me, my lord. This woman and I live in the same house, and I had a baby while she was there with me. The third day after my child was born, this woman also had a baby. We were alone; there was no one in the house but the two of us.

"During the night this woman's son died because she lay on him. So she got up in the middle of the night and took my son from my side while I your servant was asleep. She put him by her breast and put her dead son by my breast. The next morning, I got up to nurse my son—and he was dead! But when I looked at him closely in the morning light, I saw that it wasn't the son I had borne."

The other woman said, "No! The living one is my son; the dead one is yours."

But the first one insisted, "No! The dead one is yours; the living one is mine." And so they argued before the king.

The king said, "This one says, 'My son is alive and your son is dead,' while that one says, 'No! Your son is dead and mine is alive.'"

Then the king said, "Bring me a sword." So they brought a sword for the king. He then gave an order: "Cut the living child in two and give half to one and half to the other."

The woman whose son was alive was deeply moved out of love for her son and said to the king, "Please, my lord, give her the living baby! Don't kill him!"

But the other said, "Neither I nor you shall have him. Cut him in two!"

Then the king gave his ruling: "Give the living baby to the first woman. Do not kill him; she is his mother."

When all Israel heard the verdict the king had given, they held the king in awe, because they saw that he had wisdom from God to administer justice.

Evidently, the parallel Colette provided in reading us that passage was that the woman with the greater love, the true mother of the child, loved the child so much she was willing to give up the child to the other in favor of the child being divided, or cut in half. In Colette's situation, she chose to make the sacrifice in order to avoid conflict in the child's life, since reconciliation between her and the father of her baby was an impossibility. He was not a Christian, and he was unwilling to submit to the church—our church!

Obviously, we had been lied to, but many dismissed that possibility with the shocking and heartrending confession given by Colette. Obviously, the confession was intended to cover the deception, and now Colette would move on with her life without the child.

Hold on! My mother heart screamed inside of me, and I thought, *No way! This is not natural or normal in any way!*

My take was that Colette was coerced to give up the baby. No doubt Bud and Sandra Sue convinced her to take the "higher road" and give the child over to the father. Again, they provided a teaching tool to ensure control of the group. Only this time, their rigid dictates backfired, and the heads of the Royal Family ended up sacrificing one of their own with severe and unnecessary punishment.

In order to protect and uphold their faulty belief system, Bud and Sandra Sue followed through with their mind-set that the end justifies the means. Again, they made a harsh decision in order to maintain credibility.

I remember going to Colette's small duplex with Sandra Sue for some reason sometime soon after the confession, and I noted how her home and furnishings were bleak and dismal. The shades were drawn down, and there was nothing in the way of hominess or warmth to indicate the dwelling was related to that vivacious girl. Her icy-cold mother made some comment that Colette was decorating in a new way—a minimalist type of decor. Her excuse was more deception—more cover-up. The home declared loudly and clearly that Colette was in a deep depression.

I don't recall how long Colette went without being able to hold and take care of her baby, but it seemed like about seven or eight months. She became visibly thinner and more withdrawn. Then, one day, we learned that the baby's young father had died of cancer.

What? I thought.

Then we learned that Colette had custody of the child and was rejoined with her baby boy after relinquishing him for all those months. All of that culminated toward the end of the eleven years and the beginning of year twelve, at which time the final blow was about to be dealt to the fellowship.

Additionally, in a short space of time, Colette met another man outside the fellowship; planned a big, formal wedding in a church; and wore a formal white wedding gown. The event took place less than two years after a dismal wedding was inflicted on the young couple Carson and Janelle, Colette's peers, by Colette's hypocritical parents.

My interpretation of Colette's formal wedding at that juncture was that Colette was making a statement of rebellion against her parents. I learned from someone recently that the couple moved to a remote area and have been living there ever since—approximately twenty-seven years. Colette, evidently, to this day does not communicate much with her parents.

Youngest son, Cory Collins: Now we come to the youngest son, Cory. As mentioned earlier, he was reckless in nature. I am not sure if his irresponsible and impulsive actions were purposeful or if he was just one of those kids who was not careful about how he conducted himself. I recall a time much earlier—when Cory and Joe attended the same middle school—when Bud made a comment to me that caused me to believe he had no problem with his son's irresponsible behavior and, in fact, enjoyed it: "So, Makena, I hear that Joe received the middle school award for best citizen in the school. Ha! Can you imagine Cory getting such an award?"

Clearly, Bud favored his family, so his mocking eyes as he delivered that comment to me did not go unregistered. He was not complimenting Joe on his good behavior. He was mocking him and me—implying that we were too much into following society's expectations. That certainly was not the first or the last time Bud subtly put down my children, who, in many instances, were natural-born leaders and achievers. Was it jealousy on Bud's part, or was he displaying intimidating cowardly lion behavior to make sure my children stayed in subjection to him and his not-so-perfect and, in fact, unscrupulous children?

What were Cory's secret sins that weren't discovered until late in the twelve-year period or thereafter? First, as I mentioned much earlier in the narrative, as early as around eighteen or nineteen years of age, Cory was having intimacy with Tiffany, who was of the same age, on a regular basis. Tiffany left the fellowship, and we were told she was deciding whether she wanted to continue her commitment. The truth, of course, was that Bud and his wife more than likely arranged to separate the two young people to avoid any pregnancy mistakes. Of course, we members knew nothing of Cory's transgressions, and of course, there were no punishments.

However, the couple ended up getting back together on Tiffany's return and marrying. From rumor, following dissolution of the cult, we learned they had four children in a short period of time. We also learned that they divorced sometime when the children were young. I often wondered if Tiffany also covered up a pregnancy during her one-year leave and if the child was raised by someone else for a time on the outside. I can't substantiate such a possibility, but the timing lends to the likelihood.

As I have said repeatedly, dear reader, my emphasis is not on the transgressions; my emphasis is on the bullying and hypocrisy. Even now, it amazes me how that family was set out as examples and watchdogs, yet they committed transgressions that surpassed any of the members', all the while admonishing us (as Cory did with Joe) and concealing their shortcomings.

Cory, not being as astute as his older brother or as clever and manipulative as his father, followed along mindlessly to contribute to acts of violence against men who had no ill intentions toward his sister and did nothing other than respond to her charm and feminine lure. Rumors have it that Cory more than likely participated in both beatings—the young man we were told collapsed from a heart attack while jogging and the father of Colette's baby son.

Additionally, Cory's careless behavior, unchecked and, consequently, encouraged by his father, had severe consequences, as we soon discovered during the time of death and destruction.

Accidents and Fatalities

As mentioned earlier, when I came out of the cult, I read a great deal about cults, cult leaders, and their power of persuasion over devotees regardless of their educational or social backgrounds. I was amazed at discovering how Spirit took me out of the cult almost identical to my brief journaled messages, step by step, just as carefully as if I were getting my information from a wise psychologist.

As everyone knows, due to the brainwashing, it is difficult to get oneself free from the confines of a cult, particularly a religious cult. In the case of our fellowship, to leave would be to go against God himself.

Our belief system was anchored in the very Word of God, was it not?

As mentioned earlier, the best catalyst to help release the victim from cult entrapment is shock—and shock indeed came to all of us.

To reiterate, dear reader, at that point, I was nearing the end of the two-year period prior to final release. I'd received all of the evidence I needed to know that it was not only acceptable that I leave the cult but also prudent. I didn't necessarily know about all of the secret sins and hypocrisy of the cult leader and his family, but I had experienced all of the pain and suffering needed to tip the scales and deliver the last straws that broke the chains of mind control.

I'd also experienced the shock of my young nephew's early passing and the realization that our belief system was narrow and degrading. I was just waiting for the right time to address Phil about leaving and direction from Spirit on how to leave. Even those thoughts of waiting came directly from the Source of Love. Somehow, I understood secretly in my heart that I needed to get 100 percent direction and clearance in order to escape safely and with my family intact. Of course, by then, I did have one kindred spirit in Ellie, who understood as I did.

As we enter now into the space of death and destruction, I walk carefully and reverently. I can't say that young people gave up their lives in order to free the rest of us. However, if their lives' purpose was predetermined in such a direction, it causes me to weep with gratefulness and love for them as I contemplate the possibility. Our lives on this plane carry a great significance beyond our understanding, and far be it from me to draw conclusions one way or the other, but we all laud and honor that love that lays down a life for a friend.

I have asked myself, *Did God partner with these young people to be the shocking catalyst that caused more than me to question? Were their days numbered to coincide with an orchestration that resulted in an impassable roadblock to prevent further degradation of men's souls?* I can't answer these questions, but I do know that even as I write these words, I carry a special feeling of sheer joy and love for the two young women who died during that time period and are evolving magnificently on the Other Side.

The Beginning of the Shock Waves

I need to mention a prior accident that took place earlier, around the passing of my nephew. That accident was the first to jar the emotions of the young people in the fellowship. By then, besides grandparents, aunts, uncles, and a few cousins, I had experienced the deaths of my brother, thirty-one, and then my nephew, twenty-one.

I realized at the passing of my brother that most of the members were unacquainted with death, as they didn't seem to understand what I was going through. As mentioned, even my husband-to-be at that time didn't understand, and I received little solace from him as well as the church members.

So when we got word that Harris Jensen went down while piloting a private plane, the church members were deeply shocked to learn that Harris was severely injured. Harris had been up in a mountainous region, checking out property for a client. The plane didn't get enough lift when taking off from a private airstrip, and the subsequent crash landing left Harris, who was probably in his midthirties at the time, paralyzed from the waist down. He would be confined to a wheelchair for the rest of his life. Harris, though somewhat slight, was a man who cared about his health, jogged a couple miles every day, and kept active, so such a life sentence of limitation was beyond disturbing.

Edith, of course, suffered from the news and stood by him during his transition to find stability toward healing. The members were kind and supportive, and Harris made it easy on everyone by being stoic and positive, though he carried a tremendous amount of guilt for not being more careful. He'd made an unwise decision to lift from the primitive airstrip when temperatures were high and the plane gauges indicated a borderline situation. He'd ignored the risk, took off, went up several feet, and then came crashing down. The blow to his spine on impact had caused the permanent damage that sentenced him to the wheelchair.

I have often wondered if Harris's close alignment with and hero worship of Bud had something to do with his lack of judgment that day. Harris was not reckless by nature. Bud was reckless and often made light of Harris's fussy ways of doing things, such as the way he ate: pushing food carefully away on his plate so it did not touch other foods. Harris would never measure up to the football-player image the Collins males projected.

I felt that Harris was always trying to please Bud and live up to the strongman image that Bud projected. Is it possible he was trying to emulate Bud and live life a little more courageously and riskily? If this was the case, what a tough lesson he endured by denying the unique person he was designed to be.

It never works for us when we step out of our own individualization and try to copy someone else. I often think of Jesus's words "You are the salt of the earth. But if the salt loses its saltiness, how can it be made salty again?" (Matthew 5:13 NIV). We, like snowflakes, are unique, one of a kind, and it does not serve us or anyone around us to lose the essence of who we are, with our unique gifts, abilities, and purpose. Poor Harris chose to clone to Bud. In that process, he gave up a potential career as a doctor and instead became a Realtor and, while piloting a plane, took a risk that eventually limited him for the rest of his life.

Harris was one who followed Bud implicitly, and in the later years, I referred to him as Bud's "right-hand man." I got the feeling he would compromise anything to follow Bud. I ultimately lost respect for him.

I recall an occasion when Harris's parents came all the way from Harris's hometown several hundred miles distant to visit him. On the one occasion they attended the fellowship circle, Harris denounced his parents, proclaiming that his home was with his brothers and sisters and quoting the scripture that Bud repeatedly used to separate us from our families. I saw his parents' sad faces, and my heart went out to them. I understand that after Phil and I left the cult and it disbanded, Harris went back to live in his hometown.

I assume he apologized to his parents and mended the breach he caused that day.

Second Shock Wave

The second awful blow took place only months after Harris's accident and left most of the members in a state of shock. Some were more shocked than others, specifically those who witnessed the accident, as Phil did.

As mentioned earlier, one of the group activities our fellowship adopted was to gather wood during the summer to fuel wood-burning stoves for our homes in the winter. The activity allowed us, again, as a group to include each other in our day-to-day requirements for communal living. We were now dependent on conducting ourselves resourcefully and frugally since our money was taken and put in a common purse. Saving on our electric bills was one way to be responsible with the money that went into common purse.

That particular day was a Saturday, so several members were able to participate in the outing. I stayed back, as did several of the mothers with young children. The trip destination was in the lower elevations of the mountainous, forested government land. It was common knowledge that the forested areas that were clear-cut were open for anyone to gather from the piles of remaining wood. The main vehicle to carry back the gathered and loaded wood was the fellowship's old one-ton flatbed donated by Sam James. Several carloads of members went to help gather and load the wood. The driver of the flatbed was Cory Collins. He had one passenger: Edith.

Phil described the first part of the outing as a normal occurrence in our fellowship—many hands making light work. Once at the destination, everyone helped get the wood onto the truck, and once the mission was accomplished, everyone piled into his or her respective vehicle, with Cory leading the caravan, to travel back home on the two-lane highway.

Phil recalls the story told to him. Cory was driving fairly fast but noticed the traffic was picking up, so he decided to slow down. At some point in making that decision to do so, he ended up crossing into the other lane, and he hit an embankment that caused the truck to flip over and burst into flames. Unfortunately, coming from the other direction on the opposite side of the two-lane highway was a lengthy caravan of motorcycle enthusiasts making their way to a campsite to participate in a yearly event and celebratory outing.

Phil recounted, as did the other caravanning church members at the time, that they were all a distance behind Cory, when they noticed a large plume of black smoke rising ahead. Phil recalls feeling a sense of dread, and his first thoughts were of the truck in the lead. By the time the remaining members reached the scene of the accident, several motorcyclists were engulfed in flames, one was crushed beneath the truck, and several survivors were hugging each other and crying. Bodies and wood were strewn across the highway, and some reported that the scene looked like a war zone.

The accident happened quickly, as do most accidents, and evidently, the truck flipped and landed on one of the first motorcyclists, while several others slammed into the unexpected roadblock—the enflamed flatbed. Several motorcyclists died at the scene. Cory, Edith, and one of the injured motorcyclists were taken to a medical center in the main city, approximately seventy miles from the scene of the accident.

Cory and the other motorcyclist were treated for several burns and were soon released from the hospital. Edith wasn't as fortunate. She suffered severe burns over the majority of her body.

Later that evening, Monica, in a state of shock, told me the story as it had been relayed to her by Edith at the scene of the accident. She said when the truck landed, Edith noticed that Cory was not reacting quickly, and she had to scream at him repeatedly to get out of the truck—she probably saved his life. When Edith tried to escape herself, one of her feet was trapped somehow, and she did extreme damage to that leg in releasing herself from the wreckage. She hobbled to the side of the highway in flames.

I don't know how the flames were extinguished, but Monica reported that she held Edith loosely in her arms and witnessed the devastation the fire had done to Edith's body and hair. She said Edith asked Monica if she had any eyelashes. She was so badly burned that Monica only knew to reassure her that she would be okay. What a devastating, heartrending experience for those two young ladies! Only knowing that Edith is more than okay on the Other Side allows me to relive that awful event as I document this part of my narration.

On the evening of the accident, in addition to Monica, several members came to Phil's and my home. They were draped over our couches and sitting on the floor with their heads in their hands, dazed. I served them as if they had been in the accident themselves. They were in shock after witnessing such a horrific accident and experiencing the mass grieving at the site. Phil retired to the bedroom, and I would check on him occasionally, always finding him in the same position: lying on his back, staring at the ceiling.

A few days after the accident, I visited Edith in the burn center of the medical facility. The scene is vivid in my mind to this day, twenty-eight years later. Several church members were somberly waiting outside her room; one of them was Harris in his wheelchair. Having experienced a great amount of death in our family, I was not a stranger to tragedy, but I have to say, I was at a loss as to what to say to Harris. He would never walk again, and now his girlfriend—and, more than likely, future bride—was burned beyond recognition. If she were to survive, she had nothing but surgeries and pain ahead of her for a long time.

I pulled up a chair and sat across from him, holding his hand with tears streaming—no sound. It seemed irreverent to make a sound and hollow to utter any condolences, so I didn't. I just looked him in the eyes and let the emotion of tears flow gently—but not too much. Everything was already way too much.

In the room just beyond Harris was Edith, who was wrapped like a mummy from head to toe, completely covered in white bandages. By that time, she had experienced surgery involving the amputation of the irreparable leg, and she was on some type of elevated breathing machine that made her look like something surreal—surely not the beautiful Edith with the perfect white skin, clear brown eyes, and lovely golden hair.

Members came and went over the course of the next several days. We would speak to her, telling her we loved her and were praying for her. Some said they thought she made some indication she could hear, and we all hoped she at least sensed our presence somehow and knew we were there to let her know we cared.

Edith slipped away to the Other Side within a couple weeks, and I, for one, was glad she was free from any further pain or suffering.

Several members sang to her as she crossed over about two weeks after the accident. There was also some type of funeral service for her. I didn't attend either. I asked Phil if we could go to a favorite waterfall location, a place where God's creation in nature could possibly overpower our inability to reckon with such a sickening personal reality. Phil was quick to agree. No one questioned our escape or our absence. The numbing shock covered the have-tos and thou-shalts on the cult agenda like a dark, silent blanket.

Instead of dwelling on everything surrounding Edith's passing, I wanted to experience something powerful—like the magnificent cascading waterfalls I'd experienced as a young child with my parents. Waterfalls were faithful to the laws set in motion by the Source of Love. I knew there were constants provided by God, and ultimately, death has no sting.

Edith was safe and free on the Other Side. That was what I wanted to experience, and at that time, I exercised choice—I chose to remove myself from Bud and the cult environment and imagine

Edith, who was fond of horses, riding a celestial beast while she, a renewed, beautiful avatar version of herself, rode like the wind in a way she'd never experienced while in her earthly home. The powerful, repetitious pounding sight, sound, and feel of the falls embedded that vision in my mind's eye and brought me peace and solace.

I knew my time of leaving the cult was soon but somehow not yet. There were still unresolved issues, such as confronting Phil and leaving Melissa without a mother.

As time passed after Edith's death, life slowly went back to usual—that is, all of the routines of our day-to-day existence resumed. However, for some of us, though it was not talked about, the elephant in the room was a terrible blight that swirled around and among us and whispered, "Think! Open your mind, and think!"

There was the possibility of an impending trial involving Cory as the driver of the truck in the accident. We members were not necessarily privy to the details of what was happening in that legal department. It might have been that Bud's previous law enforcement connection was somehow advantageous in such dealings. After we left the cult, just prior to the entire fellowship disbanding, we heard that the judge in the case was seen coming from the Meeting Place. We heard that there were no charges against Cory, the driver of the truck.

✝ Year Twelve: In and Out

The Beginning of the End—Tell Phil

The final wake-up call took place in February 1990, just five months to the day after the awful tragedy on the wood-gathering expedition. First, I must fill you in, dear reader, on what took place prior to that February date.

During that five-month period, several important happenings took place that were instrumental in releasing me and my family from the cult. To this day, I have a deep and enduring thankfulness for God's provision—the step-by-step series of events that efficiently and expeditiously took us out of bondage. By the beginning of February, the prison gate was metaphorically swinging wide open, and we were able to walk out unscathed in May of the same year.

One of the first of that series of happenings was that I was able to approach Phil about my desire to leave the fellowship. In one of my rare times of quiet solitude, it occurred to me that it was time to approach him. After all, Phil had not been the same since the accident. He was quiet and withdrawn, more than his usual silent demeanor. I knew the accident had had a huge impact on him, but I detected more, and in the still of a moment of inquiry, in my mind and heart, I asked, *Is it time?*

I received my answer clearly and emphatically: *Yes. Tell Phil. He is ready.*

I didn't know that Phil had been unhappy for quite some time. His ideal of what it was to be part of a loving community of like-minded believers had been shattered by the tightening control, extreme legalism, and harsh punishments. For him, what had started out as a harmonious group of people living out the Christian principles taught by Bud was becoming instead a nightmare. The group was militarized to think like Bud entirely. The men's meetings were harsh and punishing, and the growing spiritual pride among the people was becoming less and less appealing, setting the tone for more rules and less freedoms. Choice diminished considerably. In fact, there was no choice or voice—period.

One of the most crushing realizations had taken place for him surrounding the wood-gathering accident. When Sam James had come to retrieve his donated flatbed truck just prior to the wood-gathering outing, Phil had told him the truck was unsafe. The wheels on the driver's side appeared to be warped, and the brakes would grab when extreme pressure was applied. Phil found out much later that the truck had been in a fire, hence the warped wheels.

At any rate, Phil had delivered his recommendation not to use the truck until a more thorough repair could be done. Sam had insisted on taking the truck as it was, unconcerned about the need to invest more money to ensure safety. The god of frugality was the overriding factor when the elders made such decisions. Saving money trumped safety. Phil was often deemed too perfectionistic. He recalls Sam reassuring him that he himself knew to be careful when applying the brakes, and the truck would work fine for the wood-gathering trip.

Whether Cory was cautioned to drive more slowly due to the brake issue is unknown. Based on Sam's character, he might have advised Cory to drive with care, particularly when applying the brakes. I am also inclined to believe that Cory did as he always did—cast caution to the wind and drove too fast for the conditions.

Just as the fellowship group disregarded my merciful input, they disregarded Phil's logic and sound reason.

This background provides the explanation for Phil's reaction the day I approached him about leaving.

It was rare that Phil and I would be driving somewhere together just the two of us, and I honestly can't remember why we were doing so, but I can vividly picture at what point on the freeway the simple exchange of words propelled us both from one position to another—from imprisonment in the cult to freedom and hope.

"Phil, I want to leave the fellowship, and I want to leave with you and Jacob," I said.

Phil's immediate response was "Yes. I do too."

I can't remember the discussion beyond that exchange of words, but I know the way was not clear yet, and we didn't have an exit plan. I probably shared what had been happening with me since the two years prior and why I was confident that we would be led out of the cult but that the timing wasn't quite right. I was still entangled in teaching school, and Melissa believed me to be her mother. Phil must have been in the same state of mind, because we returned to our home in the cult that day and kept that secret in our hearts.

Teaching Second Grade

I believe that focusing on completion of the Meeting Place was somewhat of a welcome distraction from the tragedy. The Meeting Place was easily wrapped up at that time since all of the hard labor was done. We started holding our meetings in that facility, and I was asked to teach the second graders. School was shifted to the Meeting Place.

It was necessary for me to create all of my own visual aids and curriculum and study teaching methods to ensure that six little young people aged seven to eight years old were equipped to read, write, and develop proper math skills to be successful in their later school years. I took the task seriously, and as always, I enjoyed the little ones. Typically, children in that age bracket are a joy to teach—eager for and open to instruction. That group of children was no exception. I can still remember their faces and demeanor, and these children are approximately thirty-five years old now! I have recently been in contact with one of them, and she is a delightful young lady with children of her own.

Just to quickly recall the children in that second-grade class, there were Sam and Lilith James's little freckle-faced girl, Alicia, who was cute and pugnacious; Curtis and Linda Collins's girl-and-boy twins, Thomas and Trish, who were both sweet; Kasey, the middle child of a wonderful couple not mentioned in this narrative, Jake and Norma, who was bright and attentive; Ben and Caryn Sue Weber's little boy Michael, who was also a bright and charming little guy; and Jim and Louise's third daughter, Bessie, a quiet, intelligent little girl. In those final days of struggle to hang on, God gave me one of the best gifts ever: teaching second-grade children, which had been a lifelong dream of mine.

As I mentioned much earlier, Linda would not allow me to spend time out of the classroom with her children, Thomas and Trish, though they were both only a year older than Jacob and Melissa. I didn't understand why she withheld contact, and I took it personally for a time. I thought that since I taught Linda's children, she would change her mind and allow them to play with my children, particularly since we now lived a short distance apart.

As is often the case when feelings are hurt, anger becomes the outcome. I secretly held a certain anger against Linda during that time, even though I knew something was wrong with her. Once again, I am thankful for God's guidance during that brief period, because he shed light on the situation so as to cause me to soften, even though I didn't understand. He spared me any guilt and provided a beautiful opportunity to connect with Linda shortly before her death.

Change in Household

Simultaneous to Linda's withdrawal, Bud approached Phil and I and told us that one of the singles, Marjory, would be joining our household in place of Edith. I was surprised since Marjory was part of Caryn Sue Weber's extended household. Marjory not only was an outstanding young career woman who was intelligent and wise but also was capable and gifted in any domestic application needed, including as a seamstress, a cook, a nanny—the works! Marjory not only required no instruction or counseling but also would be of great assistance in any household—it was the reason Caryn Sue had held her and another similar single young lady tightly to her household for the past five or six years—so Caryn Sue could be free to "exercise her gifts."

I was so disillusioned at the time that I didn't question the reason for the gift of Marjory from Bud, but of course, in hindsight, I realize Bud was no doubt getting nervous. At that point, unknown to us, he was hiding the secret sins of three of his children—Curtis, Colette, and Cory—and in view of the recent accident that was not yet resolved legally, he was probably feeling vulnerable. Add to that huge can of worms the fact that one of his key members, positioned centrally in the community, was questioning the church and becoming more vocal and suspicious. In his mind, I could be a real threat to the stability of the community if I should decide to leave.

His rationale could have been "Let's move Marjory to Makena's household so Makena will get some assistance and not be as tense and not rock the boat." Whereas his previous method of operation had been to work me so I could hardly think and possibly even die, he was now backpedaling like the cowardly lion and throwing favors my way—always manipulating the situation to retain control and power over the group.

Needless to say, Phil and I welcomed Marjory into our home, even though at that particular time, both of us would have liked to be somewhere on the other side of the planet, alone with our family. There was room in our home for Marjory now that Andon had married Camella and moved out, and as it turned out, Marjory was easy to be around and was especially helpful with little Melissa.

Unbeknownst to Phil and me, Marjory had taken a special liking to little Melissa. Marjory had been especially attentive to Melissa whenever Blake would include his daughter in a singles' outing when appropriate or in some of the group settings, such as the potlucks or ocean trips. Marjory had a special empathy for children who lost their natural mothers, since her mother had died when Marjory was fourteen years old. At that time, she was the oldest of four siblings. Even though Marjory's father eventually remarried after the death of her mother, Marjory was left to be the mother to her younger siblings for a couple of years—which explained her quiet, serious, and capable conduct.

It couldn't have been more than a couple of weeks after Marjory moved in when I noticed that Blake was becoming agitated around her. I didn't understand because she was so helpful with Melissa, which should have been welcomed by Blake. I certainly appreciated the help. Around that time, Phil and I were called to meet with Bud and Blake, and Blake revealed to us that he had feelings for Marjory. Blake had intended to approach Bud and the elders to ask if he could pursue Marjory in group settings for the purpose of marriage but hadn't gotten the chance before Marjory was given over to our household.

I thought, *Wow. Surprise! I didn't see this one coming at all!*

For one thing, Marjory was five years older than Blake and much more mature than he was. It also surprised me that Bud gave his immediate consent for Blake to ask Marjory if she was interested in a serious relationship—no meetings, no elders hashing everything over, no long timeframes to ensure a proper decision. Just "Go ahead and get it on!" That was not typical at all. Another shocker was that Marjory and Blake were allowed to stay in our household with adjacent bedrooms and a shared bathroom, which never would have been allowed previously.

At the end of 1989, around Christmas, Marjory and Blake were engaged and planning an April wedding. All three of my sons and Phil would be in the wedding. Per Blake's choice, Joe, Matt, and Phil would stand up with him, and Jacob would be the ring bearer. Melissa would be the flower girl. Marjory chose to have several of her single friends stand up with her, and I was to coordinate the wedding.

Amazing! I thought.

It remained a secret in Phil's and my hearts, but now we knew that immediately following the wedding, we would be making our exit.

I will no longer be Melissa's mom. Marjory will be Melissa's mom. And since school will be out of session shortly after the wedding, I can be replaced as teacher of the second-grade students. The innocent children are protected, and Phil, Jacob, and I will be free!

Oh my gosh—free! After twelve years of doubting and struggling, I will no longer be held to the confining belief system that caused so much pain to me and my children.

Thank you! Thank you for deliverance!

The only issue that remained was that we might lose our home—though we understood that would not keep us from leaving. Mind you, this home was close to being paid for and was the result of accumulated revenue from twelve years of labor with my ex-husband, Steve, not to mention the building of the current home with Phil. Yes, synergistic efforts were provided, but Phil and I had doubled those efforts back with all of our labor contributed to the fellowship over the past six years. Phil provided construction and mechanical expertise and labor. I contributed five years of teaching school and counseling, as well as cooking and caring for extended household members. Other than Blake's small rental contribution, we'd charged no rent to several young people who'd lived with us over the previous several years.

All of the money invested in the home was carried forward from the sale of my property from the divorce settlement with Steve. Phil and I were financially the most vested of all of the members in the community, other than perhaps Sam James, but because we'd signed over our property when we'd agreed to common purse, we knew we might have to relinquish it.

My thoughts at that time were *Painful? Yes! Very much so! But nothing is more painful than losing the right to make choices and feeling like your very soul is slipping away. Not even such financial loss can take away the joy I feel with the realization that my family and I are free.*

So why did Bud so quickly concede to the marriage of Blake and Marjory, when just a year earlier, the elders would have been included and more than likely would not have agreed so quickly or perhaps not at all? Certainly there were other relationship requests much more compatible that were delayed or shut down by lengthy discussions and meetings. I pondered, *Why is Bud letting this request go through without a hitch?*

Looking back and knowing what we learned later, I wonder: Was Bud looking for something positive that would add credibility to the group? A wedding is a happy occasion and would not only lighten up the members but also provide a shield from the outside world judging the recent wood-gathering tragedy. Plus, he was sitting on a time bomb with his own family. What if the truth were to get out about the sexual indiscretions of his youngest son, Cory, as well as the treatment of Colette's boyfriends and the father of her child? What if Phil and I backed out and started an avalanche of discontent?

Well, at that point, Bud hadn't even experienced the worst of it. That was soon to come—a third shock wave related to his eldest son, Curtis, and his wife, Linda.

A Compassionate Revelation

Linda, as mentioned earlier, would not sign over their home. No one knew that. At least Phil and I certainly didn't know that. We didn't learn that until quite some time after our exit from the fellowship.

Linda was showing increasingly bizarre behavior, and Bud and Sandra Sue often scowled when mentioning her. I was unhappy with Linda because she displayed a lack of trust in me, but I felt that Bud and Sandra Sue's opinion of Linda was poor and uncalled for. She was their daughter-in-law, the mother of their grandchildren. I felt they should be concerned in helping her. Their behavior toward Linda made me question more.

What exactly is the problem with Linda? What does her behavior signify? Is there mental illness? There don't seem to be any issues with her natural family or her twin sister.

In fact, we heard that her natural family was getting concerned also, though I am sure they all felt helpless, being on the outside of our fellowship.

One day when my son Matt phoned from college, I told him about Linda's behavior and the strange note she'd left on our porch for me. Matt was taking psychology courses and had immediate empathy for her. I told him I was thinking of confronting her and drawing her out—starting with my own issue of her lack of trust in me where her children were concerned. He cautioned me and said, "Mom, if she has some kind of mental illness, you could actually cause her to withdraw even more. It is better that you just love her and pray for her."

Matt's words of compassion went straight to my heart. I felt ashamed and judgmental. I had been making her withdrawal all about me. It was not about me. There was something wrong with her, and the best I could do was exactly what he'd suggested: just love her—no questions asked, no confrontation, no accusations. It's amazing how once the lights go on to move in a positive direction, God is quick and sure to provide opportunity, and that was what he did.

Makena McChesney

Imminent Angels

Once Blake and Marjory's wedding plans were announced to the fellowship, it quickly became common knowledge that come April, Melissa would be leaving our household and becoming Marjory's daughter, not mine. Marjory and Blake would start a home of their own. Everyone in the fellowship was eager to rally around and help with the wedding, and it was a common topic around the first of the year in 1990. After all, it was January, and April was just around the corner. I knew I had plenty to do myself as the coordinator, but to be honest, those couple months before and including the wedding are a complete blur in my memory. I know it was a beautiful wedding, and Marjory was a gorgeous, happy bride, but during those last few months leading up to the wedding, I could barely think. But I am getting ahead of my story.

Late in January, the fellowship group was having a Sunday potluck in the Meeting Place. I was sitting next to Linda, when her twin daughter, Trish, came up to me and, in typical childlike fashion, asked, "Is Melissa going to get a new mom?"

I smiled and said, "Yes, Trish, Marjory will be Melissa's mom." I had learned from experience that it is always good to keep answers simple with little children, particularly when an involved answer could be confusing for them, but that satisfied Trish, and no more dialogue was necessary.

However, when Trish turned to walk away, Linda grabbed her and scolded her. "No, Trish. You shouldn't ask such questions. That's not nice!"

I tried to counter with "Oh, that's okay, Linda—no harm done," but she was so distraught that she grasped Trish's hand and hurried away. I was surprised at Linda's extreme reaction. She was highly disturbed by her daughter's question.

I was thankful I had made peace with myself regarding Linda and backed off on any anger or discontent where Linda was concerned, or

I might have taken her abrupt behavior personally and not considered the alternatives. I determined to find an appropriate moment when I could explain to her that I really was okay that Melissa was going to have Marjory as her mom so she could experience a more ideal family unit. Of course, I couldn't reveal that the transfer would allow Phil and me freedom from the cult, but I wanted Linda to know that Trish had not offended me in any way.

I want to explain here, dear reader, that only after getting out of the cult and learning more about the circumstances surrounding Linda's illness did I realize that her strong reaction that day in the Meeting Place was most likely coming from her own fears.

Based on everything I came to understand later, I believe I can safely assume that Linda was concerned Bud and Sandra Sue were plotting to take Linda's children from her. After all, Bud had delivered that awful story to me when I experienced chest pains, letting me know that I was dispensable and that someone else even better could take over my children if I were to die. Of course, should that have happened, Bud would have been able to manipulate Phil and take the property as well as have sway over Jacob. In his mind at that time, I was a potential threat due to my credibility in the group. To him, it would not have been all that bad if I died.

What was different in Linda's situation? Nothing. It was the same thing. He had a daughter-in-law who could ruin his plan to take over the community completely both financially and by mind control. By not participating as a fully committed member, she was standing in the way. Hence, Bud and his wife scorned her instead of being concerned and made no efforts to help her. Curtis, of course, was trained to please and honor his father, so it was his job to get his wife under control and make sure she obeyed her husband.

Later, I also realized that fear was probably why Linda kept her children close to her and didn't trust anyone in the fellowship, including me. And why would she have? I gave no clear indication that I wasn't fully on board. After all, Phil and I had signed our home away. I was in deep, and she was struggling to get out.

A few days after the incident with Trish and Linda, some of the women met to do some quilting. I was invited and went, but quilting was the last thing I wanted to do. Ugh!

Again, I found myself sitting next to Linda. Evidently, my genuine desire to let go of any negative agenda where she was concerned and just feel love for her must have helped. She warmed up to me and said, "I am so sorry about Trish confronting you the other day." I knew that was not the place to reassure her, but told her I would come by her house one evening that week and let her know how I felt about the change in our family and our acceptance of the situation.

I was surprised that Linda accepted my offer. I visited her a few nights later. I went to her house and, standing at her front door, asked if we could talk briefly, and she cheerily agreed. At that moment, I saw the old Linda. I wanted to grab her, hug her, and tell her I missed her, but I knew that would overwhelm her and wouldn't be the thing to do.

We retired to a spare room off the hallway and sat on straight chairs across from each other. The minute I sat down, I felt something unusual. I felt as if I were there, but some part of me was put aside, as if I were an observer, not necessarily a participant. I started the conversation and heard myself say something like "I want to ease your mind about what happened with Trish the other day and her comment about Melissa getting a new mom."

Now here, dear reader, I will be unable to recount the complete conversation, but it reminded me of two little children talking to each other—one says something, and then the other says something, but the conversations are not connecting.

I recall her exclaiming, "I love my grandpa!" I had never heard her speak of her grandfather, and I had never met the gentleman. The odd thing was that somewhere in my existence, I was aware that our conversations were not connecting at all but that I was hearing

Seeking Oz

certain things from her that were important, and she was hearing things from me that were important.

I was not in the least bit concerned about the fact that something unusual was happening. In fact, I felt light, and I could see that she did too. We smiled at each other; we laughed. Though our conversation was inconsistent, something far more important was being conveyed. I also felt that something was circling over our heads, and it was manifesting love through us and for us.

I don't believe that went on for more than five or ten minutes. I am pretty sure I didn't tell her what I'd come to tell her, but it didn't matter. She jumped up and said, "Well, I have to get ready for bed, so let me drive you home." I told her it wasn't necessary; I could walk. We lived just a short distance away—in proximity. She insisted since it was dark, so I agreed. She drove me to my house. We drove up the driveway and stopped in front of my home.

I turned to her and said, "I have wondered why you haven't let me watch your children. But whether I understand or not, it doesn't matter. I trust you have your reasons, and I love you."

She giggled, hugged me, and said, "I love you too."

That was the last I saw her but not the last I heard from her.

I was glad I followed up with telling Phil about the strange occurrence that night, or I might have thought I'd imagined it. I went into the house and stood at the end of the bed, where Phil was getting ready to turn out the lights and retire for the night. I said, "The strangest thing just happened. There was something over our heads, and it was like a circle of love. Our conversations made no sense, but it didn't matter." I told him about the isolated statement that she loved her grandpa. She obviously loved him enough to interject that fact into the conversation without a context for doing so.

Now, as I write this, having gained more knowledge about the angels and a person crossing to the Other Side, I have no doubt the angels were coming to take Linda. She passed away sometime between that time and early the next morning, possibly from a seizure. We fellowship members were told that she died in her sleep.

Third and Final Shock Wave

I do need to inform you, dear reader, of the strange state of events immediately following Linda's death. That morning, I received a phone call from one of the older single ladies in our group. She said Linda was taken by ambulance to the hospital that morning, and she and a few other ladies in the fellowship were preparing to organize a helping hand by providing some food to Curtis and the young children. She asked if I would clean the house up for Curtis.

It was not uncommon for the church to rally around a difficult situation to provide any necessary or helpful comfort and relief. Helping our brothers and sisters in the church was the norm, and we always willingly complied. Without knowing any details as to why Linda had gone to the hospital, I assumed the concern was that Linda might have to remain for tests of some kind, though I didn't have much time to consider the whole situation. There was a crisis. I was asked to help, so I did.

I did, of course, wonder how Linda could fail in health to such a degree, when she'd been perfectly fine the night before—in fact, in a better state of mind than I had seen her in a long while. Some of us were aware that Linda had had a seizure in the past, but we were never given any details as to what extent or why.

I left Jacob with Phil and dutifully went to Curtis and Linda's home. No one was home, and the door was unlocked, so I went in. I cleaned up the kitchen, washed a few dishes, and put them away. I couldn't help but notice several prescription bottles on the lower shelf of the dish cupboard. I didn't read the labels but assumed they might have been some type of antidepressant and possibly medication to prevent seizures, based on what little I knew or understood of Linda's condition. I then proceeded to the back of the house to vacuum.

The master bedroom was at the end of the hall. I hesitated at the doorway when I looked in. It looked like there had been a struggle. The bed was pushed to the side awkwardly, and it looked like some of Linda's clothing had been cut up—her bra and possibly nightwear. I was taught as a young child never to enter an adult's bedroom. The parents' bedrooms were off-limits. I immediately felt like an intruder. I was taken aback at the state of the room but also compelled to follow through with my assignment.

I assumed that possibly, the paramedics had made an effort to remove all obstacles, including the bed, in order to work with Linda, who might have suffered a seizure. I reasoned that they must have quickly cut her clothing so as not to take time to remove it any other way. I put the bed back in its place, pulled the covers into place, and did my best to put things in order without being invasive. However, I couldn't help but notice several sentimental items strewn about—photos of Linda and Curtis as young romantics, probably ten or more years earlier, before marriage.

I quickly gathered everything, put it in a pile, vacuumed the room, and then moved to vacuum the remaining bedrooms and living room. In the living room, I had the feeling someone was there with me. I kept looking around, thinking maybe Linda had been brought home, and I hadn't heard her come in due to the vacuum running. I thought I probably had anxiety because I was in someone's home and not necessarily with her consent.

I finished up and went home. Someone called and asked if I would go get Thomas at the Timber House site. Someone else was watching Trish. I walked over to the construction site, where groundbreaking was commencing for Bud and Sandra Sue's new future home. A handful of men were there, working with hand shovels. I asked about Thomas, and someone said Curtis had him.

I felt a little out of place with just the men there working, but I wanted to know if anyone had heard how Linda was doing.

I went up to Sam, who was standing near Bud, whose back was to both of us. I asked him if there was any news of Linda's status—was she okay? Before Sam could respond, Bud turned on his heels violently and bellowed out angrily, "No! She is in the Chapel of the Pines!" I knew what Chapel of the Pines was—a funeral home up the road about ten miles, near the foothills hospital.

I yelled angrily back, "No!" Bud set his jaw and walked away. No one said a word. The men followed Bud's lead, avoiding any further comment or emotion. They turned their backs to me and kept working. I ran home in tears, dazed.

How could this be? Linda died? No way. Something is dreadfully and horribly wrong!

Word, of course, spread quickly, and efforts to help Curtis out increased. Within a week following, I picked up a couple of loads of laundry to take home, and there were occasions following Linda's death when Thomas would come over to play with Jacob. Little Thomas was so sad, and I was at a loss to be able to comfort the little guy. He was only eight years old, and it was visible that he was in a state of shock—quiet, withdrawn, and emotionless. I tried to comfort him the best I could without bringing anything up about the loss of his mom, but I felt like I failed him miserably.

I watched him only a couple of times, but as it turned out, Linda's mother eventually became active in helping out with her daughter's three young children. I was relieved that a natural grandmother, grieving her daughter, would be the best person to help out with the children. I was also relieved that Curtis's mother, Sandra Sue, was not the grandmother called on to help.

In that short span of time immediately following Linda's death, I had to take Thomas to the local playground in a community park, where I was supposed to meet Linda's grandfather since he was going to take Thomas for the day. I didn't know whom to look for until

I spotted an elderly gentleman sitting on a park bench. He stood up when he saw me approach with Thomas in hand. He barely uttered a word to me, and I knew why.

Linda's family blamed the church group for Linda's decline in health and probably her ultimate death. The thought struck me in the heart, and I knew to say nothing. Thomas asked to play on the playground, and the grandfather agreed and sat back down. I started to walk away, and then a small voice in my mind urged, *Let this grandpa know what Linda said the night before she died.*

Oh dear! I struggled with that thought. *This man not only doesn't know me but also most likely blames me, by association, for the death of his granddaughter.*

But I knew I had to do it. I needed to put aside self-protecting thoughts and tell him what Linda had conveyed to me that night, even though I had nothing to add to it—it was just a statement that hadn't even fit into a normal conversation. That wasn't the first or the last time I was called to follow through with something awkward relating to a person's crossing over. But those are situations beyond Oz, and by then, I had more understanding.

I took a deep breath, turned back, and sat down next to Linda's grandfather. He looked straight ahead, and so did I. I meekly said something like "Mr. Jameson, I saw Linda the night before she died. She was happy and cheerful. Though you were not a topic of conversation, she mentioned that she loved her grandpa. For whatever it is worth, I think she would want you to know that you were and are very special to her."

He mumbled something about the fact that she was his favorite grandchild and then went cold and silent. Further dialogue was unaccepted. I reverently walked away and hoped Linda's message brought some sense of comfort to her grandpa in spite of the messenger, who was affiliated with the strange group of believers who'd separated his granddaughter from him and her family.

Makena McChesney

A Message from the Other Side

The next message I received that week was not a small voice in my mind. It was audible and stopped me in my tracks. I was walking down the hallway of my home and was actually heading for the laundry I was doing for Curtis. I had Linda on my mind but wasn't prepared for what happened next. I heard her laugh out loud—her infectious laughter that couldn't be ignored and that always made me laugh along with her. She blurted out, "VA loan!" Then she laughed again.

That was it. She said, "VA loan." I stood still for a moment, trying to make sense of it, startled by the explosion of communication from Linda, who was now on the Other Side.

Why would Linda say anything about our VA loan? Phil and I took out a VA loan on our house, but why would Linda draw attention to that?

I quickly went through some logical steps in my mind. *What does "VA loan" remind me of? It reminds me of building this house and the fact that we had only six months to complete the contract for completion. It reminds me of the disappointed expression on Curtis's face when Phil and I mentioned that we had taken out a small construction loan to ensure we had enough funds to complete the house.*

Then the lights went on. Curtis and Bud wanted eventual ownership of our home and property. Our taking out a loan possibly relegated the signed document to the church as invalid in lieu of the VA mortgage, which explained Curtis's reaction when he first heard we had taken out a loan.

Something told me that if we signed our house over, the first mortgage should take some kind of precedence. I was not familiar with contractual legalities, particularly in that type of situation, but something prompted me to pick up the phone and call our mortgage company. I was too embarrassed to ask a question about my husband and I signing over our property to a church, knowing now that it was a cult and probably headed by an unstable pastor or a con man. I talked to a VA loan officer and said I had a question regarding a hypothetical situation: If someone had a VA loan against his or her home and signed the home over to his or her church, what rights did that church have to take ownership?

I never checked out legalities beyond that point, but I know the Source of Love had a hand in that, and I got the answer I needed. That answer gave me the courage to take a next step toward getting our home back.

The person on the other end of the line said emphatically and, actually, a little angrily, "No rights whatsoever. You cannot sign over something that is under contract with Veterans Affairs." I thanked the lady and got off the phone, reeling.

Oh my gosh! Linda just gave us the key to getting our house back!

Linda's gift of our home, provided in that single phrase "VA loan," took on a whole new meaning when I found out much further down the Yellow Brick Road that Linda had withheld signing over her home, which was more than likely the basis for the mental abuse she received from Curtis and his family. When I found that out, I wept. I also gained insight into how our loved ones on the Other Side can come to our aid—all under the umbrella of the Source of Love—to provide comfort and justice.

More Suspicious Behavior

I only relay this next part of my narrative to underscore the secret sins of the Royal Family and, in particular, Curtis's hypocrisy. Looking back and piecing everything together, I realized Curtis had been pushing his father's agenda for full community sharing while trying to cover up his wife's rebellion. Linda had been in a difficult place because evidently, she suffered some type of anxiety that required medical attention. The reactions from the medications might have created abnormal behavior, which in turn added credence to her husband and in-laws as to her so-called unstable condition.

In retrospect, I have no doubt there were probably threats of taking away her children, hence the additional anxiety. How sad, and how awful I felt when, further down the road, all of the pieces came together. I was actually, in her eyes, aligned with the enemy. She had no idea I was planning to leave—that is, not on this side of the veil, with the possible exception of that strange dialogue between us the night before she died.

Back to that time shortly after Linda's death, when I didn't have full understanding of Linda's predicament and before she provided the audible disclosure, Bud called a special meeting. We met in a large circle, as was often the case for all informal or impromptu group meetings. Curtis sat directly across from me, a good twenty-five feet away. At one point, he addressed the circle of members: "Who cleaned my house the day of Linda's death? I want to thank them."

I said nothing because I knew the member who'd asked me to clean the house would volunteer the information, and she did. "Makena," she said. Curtis carried it off and simply thanked me, and that was it. I wasn't suspicious at that time. I knew little other than that Linda had died suddenly and that her death might have been related to a seizure and the stress she was under in living in the cult.

About three or four weeks later, I found myself alone for some reason with Curtis, possibly when he picked up his laundry. He said to me, "Someday, Makena, we need to have a talk on the mountain." I figured he meant he wanted to tell me everything that was bothering him—possibly that he felt some guilt that Linda had died. Thank God I never had that talk with Curtis. After Phil and I made our exit, we requested complete cutting of ties with all remaining members, including Curtis.

Do I think Curtis had some direct responsibility regarding Linda's death? Was there something revealing in the house immediately following her death that I'd overlooked but that he thought I might have seen? I don't know. I don't have any evidence. But the track record is there, dear reader, and I'll let you decide.

The Wedding

Just two months after Linda's death, the fellowship supported the marriage of Marjory and Blake with a grand wedding in a lovely church in the large city twenty miles from our fellowship. As with all of our fellowship events, the wedding was beautifully decorated, choreographed, and carried out by many helpful hands. Marjory, whom I had become close to in the past few months, was a beautiful bride, and Blake was a happy and fortunate young man. He was marrying a sweet, intelligent young woman who adored his little girl.

Though Marjory and I had few conversations about Linda's death, she knew I was upset and unhappy about more than just the awful happenings of the past year. On one occasion, I inadvertently confided in her, "There is something very wrong about what's going on here in our fellowship."

She looked straight at me and said, "I know. I agree." This was a young woman who had been enslaved to Caryn Sue and Ben Weber for five years. She had her own doubts about the direction our fellowship was headed.

Shortly before the wedding, Phil and I confided in both Marjory and Blake that we would be leaving the fellowship. We felt we owed them that much. I had become accustomed to pretending that everything was okay, concealing my strong emotions that the opposite was true. However, those last few months of waiting out our situation, knowing we were almost free, were extremely difficult. I was concerned that Marjory, who was living in my household and working out wedding details with me, couldn't help but notice that I was struggling to keep focused. Marjory was quietly intuitive, and we seemed to share some unspoken bond in those final weeks before the wedding.

Phil and I trusted Marjory and Blake to keep our confidence until after the wedding, at which time we would let everyone know our intentions. We would move away from contact with everyone, including them, to leave them to create their own unit with Melissa.

There was one other person I communicated to prior to the wedding: Ellie. Though I haven't mentioned her much in this narrative, she was special to me. I felt responsible for her, as if I were an older sister to her, as I'd been instrumental in getting her and her family involved in the fellowship. Though Ellie and I were only twelve years apart, when I first met her and her family—neighbors living nearby—she was still in high school, and I was married with two young children.

When I confided in Ellie that Phil and I were leaving the cult following the wedding, she said, "Oh, Makena, I am right behind you! Brian is coming around, and we will be able to leave as a family as well." Thankfully, Ellie and Brian had no financial entanglements. They were renting a small home in proximity and had no other individuals sharing their household. They were able to move some measurable distance farther south within a few months of Phil's and my exit.

Steps and More Insights

What did I do with the knowledge and insight provided by Linda from the Other Side regarding possession of our home? I waited. I had waited for almost two years to gain freedom, and I could wait a little longer. I had to wait for the wedding to take place. As mentioned earlier, the period of preparing for the wedding and participating in the coordination is a hazy memory. I had difficulty focusing on the responsibility. Whereas I always had been capable at managing projects and event planning, it was all I could do to make a to-do list or prepare for the wedding. However, Marjory and Blake deserved my attention to the task, so somehow, I got through it.

Phil and I both knew that as soon as the wedding was over, Marjory and Blake would move out, along with little Melissa. As mentioned, Andon had married Camella and moved out earlier, and Gary had joined a singles' household some six or eight months previously, so that would leave us free to make our statement, put up the For Sale sign, and move out. But there were communications to be made.

The first communication occurred when I went alone soon after the wedding to face Bud with the conclusion to my two-year quest. I had plenty to say, so I sat at the typewriter and started typing. The list below is a summary of three typewritten pages of what I actually handed him:

> The light God shed on my predicament in answer to my questions two years ago.
>
> Questions:
>
> 1) Is there something wrong with me for desiring to leave? If so, let me know, and I will decide whether to stay or leave and take God's punishment if I leave.
>
> 2) Is there something wrong with the group's teachings? If so, let me know, and I will leave.
>
> Answers:
>
> 1) I am to follow no man but, rather, fear God over man and seek him totally in every aspect and detail in my life. This direction brings me back joy—"Joy

Unspeakable" (1 Peter 1:8 NIV), which is a result of my renewed relationship with him.

2) I will never return to the law that brings a curse (Galatians 3:10 NIV).

3) My self-worth is in God, as he is in me.

4) I no longer am open to condemnation, as I am not under the law.

What I have discovered about the group (fellowship):

1) We, the fellowship, have believed a lie—a lie that the church is sovereign and should come between the individual's relationship with God. As during the Middle Ages, when the papal system came between the people and God, the dark ages, we, as a fellowship, adopted your teachings and thereby experienced the dark years through a system that promotes

a. discernment groups or man's collective wisdom being above individual choice and discernment and

b. teachings that emphasize repetitious statements, such as "There is no such thing as 'me and God.'"

2) We, the fellowship, like the Pharisees in the New Testament of the Bible, constructed an elaborate system of law—everything from living in proximity to participating in extended households, participating in common purse, participating in common vacations, wearing special clothing, eliminating watching television, and excluding outside family, to name a few.

3) Our worth as a body has been an introspective emphasis rather than a humbling experience. Our collective experience is one of arrogance and pride.

4) The overall experience of many people in the group is fear due to brainwashing and manipulation.

What I discovered about me:

1) I allowed myself to be led by a man and his opinions and beliefs rather than by God's Holy Spirit.

2) I participated fully in a system of law rather than the true gospel of Christ (Galatians), which resulted in my never quite making it and feeling like I could fall at any time whenever you gave a directive or established a new belief or doctrine.

3) My self-worth was associated with how obedient I was to this system, as I believed I was following God's admonitions. Again, I could never attain because I was trying to live up to your and Sandra Sue's expectations rather than availing myself of the God-given freedom to obey the directives of the Holy Spirit in my own life.

4) Essentially, I discovered that I am a conscientious person who can easily be led to believe that works are where it's at, because I can also be easily condemned falsely—driven by a false guilt.

Why am I here before you today? To let you know ...

1) I cannot and will not align myself with this group any longer. Phil and I will make a brief statement to the group as soon as possible in the form of a letter. We are in need of deprogramming and healing from the past several years and will be cutting all ties with all members.

2) Phil and I are claiming our home as rightful owners. The community sharing company holds no legal ownership over the mortgage holder, Veterans Affairs. We will be listing our home on the entire five-acre parcel and reimbursing the three contributors for the two and a half acres, keeping our share of the proceeds for the home and two and a half acres.

3) You are to take immediate steps to seek your own means of providing your electricity and water. You are to remove your attachments from our home.

When I completed typing up the three-page document, I sat still at the typewriter, closed my eyes, and listened—a habit that was becoming natural and even exciting. I was never disappointed. I always got direction. Oftentimes, it was just a simple directive, step by step. Dear reader, many times I have reflected on the process of coming out of the cult, and I always experience extreme gratefulness for the help I received. I know now that I had a host of loved ones on the Other Side who heard my plea and were ready and willing to pull me and my family out of that cult. But that was a realization that came much later, exactly twenty-eight years later, and will be documented in the *Beyond Oz* narrative.

To continue, I asked for direction as to the next step in delivering

Seeking Oz

the document to Bud alone. You might ask, dear reader, why I went without Phil. Essentially, the process of coming out of the cult was my journey, and I made it through with the Source of Love. I wanted only him as my companion. Though Phil ultimately agreed with the direction I received, he had no part in my progression. The trip down the Yellow Brick Road was my trip, for which I was responsible, and for the last two years, I'd had a companion or multiple companions who, for the purpose of taking me safely to my goal, had shined light on areas difficult to discern to help me understand what it is that we all ultimately seek: the mysterious Oz.

As I listened, I heard a familiar, concise message in my mind: *Read the document to Bud, and do not make eye contact.*

That was it.

I was taught to always show respect by giving eye contact to the person before me. I was shy as a child, so sometimes that was difficult for me, but as far as the big picture goes, the outcome was positive. It helped me to relegate my self-consciousness in favor of respect to the person in front of me.

Now I was being told not to look Bud in the eyes.

At first, I thought, *Won't that make me appear guilty?* Then I thought, *Never mind. Do as I am directed.*

The message was clear.

After I came out of the cult, that command not to make eye contact made perfect sense. It also made sense to read the document aloud to Bud, not allowing any interference or exchange of dialogue from him. It is known that many charismatic leaders use their behavioral science education to manipulate, and Bud was no exception. Remember, he had a law enforcement background and was well tutored in the behavioral sciences. He used his body language and facial expressions to show disapproval, and he used the cult buzz words to pull us into his militarized belief system.

He also read our body language, such as hints of guilt or naïveté. In that case, there was no opportunity. I started out by telling him I was going to read him a document and did not want him to interfere at any point throughout to completion. I would then leave the document with him. He complied, but of course, on completion, he said the same thing he had two years earlier: "Makena, don't you think it would be beneficial to the group to hear what you have to say?"

I did not look up from my reading as he spoke those words. I said no, set the document on the table next to him, turned, and left.

As I headed back home, I was filled with a sense of peace. I didn't need to go over anything in my mind, as I might have normally done—questioning myself, trying to analyze everything that had taken place to determine if I had done anything wrong. Instead, what came to mind was a memory of when I was a little girl traveling down that alleyway years ago, confronted by a vicious, sick dog that snarled and grabbed my scarf. Something inside that little girl had told her, *Do not let go of the scarf. It belongs to you!*

I smiled to myself and said, "Thank you."

After that time, there were only two other occasions when I had a direct encounter with Bud. The first encounter took place on Treetop Lane, outside one of the singles' extended households. I don't remember why I was there, but this happenstance took place shortly after the wedding and just prior to Phil and I delivering a letter of disfellowship to all members.

Bud meekly approached me, and I immediately looked down at the ground, following through with my directive not to look that man in the eye. He came close and said almost in a whisper, "Makena, you are a good person. You are a very good person—one of the few genuine persons I have known. Do you know, Makena, how awful I feel right now? I feel so terrible I have considered taking my own life."

I have to say, dear reader, nothing should have surprised me about that man at that particular juncture. He was a master manipulator! He was capable of deceit under the guise of a godly man. However, I found his words and demeanor shocking. Such behavior was unknown to me where Bud was concerned. Never had

I heard such a compliment from him or witnessed such humility. But the flattery and false humility were not what was shocking. It was the fact that men of God who studied God's Word knew better than to commit suicide, because that would condemn them straight to the everlasting fires of hell.

First, I must mention that now, with more understanding, I don't believe people who take their lives are condemned to suffer eternally. What went through my brain like an electric charge was that this man was truly a fraud and a coward. He could punish ruthlessly and seemingly without mercy, all in the name of God, but when he met adversity, he crumbled—so much so that he would consider selfishly taking his own life. Wow! Now, whether he meant it or whether it was another manipulative tactic, it doesn't matter. This man totally fit the description of the cowardly lion when Dorothy smacked him on the nose. In Bud's own cowardly fashion, he was pleading with me to have mercy on him.

I went from a feeling of shock and confusion almost immediately to one of disgust.

I thought, *This man is really and truly a fraud! Furthermore, he is a coward. He has the audacity to request mercy of the token mercy person, whom he and his family disregarded on so many occasions. He bullied me and my family. Does he really believe I would trust him? Wow!*

Again, like Dorothy, my thoughts were *Turning point, Mr. Cowardly Lion! Fear is gone. I will have mercy—not on you but on myself and my family.* Then, in a deviation from the Oz story, I thought, *However, I will not melt with your confession. Anyone capable of deceiving an entire group of people for twelve years does not deserve my mercy. At this point, I need to be "harmless as a dove, but as wise as a serpent."*

I walked away.

The second encounter with Bud was several months later, after Phil and I had moved some distance away. I was coming out of a gym located near where I worked. He was standing near his car, which was parked in front of my car. As I approached my vehicle, he started toward me. This time, I looked directly at him and said loudly, "Stop! Don't come near me!" He did stop. I got in my car and drove off. I have never seen him since, though I've been told he lives in that same community, probably in the same Timber House.

So was the man a con artist, a pastor gone wayward, a sociopath, or, worse yet, a psychopath?

I recalled my long-distance phone conversation with Matt while he was in college, when he said, "Better that he be a con man, Mom, than a delusional man who really believes he is right—like Hitler." I determined that I didn't want to know any more about that man than necessary. Am I curious? Not really. I'm just thankful that I eventually removed myself and my family from his influence.

Three-Month Wait

In mid-May 1990, Phil and I physically hand-delivered our letter to each and every member. Some wanted to admonish us. Some wanted to plead with us to stay. Sam James cried and told us that we and our children would be in danger of hell should we leave the fellowship. I engaged, for a short time, in a defensive dialogue and then realized how futile it was to try to explain.

Whereas I had been working for two years to get away from brainwashing, he was still immersed in it. I had to just walk away. But there were many who were silent. Their downcast eyes revealed that they had been concealing the same fears and concerns—that there was something wrong, and they wanted out.

Letter of Disfellowship

It is essential that we, Makena and Phil [Last Name], sever our separate ties of membership to the group _____ Christian Fellowship and [Community Sharing Company]. We have both come to the realization that we can no longer participate in a group that adheres to beliefs contrary to what we now understand and believe as truth.

We believe the following:

God is sovereign, and Jesus Christ is Lord via the Holy Spirit in the individual life of each believer. We believe that the beliefs and practices of _____ Christian Fellowship inhibit an individual's right to listen to the Holy Spirit and freely respond, and they compromise a healthy spiritual possibility to the point of frustration or neglect not in keeping with the pure gospel of Jesus Christ.

We have also come to recognize and know that _____ Christian Fellowship is in serious error. We adjure you to put aside all you have been taught and trust the God before whom you will stand alone someday; trust him to bring you his truth. Read his Word diligently, asking the Holy Spirit to "lead you into all truth." (We recommend Galatians.)

To those of you who choose to remain members of the group _____ Christian Fellowship, we love you and will pray for you. (We certainly appreciate the prayers that have been in our behalf to date!) We do not accept your creed and do not wish to engage in any more vain arguments. We need a time of quiet and stillness before God, a time to be deprogrammed, cleansed, healed, and strengthened by his Spirit.

We point you to him, our source of hope, joy, love, and peace.

We love you very much.

Phil [Last Name]

Makena [Last Name]

May __, 1990

Out but Still Tethered

After years of pain, I was finally getting out of a bad situation. Had I continued to listen to my inner guidance early on, years ago in that little church in the foothill community, I never would have experienced any of this turmoil. I did not trust Bud at that time, but I allowed my self-doubt and ability to be victimized by false guilt to think better of a man who eventually caused an upheaval in the lives and souls of many.

However, I had something to learn. I had already been in an abusive marriage. Evidently, I needed another experience of being a victim before I really started listening carefully to my own guidance when encountering red flags. I needed to refuse fear and ask more questions—even regarding my religion.

Shortly after Phil and I delivered our letter, we listed our house for sale. I also notified my two older sons, asking to meet with them privately and separately. I let each of them know why we were leaving the church fellowship. By that time, Matt fully understood, having been closer emotionally to the disturbing events of the past year. He also had experienced some deprogramming due to his distance from Bud. Joe was immensely relieved, having questioned his being ostracized. What was most important to me in speaking with them was to apologize to them for taking them down that path with me. They were young and impressionable, and they trusted me. Consequently, they followed the religion I imposed on them.

Though both of my sons had been observing red flags and drawing their own conclusions, they still carried a residue of confusion and, in some areas, unnecessary guilt similar to the guilt I experienced having been raised in a strict Christian environment.

My two sons, being the fine young men they were and continue to be, told me they didn't place blame on me—I was faithful to what I believed in and demonstrated love to them, and that was more important to them than anything.

Now I had to let go, let them determine their own paths, and forgive myself. That took awhile, as I mentioned at the beginning of the narrative, but it is all part of discovering and evolving, something we can only do genuinely when understanding and implementing our God-given freedom of choice.

It took three months for the sale of our home to go through. We still hadn't escaped the anxiety associated with entrapment. I believe the Source of Love wanted to make sure we got the message! I actually smile at this thought now in the way a child reflects on an act of parental tough love. Living through the wait was painful, and it had a lasting impact on us—never to allow such victimization in our lives again.

If you recall, historically, 1990 marked an abrupt change in buying and selling real estate. Throughout the 1980s, under Reagan's administration, there was a great expansion of economic activity. However, the 1990s marked a time of recession in real estate. We experienced the abrupt change in the market just when we listed our home.

We were delighted when we got an offer shortly after listing from a visionary Realtor who wanted to purchase our five-acre parcel, which was already zoned to split into smaller parcels. His motivation for buying was for a gain in the future. He knew he would have to wait to make any money on the deal, as no one was buying at that time. However, the Realtor did not have the funds to complete the transaction. His offer included several contingencies—all dependent on his being able to swing the deal financially. Though the house was on the market the full three months before the offer finally went through, we did not get another single bite—no one was interested in buying our home.

In the meantime, Bud remained tethered to our home for another couple of months, using our electricity and water. He also invaded our privacy by walking across our lawn to the road connecting the other homes instead of taking the back roads to get there. The only redeeming part of his invasive attitude was a constant reminder that we had definitely made the right choice. This man was arrogant and rude.

Another upside to our painful three-month wait was that I became even more in touch with messages from the Other Side. I didn't have any interruptions. No one was knocking at our door. No one was using our laundry room, our basement, or any part of our house for meetings. No one was living with Phil, Jacob, and me. We had our home to ourselves. I didn't have to cook for several people. I didn't counsel. I didn't teach school.

I had time to take Jacob places. I took him to the park one day, and as I sat on a bench, watching him play, I closed my eyes for a moment and inwardly uttered a prayer of thanks. My gratefulness was huge. I knew I would never take that kind of freedom for granted again. (And I can truthfully say I haven't!) When I opened my eyes, I noticed that the trees were amazingly green—greener than I had ever seen them.

I thought, *Have trees always been this brilliant, with the sunlight skipping between the branches and dancing on the leaves?*

It was then I realized that I was waking up. It was as if I had been in a nightmarish dream state for the past ten years, a gradual dimming and darkening of reality as my ability to make choices kept ebbing away. It was also then I realized that my very soul had been in jeopardy. The uniqueness of who I was had been relegated and held down. I'd been losing my saltiness, as Jesus warned in the scriptures.

I asked God silently in my inner person, *Why did you allow me to get entrapped in such confinement? Especially when it is so beautiful out here in your amazing nature world?*

Quickly the answer came: *I didn't do that. You chose it. I have been here waiting for you.*

I also received two significant messages as we awaited the sale of our home. They both involved the Bible, which was an always-ready aid to provide me direction and encouragement. During that time, I kept the Bible on my nightstand before retiring, and I moved it to the kitchen counter on rising in the morning. I kept it close to me throughout the day. I didn't do that out of superstition or fear. The Bible had become my divination tool for guidance and ultimate escape.

In addition to the small voice that provided me step-by-step direction, I was often prompted to flip open the Bible randomly and read a passage. At those times, I received exactly what I needed for solace, encouragement, or direction.

Though Phil and I were essentially free from the confines of the cult, a shadow pervaded as long as we remained in proximity. We felt no guilt, of course, but we were surrounded by people we loved and had walked with for the past twelve years. It was like a gigantic divorce in which we claimed irreconcilable differences.

Some partners were angry about our decision; some were sad and confused. When you love someone, either outcome is painful. We knew we might be hurting those people, but we also knew we needed to leave with no further ado. No further explanations—just leave. I also knew from having counseled some of the members for the past couple of years that some of those people were conflicted and wanted to talk to me so they could determine what to do for themselves. That was also painful. They would have to decide for themselves.

On one morning in particular, when I felt discouraged and wondered if we were being punished and would have to eventually walk away from our home after all, since the wait was becoming excruciating, I asked God for encouragement. We were at about the one-month mark after receiving the offer, with no reassurance that it would go through.

Also, I need to mention that we also put a contingency offer on a house several miles away. It was nearing fall, when Jacob would need to attend school, and we were conflicted as to where to start him. School was starting the first of September. As it turned out, the sale did not go through until the end of October, and on faith, we enrolled Jacob in first grade in the school near the home we were hoping to

Seeking Oz

get. The hurting real estate market played in our favor on that end, as the owners were not getting any interest in their home either.

This target home was not just several miles away but also remote. It was located at a higher elevation and about halfway between two major freeways, which were about thirty-five miles and twenty miles each direction, respectively, south and north. The area was accessible by twisting, steep roads and, thereby, considered the ultimate in rural and remote locations. Our rationale in choosing that home was to be inaccessible to cult members but not removed from our grown sons and family. Needless to say, it was somewhat difficult driving several miles every day on the more primitive roads for the two months Jacob attended school, but after the twelve years in the cult, the drive was, by comparison, not a problem at all.

At any rate, that morning, after praying for encouragement, I was prompted to open the Bible. I flipped open the Bible customarily and was immediately disappointed. It appeared to be an account in the Old Testament with which I was unfamiliar. Though I knew the Bible well and had read through it from start to finish a couple of times over my lifetime thus far, I didn't necessarily retain some of the Old Testament accounts that seemed less significant than some of the more interesting stories.

The passage was in 2 Kings 25. I glanced through the passages on the page, looking for help, and again, I was disappointed. I started to close the Bible to try again—not my usual result—but something told me to put a bookmark there and come back to it to try again later. So I did and this time flipped away from the historical books of the Bible to what turned out to be Jeremiah. Better—a book in the prophecy section of the Bible.

Once again, I was disappointed. It was another historical account with which I was unfamiliar in Jeremiah 52. I placed another bookmark and closed the Bible. Sometimes, on reflecting back, I have wondered if I was somehow purposely held off from studying and reading those first passages thoroughly, because when I was prompted to open to the bookmarked passages later in the day, I was ecstatic to find that though the two accounts were several books apart in the Bible, they were the exact same account almost word for word. Not only did I receive a clear message in answer to my discouragement, but I received it twice!

> In the thirty-seventh year of the exile of Jehoiachin king of Judah, in the year Awel-Marduk became king of Babylon, he released Jehoiachin king of Judah from prison. He did this on the twenty-seventh day of the twelfth month. He spoke kindly to him and gave him a seat of honor higher than those of the other kings who were with him in Babylon. So Jehoiachin put aside his prison clothes and for the rest of his life ate regularly at the king's table. Day by day the king gave Jehoiachin a regular allowance as long as he lived. (2 Kings 25:27–30 NIV)

> In the thirty-seventh year of the exile of Jehoiachin king of Judah, in the year Awel-Marduk became king of Babylon, on the twenty-fifth day of the twelfth month, he released Jehoiachin king of Judah and freed him from prison. He spoke kindly to him and gave him a seat of honor higher than those of the other kings who were with him in Babylon. So Jehoiachin put aside his prison clothes and for the rest of his life ate regularly at the king's table. Day by day the king of Babylon gave Jehoiachin a regular allowance as long as he lived, till the day of his death. (Jeremiah 52:31–34 NIV)

I interpreted the following clear promises:

1) I would be free from imprisonment. In other words, I would no longer be entrapped and imprisoned by the cult. God would deliver Phil, Jacob, and me from our proximity location. We would be able to "put aside [our] prison clothes."

2) I would eat regularly at the king's table. This fulfillment came about approximately seven years after leaving the cult and will be relayed in a second narrative, *Beyond Oz*.

3) I would receive a regular allowance as long as I live. This fulfillment came about a year ago, when I was awarded a pension allotment that adequately covers me for the rest of my life in spite of a complete financial reversal ten years previous. Again, I will relay further details in a second narrative, *Beyond Oz*.

To further punctuate the threefold promise, prior to items two and three coming to pass, the following passage illuminated the fact that God would deliver. About six months later, after having moved away from the cult, I was reading to Jacob the story of Joseph—one of my favorite Old Testament stories. Joseph was a wonderful role model, a man of deep compassion and integrity. I came across the following scripture in a passage where Joseph interpreted Pharaoh's two dreams: "The reason the dream was given to Pharaoh in two forms is that the matter has been firmly decided by God, and God will do it soon" (Genesis 41:32 NIV).

The scripture jumped out at me, and I had to read it again aloud. I paraphrased it in my mind as "When a prophecy or promise is given by God in two forms or two times, the matter is sealed firmly by God himself, and he will follow through." The threefold promise embedded in my mind that day in my kitchen was underscored in that passage such that I never doubted that all would come to pass, even when I suffered a complete financial loss at age sixty—during the period of my life beyond Oz.

I mentioned earlier that I received two strong revelations during the three-month wait. The second revelation happened immediately following the messages relayed in 2 Kings and Jeremiah. Needless to say, I was ecstatic that I received the encouragement I needed from those passages. The God who would deliver me from the imprisoning cult would be faithful to take me all the way. I would be set on higher ground and be cared for—for the remainder of my days. That was a promise I could embrace and hold close to me. No one could take that from me.

As I closed the Bible, leaving the bookmarks in place, I heard in my mind, *Now close the book, and don't open it until later—it will have more meaning later.* In that instant, I received a rapid download of information—nothing to analyze or ponder, just an outpouring that can be summarized to something like *These scriptures you have read since you were a child have brought you joy. They have also brought you pain. The pain is in the form of guilt, shame, degradation, and fear, not necessarily love. The religion of these scriptures is exclusive, damning unbelievers to an eternity of hell. There is more. Ask questions. Start with a clean slate. Walk away from limiting doctrines and dangerous beliefs. Love is the answer. Start afresh, and I, the Source of Love, will answer all of your questions. At some point, the validation may be hidden in these very scriptures, but for now, you need only me. Listen to your inner guidance. I am there.*

I knew that closing the book was somewhat figurative. I didn't necessarily need to dismiss reading the Bible from then forward, but I knew I needed to put aside those scriptures that never really resonated with me in terms of love and encouragement. Somewhere deep within the layered interpretations, I knew that something was misrepresented or had been changed for reasons of control. The God who was really there for me—from birth and before that and onward and always—is a beautiful, mysterious Source of Love that allows choice, feeling, and discovery, not a taskmaster capable of burning his children forever if they don't believe a certain way. He takes no pleasure in sacrifice: "I don't want your sacrifices—I want your love; I don't want your offerings—I want you to know me" (Hosea 6:6 TLB).

The Wait Is Over

I would like to say that the house deal went through smoothly, and we sailed off into the sunset to our home in the hills. However, the closing sale was rough—a roller-coaster ride for the full three months. But it finally closed. We settled the amounts owed to the other participants, which were already outlined and documented in percentages relative to the full amount of sale.

We received the additional money from the sale of the Dogwood Lane property, which we had turned over to the community sharing company. We knew that the return of those several thousand dollars to us was a strong indicator that Bud was fearful of repercussions. He was running scared. There were too many negative occurrences that could prove damaging to Bud and some of his family members. We learned a few months later that the entire community sharing company had shut down.

In a short time, the members scattered, not returning to attend church meetings. We didn't look back. We were worn and weary but free—deliciously free!

* * *

So, dear reader, as we travel down the Yellow Brick Road, we all seek wholeness.

We seek to love and be loved; we seek to gain knowledge and understanding; and we seek the courage to keep going when, oftentimes, the Yellow Brick Road proves to be disappointing.

For some, religion holds all of the answers. But what if the religion proves to be an Oz—a human facsimile of something we think is powerful and capable of providing everything we need to be happy and satisfied in our various quests for truth?

And what if Oz can misrepresent what is real? What if what is real is actually inside each and every one of us? Can we question this Oz? Do we have a personal responsibility to question this Oz?

What if there is more beyond Oz?

Printed in the United States
By Bookmasters